JEWS
OF THE
AMERICAN
WEST

American Jewish Civilization Series

Editors
MOSES RISCHIN
San Francisco State University
JONATHAN D. SARNA
Brandeis University

Books in this series

Jews of the American West,
edited by Moses Rischin and John Livingston, 1991

An Ambiguous Partnership:
Non-Zionists and Zionists
in America 1939–1948,
by Menahem Kaufman, 1991

JEWS
OF THE
AMERICAN
WEST

Edited by

MOSES RISCHIN and JOHN LIVINGSTON

 WAYNE STATE UNIVERSITY PRESS DETROIT

Copyright © 1991 by Wayne State University Press,
Detroit, Michigan 48202. All rights are reserved.
No part of this book may be reproduced without formal permission.
Manufactured in the United States of America.

95 94 93 92   5 4 3 2

Library of Congress Cataloging-in-Publication Data

Jews of the American West / edited by Moses Rischin and John
   Livingston.
        p.   cm.–(American Jewish civilization series)
     Includes bibliographical references and index.
     ISBN 0–8143–2170–4 (alk. paper)
     1. Jews–West (U.S.)–History–Congresses. 2. West (U.S.)–Ethnic
   relations–Congresses. I. Rischin, Moses, date.
   II. Livingston, John, date. III. Series.
   F596.3.J5J48   1991
   978'.004924–dc20   90–44864
                                                        CIP
   Paper ISBN 0-8143-2171-2

Designer: Joanne Elkin Kinney

TO EARL POMEROY

CONTENTS

ILLUSTRATIONS

ACKNOWLEDGMENTS

Jews of the American West is the product of a conference devoted to western Jewish history held on May 19 and 20, 1986, in Denver, Colorado, sponsored by the Rocky Mountain Jewish Historical Society of the Center for Judaic Studies at the University of Denver. In addition to the Society and the Center, which played key roles in this undertaking, we are also grateful to the Colorado Endowment for the Humanities for a conference grant, to Perle Beck and Faye Schayer of Denver for matching grants, and to the Colorado Historical Society for the support of its Local Assistance Program.

Certain persons intimately associated with the conference deserve our particular gratitude. We are especially beholden to Dr. Jeanne Abrams, Director of the Rocky Mountain Jewish Historical Society, who assumed the major burdens of this scholarly enterprise. Dr. Abrams organized the conference, took primary responsibility for local arrangements, and volunteered to prepare an essay for this volume based on her meticulous research into the history of the Jewish Consumptives' Relief Society of Denver which she was unable to present at the conference itself due to the press of her other duties. We are also profoundly grateful to Dr. Stanley Wagner, Director of the Center for Judaic Studies at the University of Denver, for graciously making the resources of his Center and staff available and for generously providing a grant to aid in the preparation of this volume for publication.

Acknowledgments

We are thankful too to Bernard Wax and Stanley Remsberg, Director and Assistant Director respectively of the American Jewish Historical Society, for skillfully dovetailing the western Jewish history conference with the eighty-fourth annual meeting of the national society and doing so with grace, tact, and dispatch.

Besides the contributors to this volume to whom we are indebted above all, we should like to express our appreciation as well to those important others who participated in the conference in various capacities and whose presence, knowledge, humor, and wit enlivened our understanding of the history of the Jews of the West. They are Ralph Mann, Professor of History at the University of Colorado, Boulder; Marjorie Hornbein, veteran historian of the Jews of Denver; Ruth Rafael, Archivist of the Western Jewish History Center of the Judah L. Magnes Museum, Berkeley; Harriet Rochlin, historian and novelist, Los Angeles; Kenneth Libo, Curator of the National Museum of American Jewish History, Philadelphia; and a host of engaged others whose spirited attendance made the conference a memorable event.

Finally, we should like to express our appreciation to Stanley Chyet, Martin Zinkow, and Nora Contini for aiding us in securing a number of the illustrations and to Yehudit Goldfarb for preparing the index.

CONTRIBUTORS

JEANNE ABRAMS, Director of the Rocky Mountain Jewish Historical Society, has written primarily on the Jews of Denver.

LEONARD DINNERSTEIN, Professor of History at the University of Arizona, has written extensively on the history of the Jews of the South, ethnic and immigration history, and anti-Semitism. He is the author of *The Leo Frank Case*, *Ethnic Americans*, *Natives and Strangers*, *America and the Survivors of the Holocaust*, and *Uneasy at Home: Antisemitism and the American Jewish Experience*.

ROBERT A. GOLDBERG, Associate Professor of History at the University of Utah, is the author of *The Ku Klux Klan in Colorado* and *Back to the Soil: The Jewish Farmers of Clarion, Utah and Their World*.

JOHN LIVINGSTON is Associate Professor of History at the University of Denver, Chairperson of the Academic Council of the American Jewish Historical Society, and the author of *Clarence Darrow: The Mind of a Sentimental Rebel*.

EARL POMEROY is both Beekman Professor Emeritus at the University of Oregon and Professor Emeritus at the University of California-San Diego. The author of *The Territories and the United States 1861–1890: Studies in Colonial Administration*, *In Search of the Golden West: The Tourist in Western America*, and *The Pacific Slope: A History of California, Oregon, Washington, Idaho, Utah, and Ne-*

vada, he is completing a long-awaited volume on the West in the twentieth century for the New American Nation series.

MARC LEE RAPHAEL, the Nathan and Sophia Jumenick Professor of Judaic Studies at the College of William and Mary and editor of *American Jewish History*, is the author of *Jews and Judaism in a Midwestern Community: Columbus, Ohio 1840–1975, Profiles in American Judaism: The Reform, Conservative, Orthodox, and Reconstructionist Traditions in Historical Perspective, Abba Hillel Silver: A Profile in American Judaism*, and other works.

MOSES RISCHIN is Professor of History at San Francisco State University, Director of the Western Jewish History Center of the Judah L. Magnes Museum, and a past President of the Immigration History Society. His books include *The Promised City: New York's Jews, 1870–1914, The Jews of the West: The Metropolitan Years, Grandma Never Lived in America: The New Journalism of Abraham Cahan, Like All the Nations? The Life and Legacy of Judah L. Magnes*, and *The Jews of North America*.

FRED ROSENBAUM, Director of Lehrhaus Judaica, the school for adult Jewish education in Berkeley, San Francisco, and Stanford, is the author of *Free to Choose: The Making of a Jewish Community in the American West: The Jews of Oakland, California, from the Gold Rush to the Present Day* and *Architects of Reform: Congregational and Community Leadership, Emanu-El of San Francisco, 1849–1880*.

WILLIAM TOLL, who teaches at Oregon State University, is the author of *The Resurgence of Race: Black Social Theory from Reconstruction to the Pan-African Congresses* and *The Making of an Ethnic Middle Class: Portland Jewry over Four Generations*, and is at work on an intellectual biography of Horace M. Kallen.

INTRODUCTION

John Livingston

"The West," remarked a distinguished visiting statesman and savant a century ago, "is the most American part of America."[1] Reiterated and elaborated into a deeply felt turn-of-the-century American national idiom—and promptly canonized by Frederick Jackson Turner—James Bryce's offhanded perception of the West was to inform the single most renowned and most resonant essay ever penned by an American historian. As much attitude and state of mind as it was poetic response, Turner's symbolic frontier statement, however ethnocentric, racist, and sexist by later standards, linked American democracy to American geography with an almost metaphoric simplicity that continues to inhabit the American imagination.[2]

America's Jews, in untold numbers, have behaved as if the West, whether as frontier or postfrontier, has been "the most American part of America" for them too. Yet historians, understandably, have been slow to recognize the critical importance of this dimension of the American Jewish experience. For so many reasons, American Jewish history, even more than American history, has been heavily weighted toward the older metropolitan centers of the East and Middle West. There a colonial and mid-nineteenth-century Jewish presence, magnified tenfold by the transforming energies of the great Jewish migration, was for a century continually giving a whole array of national developments an implicitly nonwestern focus that went virtually un-

15

challenged. Because the maintenance and reconstitution of a whole ethnic and religious tradition was also reflexively associated with the most proverbially Eurocentric regions of the country, the history of Jews in the "most American part of America" long was perceived to be peripheral to mainstream Jewish America, at best tributary and derivative, and of little serious interest. As a result, the question as to whether the history of the Jews in the West, and the South as well, had a distinctiveness and importance for an understanding of America and its Jews did not seem worthy of major scholarly attention and went virtually unexplored.

Yet, however tentative, serious studies in western Jewish history did begin to emerge in the 1960s. Several factors account for this growing interest. Surely the vitalization and expansion of graduate study stand first and foremost. Just as so many other areas of Jewish life underwent professionalization in the years after World War II, so too did the writing and teaching of American Jewish history increasingly attract the attention and talents of professionally trained historians. Although the precise definition of *profession* is subject to dispute among both sociologists and in the popular mind, a committee of the American Historical Association has recently agreed, not surprisingly, that the profession of history comprises "those individuals who have graduate degrees or some formal training in history and who practice or have practiced history either in teaching or research or both."[3] A survey of the authors whose articles have appeared in *American Jewish History* and the *American Jewish Archives* over the past twenty-five years leaves no doubt that American Jewish history has become the preserve of just such scholars. In sharp contrast with the amateurs and antiquarians who once dominated the field, their successors have been professional historians. Thoroughly schooled in American history, they have selected American Jewish history as one of their specialities and have been committed to relating the history of Jews to the experiences of other groups and to integrating Jewish history into the nation's larger story. The contributions to this volume reflect these changes in the field.

An additional factor that has drawn attention to the history of Jews in the West has been the recognition given by historians to ethnic and religious history as integral to the larger American experience. Propelled by the Civil Rights Movement, the reform in the immigration laws, the upsurge of black and other ethnic prides, and the drive to introduce courses in the history of diverse ethnic groups—including Jews—into the college and univerity curriculum, historians began to look afresh at the whole conceptual structure of their discipline. The resultant academic response led to an unprecedented acknowledgment and acceptance of the pluralistic realities of American cultural life. However belatedly, western historians came to perceive that the West had been settled by immigrants as well as migrants, that theirs was a multiracial and multicultural society even more varied and more complex than in other regions, and that interethnic, interracial, and interreligious relations called for major new scholarship.[4]

Reinforcing the emphasis on ethnic and religious pluralism and further stimulating interest in American Jewish history was the rise as well of a social history with its stress on racial, ethnic, religious, and sexual diversity that has come to dominate the discipline. Spurred by the radical and revolutionary impulses of the sixties, American history was criticized for its focus on elites, notably white middle-class men, to the virtual exclusion of all others. In response, a younger generation of American historians pioneered new approaches and methodologies that made possible the exploration of the lives of anonymous Americans. In their studies of "history from the bottom up," these historians tracked the lives of those who left few if any written remains. They ransacked county courthouse records; studied federal and state manuscript census schedules, city directories, and voter registration lists; and examined birth, marriage, naturalization, and death registers. Thus they were able to diagram occupational, family, residential, and voting patterns with meticulous veracity. Armed with sociological savvy, blessed with an abundance of documents amenable to quantification, and aided by computer technology, the new social historians have generated a new people's history as women, children, workers, blacks, immigrants, and many others have been portrayed as they never have been before. Indeed, over a decade earlier, the pioneering application of the methods of the New Social History to local history—to test Turner's claims to frontier democracy appropriately—had been undertaken by Turner's last student, Merle Curti, in his now-classic study of Trempeleau County.[5] Younger historians of the Jewish experience in America soon followed suit as they applied quantification and the techniques of statistical analysis to the study of social, occupational, and geographical mobility patterns as well as to demographic and family changes over the generations in order to recover dimensions of the heretofore inaccessible Jewish past.[6]

A sign that professional historians were turning their attention to ethnic history in the West was flashed in 1968 when the *Journal of American History* published an article by Moses Rischin titled, "Beyond the Great Divide: Immigration and the Last Frontier." A recognized authority in American ethnic, immigration, and Jewish history,

Rischin first called attention to "an upsurge of historical scholarship [that reflected] a growing interest in the plurality of origins, institutions and group memories that have been native to the West."[7]

Yet, in surveying the historical literature of the West two decades ago, Rischin could cite only one published monograph of distinction that related to Jews. Since then the developments in the field of western Jewish history have been far more impressive. Important works that cannot be ignored are: (1) Max Vorspan and Lloyd P. Gartner's history of the Los Angeles Jewish community; (2) a collection of essays on the Jews of the metropolitan West, edited by Moses Rischin, based on papers presented at the First Conference on Western Jewish History held in 1977 in Berkeley, California, and cosponsored by the American Jewish Historical Society, the Bancroft Library, and the Western Jewish History Center of the Magnes Museum; (3) Fred Rosenbaum's studies of the Jews of Oakland and of Temple Emanu-El of San Francisco; (4) a monograph on the Jews and the California gold rush by Robert Levinson; (5) a work on the making of the Jewish middle class in Portland, Oregon, by William Toll; (6) and a history of Utah's Clarion agrarian community by Robert A. Goldberg.[8] In addition, imaginatively researched popular works by Harriet and Fred Rochlin and by Kenneth Libo and Irving Howe have contributed to a wider public interest in western Jewish history.[9]

If the professionalization of American Jewish history and western Jewish history has reflected a concern with ethnicity and the adoption of the methods of the regnant New Social History, the developments in the lives of American Jews in the West in the closing decades of the twentieth century have spurred a search for a regional Jewish identity rooted in both a regional as well as a larger American and Jewish past. As a number of contributors to this volume have noted, the new migrations to the West associated with World War II and after carried with them a greater proportion of America's Jews than ever before. Transforming the contours of American Jewish demography, these migrations have led to the dramatic expansion of older Jewish communities and the establishment of centers of Jewish settlement where none had existed before. The tilting of the balance of America's Jewish population away from the North Atlantic and Great Lakes regions toward the Pacific was especially dramatized by the emergence of Los Angeles as the second most populous Jewish city in the United States, trailing only New York.

As the Jews of the West grew in importance, numbers and maturity, they sought legitimation in a regional Jewish historical presence by founding local and regional historical societies, museums, and archives to preserve the records of the past and oral history programs to salvage the memories of an older generation about to pass from the scene. It has been these institutions, beginning in 1967 with the founding of the Western Jewish History Center in Berkeley, that have provided the splendid resources that have made serious research into the history of the Jews of the West possible for the first time. Not to be overlooked is the establishment of the quasi-scholarly but useful *Western States Jewish History,* formerly the *Western States Jewish Historical Quarterly,* founded in 1968 in southern California.

Encouraged by the new importance of the field, in 1986, the Rocky Mountain Jewish Historical Society—founded in 1976 in response to the new-felt needs—organized the second Conference on Western Jewish History, of which *Jews of the American West* is the proud product. A volume of fresh interpretative essays—ranging over the whole field—by mostly older historians along with more sharply focused topical essays by mostly younger historians, this collection is aimed at readers with diverse needs, interests, and tastes. From Moses Rischin's telescopic view—extending across five generations—of the relationship of the western Jewish experience to the American Jewish mainstream and from Marc Lee Raphael's conspectus of the Jews of the West as seen by a scholar focusing on contemporary American Jewish history to Earl Pomeroy's comparative overview of the common experiences shared by American migrants and diverse immigrants (Jews and others), the reader is invited to share in a variety of perspectives. By highlighting long-term patterns, we trust that the history of the Jews of the West is at last given the epical dimension that it merits. On the other hand, the tightly focused studies of agrarian socialism in Clarion, Utah, by Robert A. Goldberg; of the health seekers of Denver by Jeanne Abrams; and of the San Francisco Jewish elite's response to Zionism and the founding of the State of Israel by Fred Rosenbaum lend both a thick historicity and a local specificity to important episodes and manifestations of Jewish life in the West. Finally, the extended profile by Leonard Dinnerstein of the Tucson, Arizona, Jewish community—from its founding to the present, with special attention to its support for Israel—and the careful study by William Toll of intermarriage patterns and their implications for the Jewish communities of the West are valuable inquires into contemporary issues of deepest concern.

Although each essay stands on its own merits, taken together they may call for a reinterpretation of western Jewish history in distinctively regional terms. The first area compelling reconsideration is the traditional periodization of American Jewish history that has been pegged to the successive major streams of Jewish immigration: (1) an initial period, 1654–1820, dominated, it was once thought, by Sephardic Jews; (2) a middle period, 1820–1881, associated with the coming of Jews from the German states; (3) a third period, 1881–1924, when Eastern European Jews overwhelmed their predecessors; and (4) a final period, 1924 to the present, characterized by the end of major immigration, the consolidation of a greater American Jewish community, and the commitment of that community to its own transformation and renewal as well as to the survival of the State of Israel. For the history of the Jews in the West, this scheme of periodization clearly is inappropriate and needs either to be drastically modified or discarded. The Sephardic period obviously is irrelevant to the West; the German period must be seen as broadly Central, if not all, European. The vast East European migration in the third period, which atlered the structure of Jewish communities in the Northeast and Midwest, did not have the same impact in the West, for, with a few notable exceptions, Eastern Europeans did not move West in great numbers, and when their children and grandchildren did, in the post–World War II years, they would come to play a very different role.

A number of essays in this volume, most notably Moses Rischin's, dismiss the traditional periodization as unsuited to the West. What appears more significant for periodizing western Jewish history than the national or regional origins of the newcomers is the extent of the migration from east to west. Western Jewry, it would appear, has moved through three stages of development: (1) an initial period, 1848–1890, in which large numbers of Jews moved westward and established a critical demographic presence relative to the total Jewish population of the United States; (2) a second period, 1890–1941, when Jewish migration to the West declined even when multitudes of Eastern European immigrants, followed by their numerous children, came to people the cities of the industrial Northeast and Midwest; and (3) a third period, 1941 to the present, when a second westward migration contributed to a renewed Jewish presence in the West. Although this scheme of periodization is linked to demographic trends, numbers alone do not tell the whole story, for quantity potentially affects life quality and the nature and character of Jewish communal organizations and institutions. Although the history of Jews in the West was conditioned by the social and economic environment they encountered within the region, the specifically Jewish dimension of western Jewish history has been related in many important ways to their numbers. Further research in western Jewish history may lead historians to arrive at a more complex and highly differentiated scheme of periodization than the one proposed here, but it appears undeniable that the ebb and flow of Jewish life in the West have been shaped by patterns distinctive to the region, patterns to which scholars ought to be sensitive and alert.

A second differentiating feature of western Jewish history that must be reckoned with is the relative absence of Eastern European immigrants at just the time when vast numbers of these newcomers were establishing a formidable presence in the metropolitan centers of the East and Midwest. As a result, in the early twentieth century, Jewish communities in the West were less diverse, less affected by the emergent culture of Yiddishkeit, and, as Marc Lee Raphael contends, less European in sensibility and ambience. By contrast with the American East during the era of the great Jewish migration, Jewish socialism, Zionism, and Orthodoxy had far fewer adherents and a smaller voice in the West whereas utopian efforts to create idealistic agricultural communities there, as elsewhere, were doomed to fail. It is true, however, that where Eastern Europeans clustered in ethnic neighborhoods (namely in the Fillmore in San Francisco, in Boyle Heights in Los Angeles, and in Denver's Colfax district), they mustered the "critical mass" that enabled them to recreate the socialist, labor, Zionist, and Orthodox institutions and organizations that linked them with the world of the Jewish Lower East Side and its counterparts in the older regions of the nation. In Los Angeles, for example, the employment of Jews in the garment industry led to the formation of West Coast locals of the International Ladies' Garment Workers' Union (ILGWU).[10] During the Great Depression, in the West no less than in the East—although few relative to the total Jewish population—Jews were disproportionately represented in the Communist party.[11] Yet the significant story of Jewish radicalism in the West, postdating as it did the high tide of Jewish radicalism in the East, registered the emergence of a second and third generation associated with a genre of radicalism that may be distinctive to the West and that has yet to be explored.

A third theme calling for attention has been the relative absence of anti-Semitism in the West. For quite understandable reasons, the persistence of anti-Semitism has been accepted implicitly by most Jews, even if scholars who have studied this phenomenon have not always done so. In his recent survey of the literature, David Gerber has identified three interpretations of the significance of anti-Semitism for an understanding of American Jewish history. The earliest students of anti-Semitism in the United States viewed anti-Jewish prejudice as exceptional and regarded it as an aberration from the general pattern of the acceptance of newcomers and strangers, that is, when their skins were "white." A younger generation of historians, living in a post-Holocaust world and reacting to the negative image of the United States as a racist and imperialist nation which arose with the tide of the racial revolution and radical politics in the 1960s, have argued that anti-Semitism was as endemic to the United States as it was to Europe. These revisionists have, in turn, been challenged by others who contend that manifestations of anti-Semitism in the United States, which surely can be enumerated, have never received the historic sanction of the national state, of national law, or of national institutions as they have in Europe.[12]

Although it is unlikely that scholars will resolve the question readily, several of the essays in this volume do contend that anti-Semitism was less prevalent in the West than it was elsewhere in the country, particularly in the Northeast. It is suggestive that Jewish pioneer merchants in the West were welcomed by their neighbors far more equitably than were their counterparts in the East; that Jews were elected to public office at every level in the West, where they formed an insignificant part of the electorate, long before Jews attained such recognition in the East; and that in an era when Jews were still being accepted into elite circles in San Francisco, they were being excluded from New York society. Whatever the reasons, whether the West's reception of Jews reflected the region's initial cosmopolitanism, the Jewish pioneer role in the founding of many western towns, or the absence of large numbers of Eastern European immigrants, this is a subject that warrants further attention.

Finally, all the authors have incorporated a comparative perspective into their discussions, and this is especially important. Essential as it is to ground the history of the Jews in the West in the particulars of the local Jewish communities, the imaginative historian must always reach out for a larger comparative framework. What is specifically western about western Jewish history can be discerned clearly only when compared with the experience of Jews in other regions, and, in some instances, in other countries. On the other hand, what is uniquely Jewish about the history of Jews in the West can be understood only by comparing their history with the histories of westerners of other ethnic and religious origins. The first and last essays in this book illustrate the virtues of these two comparative approaches. Moses Rischin compares and contrasts the history of the Jews in the West with the history of the Jews in the Northeast, whereas Earl Pomeroy explores the history of the Jews of the West alongside the histories of other groups who have peopled "the last frontier." The other contributors have highlighted other frameworks of comparison. All demonstrate that the history of the Jews in the West, if it is to avoid the pitfalls of parochialism and antiquarianism, must be understood in relation to the history of Jews in other regions of the United States and, at times, in other places in the world.

If the authors of these essays have generated new perspectives and placed previously explored matters in new contexts, there are aspects of the history of the Jews of the West that of necessity have gone unmentioned. Most sorely missed in a volume of this kind is a discussion of intergroup relations. Although a few important studies have appeared that analyze group relations elsewhere in the nation,[13] the interaction of western Jews with their varied neighbors has gone virtually untold. The theme may be especially fruitful in the Southwest and in southern California where the encounter between Jews and Hispanics may offer a different perspective on the patterns of intergroup relations than those already portrayed.[14]

Despite the many gaps in our knowledge, the great strides made in the last few decades in the study of what might be called the New American Jewish History as well as the phenomenal expansion in the parameters of the whole field of American history hold out the promise of rich new syntheses for both. We trust that this will also be true for the histories of the West and of its Jews. Hopefully, the essays in this volume will contribute to the furtherance of these important goals.

Notes

1. James Bryce, cited in Howard R. Lamar, "Frederick Jackson Turner," in Marcus Cunliffe and Robin Winks, eds., *Pastmasters: Some Early Essays on American Historians* (New York, 1969), 84.

2. Frederick Jackson Turner, "The Significance of the Frontier in American History," *Report of the American Historical Association for 1893* (Washington, DC, 1894), 199–227. For scholarly efforts to review and revive the Turner thesis, see Jackson K. Putnam, "The Turner Thesis and the Westward Movement: A Reappraisal," *Western Historical Quarterly*, 7 (October 1976), 377–404, and William Cronon, "Revisiting the Vanishing Frontier: The Legacy of Frederick Jackson Turner," *Western Historical Quarterly*, 17 (April 1987), 157–76. Two extremely valuable volumes of collected essays that assess the entire field of western history are Michael P. Malone, ed., *Historians and the American West* (Lincoln, NE, 1983), and Roger L. Nichols, ed., *American Frontier and Western Issues: A Historiographical Review* (New York, 1986). More recent works on western history include the controversial and provocatively entitled *The Legacy of Conflict: The Unbroken Past of the American West* (New York, 1987) by Patricia Limerick; Clyde A. Milner II, ed., *Major Problems in the History of the American West: Documents and Essays* (Boston, 1989), which reflects the latest historiography; and for the twentieth century Michael

P. Malone and Richard Etulain, *The American West: A Twentieth-Century History* (Lincoln, NE, 1989) and Gerald Nash and Richard Etulain, eds., *The Twentieth Century West: Historical Interpretations* (Albuquerque, 1989).

3. American Historical Association, "We Have Seen the Future and It Needs Work: Report of the Ad Hoc Committee on the Future of the AHA," *Perspectives,* 26 (September 1988), 6.

4. For general treatments of ethnic pluralism in the West, see Frederick C. Luebke, "Ethnic Minority Groups in the American West," in Malone, *Historians,* 387–413; Carlton C. Qualey, "Ethnic Groups and the Frontier," in Nichols, *American Frontier,* 199–216; and Frederick C. Luebke, *Ethnicity on the Great Plains* (Lincoln, NE, 1980).

5. Merle Curti, *The Making of an American Community: A Case Study of Democracy in a Frontier County* (Palo Alto, 1959). For an assessment of Curti's attempt to apply the methods of the New Social History to the history of the West in a test of the Turner thesis, see James A. Henretta, *"The Making of an American Community: A Thirty-Year Retrospective."* *Reviews in American History,* 16 (September 1988), 506–12.

6. William Toll, "The 'New Social History' and Recent Jewish Historical Writing," *American Jewish History,* 69 (March 1980), 325–41; Deborah Dash Moore, "The Construction of Community, Jewish Migration and Ethnicity in the United States," in Moses Rischin, ed., *The Jews of North America* (Detroit, 1987), 105–17.

7. Moses Rischin, "Beyond the Great Divide: Immigration and the Last Frontier," *Journal of American History,* 55 (June 1968), 42–53.

8. Max Vorspan and Lloyd P. Gartner, *History of the Jews of Los Angeles* (San Marino, CA, 1970); Moses Rischin, ed., *The Jews of the West: The Metropolitan Years* (Berkeley, 1979); Fred Rosenbaum, *Free to Choose: The Making of a Jewish Community in the American West: The Jews of Oakland, California, from the Gold Rush to the Present Day* (Berkeley, 1976); idem, *Architects of Reform: Congregational and Community Leadership, Emanu-El of San Francisco, 1849–1980* (Berkeley, 1980); Robert Levinson, *The Jews in the California Gold Rush* (New York, 1978); William Toll, *The Making of an Ethnic Middle Class: Portland Jewry over Four Generations* (Albany, NY, 1982); Robert A. Goldberg, *Back to the Soil: The Jewish Farmers of Clarion, Utah, and Their World* (Salt Lake City, 1986).

9. Harriet Rochlin and Fred Rochlin, *Pioneer Jews: A New Life in the Far West* (Boston, 1984); and Kenneth Libo and Irving Howe, *We Lived There Too* (New York, 1984). Two other works of popular western Jewish history also deserve mention: Irene Narell, *Our City: The Jews of San Francisco* (San Diego, 1980) and Bernice Scharlach, *House of Harmony: Concordia-Argonaut's First 130 Years* (Berkeley, 1983). For the holdings of the major repository for western Jewish history, see Ruth K. Rafael, *Western Jewish History Center: Guide to Archival and Oral History Collections* (Berkeley, 1987.)

10. See John Laslett and Mary Tyler, *The ILGWU in Los Angeles 1907–1988* (Los Angeles, 1989) and the as yet unpublished paper by Laslett, "Gender, Class, and Race: The Role of Rose Pesotta in the Los Angeles ILGWU, 1933–1942." A popularly written collection of essays on the Jewish role in the clothing industry in southern California, including one on Los Angeles's ILGWU locals, is "Two Pair of Pants Come with This Coat—A Perfect Fit: History of the Jews in the Southern California Apparel Business," *Legacy,* 1 (Spring 1988), 1–76.

11. There is no study of the role of Jews in the Communist party in the West. Howard Suber, "Politics and Popular Culture: Hollywood at Bay, 1933–1953," in Rischin, *The Jews of the West,* focuses on the Hollywood Ten. Also see David Caute, *The Great Fear: The Anti-Communist Purge Under Truman and Eisenhower* (New York, 1978), 487–520; Victor Navasky, *Naming Names* (New York, 1980); and Larry Ceplain and

Introduction

Steven England, *The Inquistion in Hollywood: Politics in the Film Community* (New York, 1980). Harvey Klehr, *Communist Cadre* (Stanford, CT, 1978); and idem. *The Heyday of American Communism: The Depression Years* (New York, 1984) cast some light on the California scene, as does an oral history edited by Kenneth Kann, *Joe Rapoport: The Life of a Jewish Radical* (Philadelphia, 1981).

12. David Gerber, "Anti-Semitism and Jewish-Gentile Relations in American Historiography and the American Past," in David Gerber, ed., *Anti-Semitism in American History* (Urbana and Chicago, 1986), 3–56.

13. Indispensable for interethnic relations is Scott Cline, "Jewish-Ethnic Interactions: A Bibliographic Essay," *American Jewish History,* 77 (September 1987), 135–54. Especially valuable are the works of Rudolf Glanz, the pioneer historian of the relations between Jews and other ethnics. See, for example, "Jews and Chinese in America," in his *Studies in Judaica Americana* (New York, 1970), 314–29. For relations between Jews and blacks see Hasia Diner, *In the Almost Promised Land: American Jews and Blacks, 1915–1935* (Westport, CT, 1977). Ronald Bayor, *Neighbors in Conflict: The Irish, Germans, Jews and Italians of New York City, 1929–1941* (Baltimore, 1979) is thus far the most ambitious study of interethnic relations.

14. For first-rate studies of the Hispanic communities in southern California and Tucson, see Leonard Pitt, *The Decline of the Californios: A Social History of the Spanish-Speaking Californias, 1846–1890* (Berkeley, 1966); and Thomas E. Sheridan, *Los Tucsonenses: The Mexican Community in Tucson, 1854–1941* (Tucson, 1986). A superb monograph that does discuss Jewish-Hispanic business relations in the nineteenth century in detail is William J. Parrish, *The Charles Ilfeld Company: A Study of the Rise and Decline of Mercantile Capitalism in New Mexico* (Cambridge, MA, 1961).

25

Chapter 1

The Jewish Experience in America:

A View from the West

MOSES RISCHIN

Introduction

The initial essay in this collection offers a broad overview of Jewish history in the West. Perched on the hills of San Francisco and gazing back across the continent as have so many westerners, Moses Rischin reflects on the westward movement, the settlement patterns, and the incorporation of the newly peopled region into the greater American society. Continentalization, as he has called it, and the critical role the West, of course, has played in that process is the theme he has chosen to illuminate the history of the Jews of the region.

Approaching western Jewish history as a species of western and of American Jewish history, Rischin demonstrates that shifts in the centrality of the West to American patterns of development have their parallels in American Jewish history. Because the Jews of the West have been so far separated by geography from the centers of American Jewish culture in the Northeast, all too often western Jewish history has been ignored, viewed as "an anomaly," and regarded as "of little significance." But, as Rischin argues, such was not always the case. In the latter half of the nineteenth century, when the West loomed large in the American imagination, it appeared equally attractive to Jews.

The West of the late nineteenth century, the scene of boom and bust and boom again, was a region of phenomenal expansion gauged by any index of growth, whether demographic, economic, or political. The opportunities offered by the West in these years attracted a polyglot mix of emigrants from almost every corner of the globe. The Jewish presence in the West in the third quarter of the nineteenth century was important, Rischin insists, even when measured against the far larger Jewish presence in the East. As evidence he points to the fact that in 1877 California had more communities where Jews were to be found than did any other state in the Union, including New

York, whereas the Far West accounted for 8 percent of all Jews in the United States.

As the final stages of the peopling of the continent reached its farthest rim along the California and Pacific shore and the continentalization of the United States became a reality, a world-centered cosmopolitanism was fashioned by people of diverse ethnic, religious, national, and racial backgrounds. It was, according to Rischin, a cultural outlook that looked back to the East from which so many of the newly arrived had come, but it also looked west across the Pacific, from which other immigrants had journeyed, as well as south to Mexico and beyond to Latin America. For Jews, the loose-jointed cosmopolitan society of the West offered not only economic opportunity but social acceptance and political place markedly in advance of other regions of the country.

If the West was cosmopolitan in the closing decades of the nineteenth century, as Rischin contends, California was its most cosmopolitan state and San Francisco its most cosmopolitan city, ranking second only to New York City as the largest and the most cosmopolitan Jewish community in the nation. Yet, Rischin observes, the Jewish "cultural and intellectual life [of San Francisco] has not yet even quite begun to be identified, no less understood."

From the 1880s until World War II, the expansion of the West slowed and the booming industrializing centers of the Northeast and North Central regions attracted the new Jewish immigrants from Eastern Europe. As a result, the Jewish population in the West increased only moderately declining in proportion to the nation's total Jewish population and relegating western Jewry to the periphery of American Jewish life. If in the era of the first migration Jews flocked westward along with so many others in pursuit of the American dream, by the first years of the twentieth century, the dream had paled, immigration had slowed, and the failure of the utopian agricultural colonies at New Odessa, Oregon, and elsewhere signified the West's limited capacity to attract great numbers of immigrants.

World War II revitalized the West, revived its cosmopolitanism, and restored its place of centrality in the nation. For Jews and others the West again became a magnet promising a better life, a freer atmosphere, and an openness to experiment and innovation. In short order, Los Angeles became the second most populous Jewish city in the country, national Jewish leadership increasingly came to be drawn from the West, and western Jewry reemerged as a major force in American Jewish life. The new role enjoyed by the Jews of the West on the national Jewish scene leads Rischin to conclude his essay with the challenge that others take up "the need to understand the historic implications of the continentalization of the Jewish experience. . . . So formidable a theme . . . has ramifications that extend into every aspect of American and Jewish life, both at home and abroad. Hopefully, it is a theme that ought to strike a responsive chord and be pursued by historians eager to comprehend the Jewish experience in the West in its broadest and most rewarding terms."

THE JEWISH EXPERIENCE IN AMERICA

The overarching theme of this volume, and most certainly of this essay, inevitably arouses expectations of a realignment of historical sights as well as of direction. "The Jewish Experience in America: A View from the West" appears to imply that geography is not merely an important factor in any interpretation or understanding of the Jewish experience in the West, but that it is a key factor. It assumes as well that the West has been radically different from the South, the Midwest, and most notably from the Northeast, for so long the hub of American Jewish life. The thinness and brevity of the West's history by Eurocentric standards—what William James on a brief sojourn in California in 1905 spoke of as "the great historic vacuum . . . absolute silence before fifty years ago"—the awesomeness of its distances, and its seeming isolation all would appear to add up to a presumption of western Jewish exceptionalism, to the seeming ultimate in American and Jewish geographical mobility and historical discontinuity. In the West, where Judaism like Puritanism may appear to have gone on an extended holiday, older American time and historic Jewish time also may seem to have experienced an extraordinary lapse from commonly honored patterns.

This reading of the role of the West in the American Jewish experience as a tale of vanishing Jews and of a crepuscular Judaism is understandable and is not without basis. It fails, however, to take account of the precise historical circumstances that shaped the Jewish experience in a region that from the beginning occupied a vaunted place in the American Jewish imagination, even as it did in the American imagination. It may be that so little has been written along these lines because the West has seemed inseparable from the greater idea of America; because it has been associated with the repeated failure of agrarian dreams; because for many decades it was overshadowed by far more compelling developments elsewhere; or simply because the West, more than any other region in the nation, for long seemed so far distant from the fertile cultural crescent of Jewish life in the Northeast that it came to be viewed by default or in absence of mind as an anomaly and of little significance for an understanding of the larger American Jewish experience.

This certainly was not so in the mid-nineteenth century when the West veered into the center of American Jewish consciousness, and it has not been so in our own time when a greater proportion of America's Jews have come to live in the region than ever before. It is not mere chance that in the first wide-ranging account of America to be written by a Jewish traveler—and still the most ambitious effort of its kind—the Jewish experience in the West so calculatedly dominates the almost six-hundred-page text that it well warrants the title, *My Years in California and the West, with a Brief Report on the United States of America*, rather than the more general title the author chose to give it. Published in German in 1862, Israel Joseph Benjamin's *Three Years in America*, which waited nearly a century to be translated into English, caught the western experience near flood tide.[1] At a time when the American West, most notably California, captivated the world as did virtually no other spot on earth, the author's name might well have become a legend, certainly in Jewish circles, if not for the outbreak of the Civil War and his own untimely death in 1864 at age forty-six shortly after the book's publication. Crammed with facts, observations, and often superficial and pungently prejudiced assessments of people and motives as well as with a rich miscellany of information garnered from a wide variety of sources and incorporated bodily into the text, the two volumes still make fascinating reading. Especially arresting is Benjamin's portentous and almost apocalyptic preface. Imbued with a vein of messianic mid-nineteenth-century nationalism—akin to mission, not to manifest destiny—he ascribes almost redemptive propensities to his fellow Jews. In free America, most especailly in California, he sees them destined at last to fulfill their providential role, as it were, of bringing all the peoples of the world together.

> Where everything was just beginning [wrote Benjamin,] and in the pro-
> cess of becoming—and, to a certain extent, still is in that condition; where
> it is still possible to plant the seed of civilization in virgin soil; where the
> foundation of the structure of the new state of necessity implied the
> acknowledgment of the common origin of all men and their common
> right to equality, there the example and activity of that race which knew
> how to use the delicate ties of family and the firm bonds of the religious
> community in order to unite into a single whole the cultures of the earth's
> varied areas would be of great and telling significance. In our day the
> development of California bears witness to this very situation.[2]

Benjamin's rhapsodic postulations, however romantic and extravagant, focused attention for the first time on a region and a state that
more than any other appeared from the outset to project—as seen
from a Jewish perspective—a sense of America at its most promising,
open, and refreshing. Surely that vision, despite its anachronous tenor,
still merits a place at the center of both the American and the American Jewish consciousness, not alone because it is significant in its
own terms, but because it was a harbinger of developments that have
come to a focus in our own time when the Jews of the West, and most
notably of California, again loom forth as central rather than peripheral to the life of the nation and to Jewish life. Although coming
a century apart, in both eras the West appeared to be an immediate
presence, close at hand, and a ready and vital extension rather than
a remote colonial appendage of a far-distant, older America. Above
all, the West proved to be a magnetic new epicenter, dramatizing what
might be called the continentalization of the American and the American Jewish experience, the emphatic projection to its Pacific limits
of that expansive American impulse that gave the third quarter of the
nineteenth century in the West a raw cosmopolitan world-centeredness
that was to be recapitulated a century later on an infinitely vaster and
more sophisticated scale.

The opening of California and the West to mass settlement in the
mid-nineteenth century came at a critical juncture in American, Jewish, and world history. The cresting of the first great wave of mass immigration from Europe, including the first large and variegated Jewish
immigration and the Chinese and Latin American migrations; the failed
revolutions of 1848; and the westward surge of American settlers and
adventurers from virtually every American state and territory precipi-
tously turned California in particular into the most multiethnic instant
commonwealth in the nation's history. The irrepressible lure of gold
and prosperity on the nation's first self-financing frontier, the near instant certification of European immigrants—if not of others—as Amer-

icans in a still unstructured and totally new society, and the completion in quick succession of the transcontinental telegraph and the first transcontinental railroad gave momentum, exuberance, and a sense of inordinate self-importance to the nation's newest region with its regnant American thrust. Directly tethered neither to pre-revolutionary nor to pre–Civil War America—for the West did not experience the American Revolution and was touched only obliquely by the Civil War—the West tendered pioneers (when they were Caucasians) a rough-and-ready American welcome that served to unite diverse newcomers in bonds of fraternity and solidarity with an ease, liberality, and independence not matched elsewhere in the country.[3]

From the beginning, the West attracted a decidedly youthful, mobile, adventurous, energetic, and eager-to-prosper throng of newcomers. The distances to be traversed and the costs and problematics of the journey of necessity proved to be self-selecting. If most immigrants traveled directly to their destinations in the West, particularly in the gold rush years, almost as many appear to have been transmigrants who moved in successive stages and who were apprenticed to American life along the way. Succeeding in good times, failing in bad, they rapidly learned to cope with the strange and unfamiliar. As a consequence, by the time these seasoned adventurers reached their final destinations, they were undoubtedly more schooled in American ways than the majority who had remained behind in the older regions of the country. Readily entering into the everyday rhythms of American life in places large and small, they often found themselves virtually on a par with the native-born. Whether in Roseburg, Grass Valley, or Nevada City, . . . whether in Denver, Portland, San Francisco, or in scores of smaller towns, Jews along with others from the German lands appear to have been among the best organized of the newcomers.[4] Undoubtedly, their frequent role as public officeholders also reflected the easy acceptance of able and energetic first-comers in an unstructured region where all outsiders were potential insiders whose private interests were inseparable from their public concerns.[5]

Whether earlier or later, California inevitably attracted the overwhelming majority of Jews, as it did of other migrants. When the founder of American Reform Judaism toured the West in quest of support for his new religious movement in 1877, a census of the Jews of the United States taken that year revealed that 84 percent of the Jews of the region were in California. As elsewhere in the country and the West, the new arrivals were widely dispersed, thus reflecting the diffuse pattern of settlement and commerce of the era of westward expansion. Indeed, California stood first in the nation in the number of places where Jews were to be found—eighty-nine in all. New York stood second with seventy-three, followed by Pennsylvania with seventy, and Illinois with sixty-eight, whereas fourteen other states each reported from twenty-seven to fifty-nine localities where Jews were to be found. Elsewhere in the West, Oregon, Nevada, Colorado, Utah, Idaho, Washington, Arizona, and Wyoming reported an additional three score communities with Jewish inhabitants and surely there were more, for New Mexico with a significant scattering of Jews went surprisingly unreported. With the West as a whole accounting for one-tenth of all communities in the United States with Jews and comprising over 8 percent of the Jews in the nation, the region had attained a high watermark that would not be surpassed for nearly a century.[6]

Equally striking was the singular place of the metropolis in the western Jewish experience. In these years, the metropolis like no other in the West was, of course, San Francisco, "one of the wonders of the nineteenth century," exulted Isaac Mayer Wise, proud trumpeter of his beloved Cincinnati—renowned as the Queen City of the West—and thus no mean judge. In San Francisco Jews of all origins and persuasions could hope to enjoy the freedom to pursue varied opportunities and lead vibrant lives, to assimilate the best of modern America and the modern world, and to satisfy their special needs as Jews, which they could not readily do in small towns. With its unsurpassed harbor appointed to shelter the fleets of all the world's nations and with the great California Valley—if effectively watered—potentially able to supply the grain needs of all the world's peoples, San Francisco emerged an instant world city. In so immense, sparsely settled, and far-flung a region that extended over one-third of the continental land area of the United States, the city was strategically situated, as was no other for a thousand and more miles around—north, south, east, or west—to serve, above all, as the portal to world civilization. Indeed, for a vast hinterland isolated from the rest of the country and world by forbidding mountains, endless deserts, awesome distances, and an otherwise near harborless coastline, it was civilization itself. In the 1870s, with one-third of the population of California living in San Francisco, Jews made up 7 to 8 percent of its inhabitants.[7]

Virtually on first coming to San Francisco, Jews, like so many newcomers from every state in the Union and all the world's continents, sensed themselves to be in a singularly cosmopolitan city. Most of them would have agreed with the favored sojourner, Henry George, that San Francisco was "New York, Boston, Portland, Philadelphia, Richmond, and Charleston . . . rolled into one."[8] To many others it was the hoped-for New York of the Pacific. As an earnest of their faith

Temple Emanu-El, San Francisco, 1867, "attracts the eye before all the Christian churches." (Courtesy of the San Francisco Public Library.)

in the city's unlimited prospects, the founders of San Francisco's two charter synagogues named them in 1851 after New York's best, Shearith Israel and Emanu-El, and they were not to be disappointed. Within a generation, San Francisco's Jewish population was to become second only to that of New York City, if admittedly only a distant second, just as California's Jewish population briefly was to stand second to that of New York State and slightly ahead of that of Pennsylvania, with Ohio and Illinois lagging considerably behind.

With 16,000 Jews in the 1870s, San Francisco more than any other city west of the Hudson became the natural site for an embryonic Jewish cultural and intellectual life that has not yet even begun to be identified, no less understood. Without equal in the country in proportion to its population in its support for writers and newspapers of all kinds in those years, San Francisco briefly even challenged New York as a center of Jewish journalism. With four Anglo-Jewish weeklies—the *Hebrew* (1863–1887), the *Hebrew Observer*, (1856–188?), the *Progress* (1877–1896), and the *Voice of Israel* (1870–1874)—appearing almost simultaneously, the city lacked only a proto-Yiddish journal to bring it abreast of New York's five weekly newspapers, and it surpassed Cincinnati, the midwestern Jewish metropolis of the old West, most especially of Reform Jewish America. Alone among American cities, San Francisco also took singular pride in its Jewish library. With no less than twenty-five hundred volumes, which increased more than fourfold before the 1906 earthquake and fire destroyed books, library, and all, it had been founded by the Independent Order of B'nai B'rith, with no less than seven lodges, including well-named Ophir No. 21, the most affluent B'nai B'rith lodge in the country.[9]

Vital, free-wheeling, and cosmopolitan, San Francisco's renowned instant subculture of literary journalism also spawned the first satirist of America's Jews. For two decades beginning in 1873, in weekly penny-a-line letters to Cincinnati's national Jewish weekly, the *American Israelite*, its San Francisco correspondent, I. N. Choynski, regularly twitted his fellow Jews unsparingly. Over the byline "Maftir," the last one called to the synagogue dais on the Sabbath to read the weekly portion from the prophets, he, indeed, appeared to have the last word, at least in his column. Journalist, printer, antiquarian bookseller, and much else, this son of a learned rabbi and father of a noted heavyweight boxer proved to be the Pacific seaboard's first seriocomic voice of the Hebrew enlightenment as it was modulated by the unencumbered frontier metropolis.[10]

As a matter of course, San Francisco also prided itself on the West's most renowned Jewish edifice. Like no other building in the nation, the region's cathedral synagogue dramatically came to symbolize the freedom, equality, openness, and fraternity of America and of the West for Jews and others. Completed in barely eighteen months in 1866, the new twin-spired Sutter Street Temple was promptly hailed as the city's "most sumptuous ecclesiastic edifice" that "attracts the eye before all the Christian churches." By contrast, the magnificent Mormon Tabernacle and the Mormon Temple in Salt Lake City were to be erected in a remote Utah valley where the Church of Jesus Christ of Latter-day Saints, the West's most indigenous religious sect, found the seclusion and isolation where "the pure in heart do flow" that Jews did not seek.[11]

A pioneer identification with both the extraordinary metropolis of San Francisco and with over 150 communities throughout the West in the first era of American Jewish continentalism would establish the vaunted tradition of the founders. These later-mythicized Jewish westerners, who were to play significant roles in city, state, and region, derived their important place in the West and in Jewish life from their standing as pioneers in the watershed years of the West, years that are only beginning to be understood. Despite the impressive scholarship of the past generation, this era has spurred no authoritative studies that portray with intellectual discernment and sociological imagination either the long-term generational continuities or the discontinuities in the western Jewish experience in the course of the last century.

Our understanding of the first era of Jewish continentalism would be incomplete, however, without some appreciation of the most dramatic, inspiring, and disastrous venture in the whole history of the Jewish westward migration: the founding of agricultural colonies, exemplified especially by the utopian community of New Odessa, Oregon, at the West's Pacific edge. No other expression of Jewish pioneering appeared to be so in accord with classic frontier models, if not quite the Turnerian one, and none was as symbolic of the disjuncture between the first era of westward Jewish migration and the one that followed. Better than any other single episode, the rise and fall of New Odessa signalized the passing of the first era of continentalism and the posting of limits to mass Jewish migration westward by East European newcomers.

If the Edenic myth of an American terrestrial paradise never quite gained an equivalence in the Jewish imagination,[12] it came close to doing so in the 1880s. If ever immigrants entertained a grand vision of themselves as latter-day pilgrims destined for the promised land, the Am Olamites from Russia of the "heroic era of 1881 and 1882" certainly stood among the foremost. With the passion of the earliest Zionist pioneers who went to the malarial swamps and torrid deserts of Palestine in precisely these years, *livnot ulehibanot*, to build and to be rebuilt, as later Zionists would proclaim their mission, the Eternal People, implicitly Jewish in impulse even as their ideology strained for the universal, came to repossess the land and to reconstitute themselves into new people, into children of the soil like their ancient ancestors. So redolent with the fever of agrarian utopianism were the 1880s that a leading pioneer predicted that half a million Jewish farmers would in time derive their livelihoods from the land.

Of the score of Jewish colonies founded between 1881 and 1883 from Sicily Island, Louisiana, to Bethlehem–Yehudah and Painted Woods in the Dakotas to Cotopaxi in the Rockies, New Odessa — seven thousand miles away from the Russian city to which it owed its name —

was regarded as the most exemplary of their number. "Most promising of all—strong by the tried endurance and fortitude of its youthful members—is the remotest of the Russian colonies, New Odessa," rejoiced Michael Heilprin, forty-eighter, abolitionist, and the colonists' most stalwart friend from the community's founding early in 1883. Not only did New Odessa's leaders plan to build steamships on the Pacific shore so that they might liberate Russian exiles in Siberia, but they cherished a vision of a colony ultimately of two thousand strong, one that would make a genuine impact on the world. "This was the only attempt of the members of the Jewish intelligentsia to establish a colony through their own means," wrote an admiring contemporary, "the only group which maintained its identity" from its founding in Brody in 1882, as the so-called Odessa commune, until its final dissolution a decade later.[13]

Of all the immigrants who came to America with the aim of building a new society on the land, the youth of New Odessa comprised a self-constituted elite. Led by the repentant Russian nobleman and positivist preacher of the religion of humanity, Vladimir Konstantinovich Heins, better known by his adopted new libertarian American name, William Frey, they were passionately dedicated to "mutual assistance in perfecting" and developing the "physical, mental, and moral capacities," as they put it, of their members and to becoming new people. Only the absence among them of a gifted novelist deprived the plain living and high thinking Odessa Society of Ploughmen, as they called themselves, of the legendary renown that Nathaniel Hawthorne Ploughman conferred on the transcendental votaries of Brook Farm in *The Blithedale Romance*. The tribute paid to New Odessa's veterans by their earliest chronicler in 1904, over a decade after the commune's official demise, must, therefore, suffice. "They are," wrote Herman Rosenthal, "currently fighting with one another, and indeed the entire world, on behalf of their ideas and opinions. In spite of the graying hair on their heads, each and every one of them still has his own unique ideas. Each of them wears tinted glasses through which only he can gain the 'true' perspective on the occurences and past events of the setttlement. . . . The majority of the participants in this tragi-comedy are still alive. They are still hoping for the day when their dream will come true."[14]

Perhaps the best test of the potency of the New Odessa dream may be measured by the lifelong devotion to it of its most successful alumnus, at least by worldly standards, the president and most long-lived of the Odessa Society of Ploughmen, Peter Fireman (1863–1962). A renowned scientist and manufacturing chemist, the oldest member

Twenty members of the New Odessa Farm Colony shortly after their arrival from Russia, c. 1885. (Courtesy of the New York Public Library.)

of Washington's prestigious scientific Cosmos Club, who was listed in *Who's Who in America* from its inception until his death sixty-three years later, just short of his centennial, Fireman never quite relinquished the badge of heroic distinction that he associated with his New Odessa years. From the laconic phrase, "farmed in western Oregon for several years," which he included in his biographical sketch in *Who's Who* in the first dozen years, to his virtual epitaph, in which he attempted to reconcile Plato with Marx, *Justice in Plato's Republic*, published privately in his ninety-fifth year, Fireman never shook off the vision of the perfect society inseparable from the New Odessa of his youth.[15]

Clearly, the era of continentalism for the immigrant generation had come to a close. In the early decades of the twentieth century, the great majority of the nation's Jews would become ever more rooted in the northeastern quadrant of the country, where the greatest industrial economy in the world was providing millions of newcomers with opportunities for employment and allowing for the establishment of the varied religious, social, and cultural institutions and associations that they would require to serve their complex needs. The unequaled industrialization of the Great Lakes region—the only area in the country that showed a greater rate of population growth in the century's second decade than it did in the first—more than confirmed the place of the nation's industrial heartland in the lives of immigrants and their children. At a time when from 90 to 92 percent of America's Jews were to be found in the Northeast and East North Central states, the West appeared out of range for all but a small minority. As a result, the percentage of the nation's Jews in the region fell from over 8 percent in the 1870s to 3 to 4 percent half a century later. The disappointing rate of growth in the opening years of the twentieth century of the West's greatest city and the only western city comparable to the great eastern centers was symptomatic not only of the falloff in immigration to the West from Europe but of its limited possibilities for industrial expansion. San Francisco's population had grown at an inspired 31 percent clip annually between 1900 and 1906, including a few thousand Russian Jewish immigrants, but declined 7 percent in the next four years in the wake of the 1906 earthquake and fire, the all-time peak year of Jewish immigration.[16] Predictions that San Francisco was destined to stand among the nation's supreme urban centers, ranking just below New York, Chicago, and Philadelphia, proved ill-timed. Elsewhere in the West, modest growth and low wages prevailed in those industires where semiskilled and unskilled Jewish immigrants might expect to secure employment and gain ready entry into the labor force—even booming Los Angeles in the 1920s would offer them only limited opportunities. Although a significant number of immigrants, induced to go west by the Industrial Removal Office and other Jewish social agencies, provoked a mild chain migration, bringing a significant number of Russian Jews to Denver, Portland, and Los Angeles, particularly, the distant, underpopulated, and underdeveloped West could not satisfy the cravings of great numbers of immigrants for a vibrantly immediate Jewish society resonating with the energy of a magnetic new metropolitan culture.[17] In an intimidating strange new world, the immigrants' yearning for group and personal fulfillment on their own terms, in one of the most wrenching periods in Jewish history, had to be braced, refreshed, and fortified by the power of place and the strength of numbers. In these years, mounting anti-immigration sentiment in the West, without equal elsewhere in the country, may further have inhibited Jewish immigrants from venturing westward. In any case, the number of "Russians" enumerated in the census, not all of them Jews by any means, rose from 1,500 in 1900 to a mere 5,800 in San Francisco in 1920.[18]

No more poignant evidence of the disjuncture in Jewish life in the West in the early twentieth century between the earlier cosmopolitanism and a growing provincialism is likely to be found than in two revealing letters. Of a mere handful that survived the 1906 earthquake and fire, they were written by the West's leading rabbi to his gifted protégé, Judah Magnes, who was to become the region's first native-born rabbi, founder and first chancellor and president of the Hebrew University, and America's first "totally free" Jew. Like most of his Reform colleagues of the late nineteenth and early twentieth centuries, Jacob Voorsanger was a militant Americanist, ever embattled and unsparing in his denunciation of virtually all Jewish customs and traditions that might make Jews appear oriental and unwestern.[19] Yet in his relations with the younger man, who certainly did not have to be Americanized, Voorsanger shed the mask of the public man and revealed himself in an entirely different light. Shortly before young Magnes's ordination at the Hebrew Union College, Voorsanger not only counseled his protégé to go on to higher Jewish studies and promised to secure financial assistance for him so that he might do so but commended a course of study to Magnes that smacked as much of counter-reform as it did of reform, as much of going back to oriental Talmud as it did of going forward to occidental *Wissenschaft*. Voorsanger wrote to Magnes:

> I know somewhat of the Cincinnati atmosphere, or rather the lack of it. You need the mellowing influence of the European universities and the steadying processes of some old Yeshiba [sic]. I want you to have them both. Cincinnati has been a training school for ministers, not a home for scholars as yet, and of its sixty odd graduates not one could make a showing in a conversation of learned scholars. . . . I want you to become a scholar. I want you to have these years in Germany and a Ph.D. degree, and if possible a *Semicha* from a European college. One of the great weaknesses of the present period is that the pew is outgrowing the pulpit in intellectuality. We are not keeping track of that splendid university bred generation that finds nothing in the Synagogue to attract them. We need eminent scholars for such people, not mere readers of the scriptures and composers of flat and stale sentences. If the message of God is to [enter] into these young American Jews it can only be done by men whose life was touched with the coal of fire that the angel laid on Isaiah's lips, men who are at the same time permeated with the genuine, not the

counterfeit spirit of Judaism. I have always hoped great things for you, and your going to Europe has always been part of my plans.[20]

Five years later, when Magnes emerged as the nation's leading young Zionist, Voorsanger, the unrelenting anti-Zionist, not only bestowed his personal blessings upon the young rabbi but revealed the depth of his ambivalence no less than his commitment to a pluralistic Judaism that was notabley absent from his public utterances. He wrote:

> You have the future before you. If Zionism is your aim, concentrate; we in America need the vigorous touch of association; and it has not yet marked us. I have heard of your successes at the Congresses and I have rejoiced in them, little as I sympathize with the movement; for as I conceive it, its territorial aspects are chimerical, while its moral aspects are in no wise moral. . . . Still I can see when Judaism needs the great lever of ambition and loyalty, of attributes of persistence grafted on the [constitution] of every Jew, and if you once pull and work those levers you will become a great man, as in my obscurity I hope and pray you may become. I cannot be a Zionist, but I can admire . . . the persistency that seeks to regenerate Israel, to resuscitate its soul, to restore its honor, to rejuvenate its inheritance and I will quarrel with no adjectives in my anxiety to do honor to the man or men who will achieve this hope.[21]

However, the sorry demagogy to which Jacob Voorsanger and some of his contemporaries of the late nineteenth and early twentieth century felt driven in their public efforts to reconcile the American, Jewish, and western elements in their conception of themselves as American Jews, scored the growing provincialism of the West and set limits to the region's capacity for Jewish leadership and the acceptance of newcomers who were different.

Only with the social, economic, and technological transformation set in motion during World War II, wrought by nearly a half-century of change in every aspect of American and Jewish life, would the West enter upon a second great era of continentalism that would catapult the region into the role of potential pacesetter in American and Jewish life. In the 1960s and 1970s the precipitous decline of the industrial Northeast and Midwest and the deterioration of their aging central cities further contributed to an increasing shift in the nation's center of gravity and a radical regional realignment that would bring the periphery ever-closer to the center. The high-speed automobile; the sleek interstate highway network; the jet plane; instant electronic, telephonic, and satellite communication; the massive migration of Asians and Mexicans; and the unprecendented challenge of the Pacific Basin to the proverbial hegemony of the North Atlantic revolutionized the American perception and experience of time, space, direction, and society. By the early 1970s when San Francisco's Levi Strauss Company zoomed past Chicago's Hart Schaffner & Marx on *Fortune's* 500 list of the largest industrials, the West appeared to have displaced the older American heartland as standard-bearer of the nation's and the world's postindustrial life-styles. Not since Henry Ford's Model T had an American product become so associated in the public mind with the "American way" as had the ubiquitous Levis.

In the third quarter of the twentieth century, the West, and most notably California—where in April 1945 in San Francisco as if in anticipation of a new Pacific parity the United Nations was founded—reemerged uncontestably as a world center. In California, particularly, almost overnight an array of business, educational, scientific, and cultural institutions of world stature conspicuously registered levels of aspiration and accomplishment second to none. A region once celebrated for its remoteness from the original thirteen states and designated the Far West by cartographers seated at drawing boards closer to the prime meridian than to the 120th called forth a new nomenclature. If Santa Barbara, Whittier, and Palo Alto have yet to rival Hyde Park, Monticello, and Mount Vernon as national shrines, and if Denver no longer seems destined to become the nation's summer capital, there was no doubting that in the 1980s the West, with nearly 20 percent of the nation's population and one-sixth of its Jews, had come to play an unprecedented role in American life.

Inevitably, Los Angeles, the nation's second city and its unrivaled neometropolis, has become the most spectacular expression of the Jewish no less than the American westward tilt. To that impelling boom metropolis the newcomers of the mid-twentieth century, primarily native-born professsionals with college and university degrees, brought with them cosmopolitan perspectives that were in a short time to transform Jewish communal life in the region. It comes as no surprise that many of that city's boosters have viewed Los Angeles as the most dynamic center of Jewish life in the nation, the showcase and harbinger, for better or worse, of American and American Jewish life in the years to come. With a critical mass of some six hundred thousand Jews, numbers surpassed only by New York City, the Jews of Los Angeles in a remarkably short time have generated a host of religious and secular institutions that extend across the whole spectrum of American Jewish life. They also appear to have unselfconsciously infused the greater cultural, political, and institutional life of that region with something of their distinctive elan and expressiveness. Indeed, it even has been suggested that America's Jews, who traditionally face east when they pray, increasingly have been facing west when they seek new ideas and leaders with a continental American outlook, as is attested by the array of national organizations whose presidents have been drawn from southern California.[22]

In our time, Americans and Jews and westerners have come to see themselves as inhabitants of a universe and a nation that is pluralistic in impulse, expression, and consciousness, whether in ethnic, racial, religious, or sexual terms, to a degree unparalleled in American and world history. If anything, the American Jewish experience in the West in the late twentieth century may yet demonstrate that space is compatible with the cultivation and refinement of Jewish identity in ways heretofore not quite fully imagined. However "problematic—post-Judaic, post-secular, and remote even from an earlier subculture of Jewishness" are so many manifestations of Jewish life in the West, Jewish perpetuation and renewal appear intrinsic to the Jewish as to the human condition. Both in the nineteenth century as a heralded new region of the United States and again a century later when it emerged as a dynamic regional center of national and international dimensions, the West may yet extend and revitalize historic Jewish continuities to a degree and on a scale that has yet to be fully understood.[23]

It also may be that I. J. Benjamin's vision of a providential Jewish mission in the West, "to unite into a single whole the cultures of the earth's varied areas," no longer appears so extravagant and chimerical in a multiethnic America in search of ever-larger expression. In this process, the thirteen western states, most notably California, may become a fulcrum for an ever-newer America where Jews and their diverse fellow westerners may better come to appreciate the challenge to all that a historic American Jewish tradition in the making affords to the fulfillment and mutual reinforcement of a pluralistic American, no less than of a pluralistic Jewish life. In a nation that is in continual need of examples and reminders of the complexity of human relations, of the complementarity of peoples, of the fragility of civilization, and of the sanctity of all persons, the Jews of the West have come to inhabit a new world, not alone a new region, of the spirit. Still unfolding, that world region more than ever calls for historic guideposts.

The need to understand the historic implications of the continentalization of the Jewish experience has barely been suggested in this paper. So formidable a theme of course has ramifications that extend into every aspect of American and of American Jewish life, both at home and abroad. Hopefully, it is a theme that ought to strike a responsive chord and be pursued by historians eager to comprehend the Jewish experience in the West in the broadest and most rewarding terms.

Notes

1. Israel Joseph Benjamin, *Three Years in America, 1859–1862* 2 vols., trans. by Charles Reznikoff (Philadelphia, 1956), vol. 1; see pp. 1–9, vol. 1 for Oscar Handlin's summary. Curiously, Ray Billington's superb, *Land of Savagery, Land of Promise: The European Image of the American Frontier* (New York, 1981) fails to mention Benjamin's travel account.

2. *Three Years*, v. 1, 41.

3. Rodman W. Paul, *The Far West and the Great Plains in Transition 1859–1900* (New York, 1988), esp. Chap. 6, "Many Peoples," 121–68; and Moses Rischin, "Immigration, Migration, and Minorities in California," *Pacific Historical Review*, 41 (February 1972), 78–80. Also see Tony Fels, "Religious Assimilation in a Fraternal Organization: Jews and Freemasonry in Gilded-Age San Francisco," *American Jewish History*, 74 (June 1985), 369ff.

4. Moses Rischin, ed., *The Jews of the West: The Metropolitan Years* (Berkeley, 1979), 8; Peter Decker, *Fortunes and Failures* (Cambridge, MA, 1978), 81–84; Ralph Mann, *After the Gold Rush: Society in Grass Valley and Nevada City, California, 1849–1870* (Standord, CA, 1982), 50, 90, 120, 159, 173–74, 214–16; Stephen J. Leonard, "Denver's Foreign-Born Immigrants" (Ph.D. diss., Claremont Graduate School, CA, 1971), 90, 97–98, 104–5; cf. R. A. Burchell, *The San Francisco Irish, 1848–1880* (Berkeley, 1980); Timothy Sarbaugh, "Exiles of Confidence: The Irish-American Community of San Francisco, 1880–1920," in Timothy J. Meagher, ed., *From Paddy to Studs* (Westport, CT, 1986), 161–79; and Dino Cinel, *From Italy to San Francisco* (Stanford, CA 1982).

5. Harriet Rochlin and Fred Rochlin, *Pioneer Jews: A New Life in the Far West* (Boston, 1984), 158–59; William Toll, *The Making of an Ethnic Middle Class: Portland Jewry over Four Generations* (Albany, NY, 1982), 80–83.

6. See *Statistics of the Jews of the United States* (Philadelphia, 1880), passim. See Marc Lee Raphael, *Jews and Judaism in a Midwestern Community: Columbus, Ohio, 1840–1975* (Columbus, 1979), chap. 1, "Familiar Faces and Familiar Names: German Jewish Emigration," 9–16, for his astute estimate of the distinctive dynamics and geographical mobility of mid-nineteenth-century German Jewish immigrants.

7. William M. Kramer, ed., *The Western Journal of Isaac Mayer Wise, 1877* (Berkeley, 1974), 16; Earl Pomeroy, *The Pacific Slope: A History of California, Oregon, Washington, Idaho, Utah, and Nevada* (New York, 1965), 120ff.; Gunther Barth, *Instant Cities* (New York, 1975), 131; Moses Rischin, *The Promised City: New York's Jews, 1870–1914* (Cambridge, MA, 1962), 94. See Peter B. Hales, *Silver Cities: The Photography of American Urbanization, 1839–1915* (Philadelphia, 1984), pp. 33–34, 48–57, and William H. Goetzmann and William N. G. Goetzmann, *The West of the Imagination* (New York, 1986), pp. 127–41, for a record of the instant fame granted San Francisco by photographers and artists.

8. Quoted in Barth, *Instant Cities*, 219; William Issel and Robert W. Cherny, *San Francisco 1865–1932: Politics, Power, and Urban Development* (Berkeley, 1986), 23ff.

9. Pomeroy, *The Pacific Slope*, 158; *Statistics of the Jews of the United States*, 59; Sara G. Cogan, comp., *The Jews of San Francisco and the Greater Bay Area 1849–1919: An Annotated Bibliography* (Berkeley, 1973), 18; *Journal of Proceedings of the Forty-*

Third Annual Session . . . District Grand Lodge No. 4 (San Francisco, 1906), 69; David A. D'Ancona, *A California–Nevada Travel Diary of 1876*, ed. W. Kramer (Santa Monica, 1975), 18.

10. See Rudolf Glanz, *The Jews of California* (New York, 1960), 111–13, 133–37, 150ff.; Fred Rosenbaum, *Architects of Reform: Congregational and Community Leadership, Emanu-El of San Francisco, 1849–1980* (Berkeley, 1980), 136–41. Robert Singerman is at work on an annotated edition of Choynski's selected letters.

11. See Rosenbaum, *Architects of Reform*, 32–36; Oscar Handlin, ed., *This Was America* (Cambridge, MA 1947), 319; and Karen Lynn, "The Mormon Zion and the Jewish Golden Land," *Yiddish*, 5 (1984), 111.

12. Thomas A. Krueger, "The Historians and the Edenic Myth: A Critique," *Canadian Review of American Studies*, 4 (Spring 1973), 8–9.

13. *American Hebrew*, April 29, 1883, pp. 110–111; George M. Price, "The Russian Jews in America," in Abraham Karp, ed., *The Jewish Experience in America* (New York, 1969), 4, 311; Robert V. Hine, *Community on the American Frontier: Separate but Not Alone* (Norman, 1980), 82–83; Uri D. Herscher, *Jewish Agricultural Utopias in America: 1880–1910* (Detroit, 1981), 39 ff.

14. Malcolm Cowley, ed., *The Portable Hawthorne* (New York, 1948), 617; Lindsay Swift, *Brook Farm* (New York, 1900), v–vi, 47; Herman Rosenthal, ed., *Chronicles of the Communist Settlement Known by the Name "New Odessa,"* trans. by Gary P. Zola (Cincinnati, 1979), 1, 11.

15. Moses Rischin, "Am Olam: From Odessa, Russia, to New Odessa, Oregon, in the Ardent Eighties," (unpublished paper in author's possession); see *Who's Who in America, 1899–1963* (Chicago, 1963) and *National Cyclopedia of American Biography* (New York, 1970), v. 52, 271–72.

16. Gladys Hansen and Emmit Condon, *Denial of Disaster: The Untold Story and Photographs of the San Francisco Earthquake and Fire of 1906* (San Francisco, 1989), the most authoritative study to date, demonstrates that earthquake rather than fire caused an estimated three thousand deaths rather than the conventionally reported figure of five hundred.

17. *World Almanac 1947* (New York, 1947), 220; Herbert Croly, "The Promised City of San Francisco," *Architectural Record*, 16 (June 1906), 424; Max Vorspan and Lloyd P. Gartner, *History of the Jews of Los Angeles* (San Marino, CA, 1970), 109ff.; Bernard Marinbach, *Galveston: Ellis Island of the West* (Albany, NY, 1983), 182ff.; John Livingston, "The Industrial Removal Office, the Galveston Project, and the Denver Jewish Community," in Rischin, *Jews of the West*, 50ff.; and the unpublished paper by George J. Sanchez, "The Other Los Angeles: Chicanos, Jews, and Japanese on the Eastside, 1925–1945."

18. John Higham, *Strangers in the Land* (New York, 1955), 73–74, 165–66, 168, 174; Robert G. Athearn, *The Mythic West in Twentieth-Century America* (Lawrence, KS, 1986), 53–57, Michael Kazin, *Barons of Labor: The San Franscisco Building Trades and Union Power in the Progressive Era* (Urbana, 1987), pp. 19–20.

19. See Marc Lee Raphael, "Rabbi Jacob Voorsanger of San Francisco on Jews and Judaism: The Implications of the Pittsburgh Platform," *American Jewish Historical Quarterly*, 63 (December 1973), 185ff.; Rosenbaum, *Architects*, 45ff.; Marc Lee Raphael, *Profiles in American Judaism: The Reform, Conservative, Orthodox and Reconstructionist Traditions in Historical Perspectives* (San Francisco, 1984), 20–32.

20. J. Voorsanger to J. L. Magnes, January 3, 1900, Voorsanger Papers, Western Jewish History Center, Berkeley. Fred Rosenbaum, "San Francisco–Oakland: The Native Son," in William M. Brinner and Moses Rischin, eds., *Like All the Nations? The Life and Legacy of Judah L. Magnes* (Albany, NY, 1987), 19–27.

21. J. Voorsanger to J. L. Magnes, October 19, 1905, Voorsanger Papers, Western Jewish History Center, Berkeley.

22. See Steve Zipperstein, "The Golden State: An Introduction," *Present Tense*, 9 (Spring, 1982), 28. The founding in 1986 in Oakland, California, of the intellectual national bimonthly *Tikkun*, the first of its kind in the American West, is symptomatic of the westward Jewish tilt. The emergence of Hollywood in the 1920s as the film capital of the nation that was to a great extent pioneered by Jews is a special case long antedating the mass Jewish migration westward. See Neil Gabler, *An Empire of Their Own: How the Jews Invented Hollywood* (New York, 1988) and A. Scott Berg, *Goldwyn: A Biography* (New York, 1989) for the latest efforts to depict that role.

23. Eldon G. Ernst, "American Religious History from a Pacific Coast Perspective," in *Religion and Society in the American West: Historical Essays*, ed. Carl Guarneri and David Alvarez (Lanham, MD, 1987), 22–23; see Moses Rischin, Foreword to Sara G. Cogan, comp., *The Jews of Los Angeles 1849–1945: An Annotated Bibliography* (Berkeley, 1980), viii; Steven M. Cohen, *American Modernity and Jewish Identity* (New York, 1983), 99, 108; Charles Silberman, *A Certain People: American Jews and Their Lives Today* (New York, 1985), 221ff.; and Deborah Dash Moore, "The Construction of Community: Jewish Migration and Ethnicity in the United States," in Moses Rischin, ed., *The Jews of North America* (Detroit, 1987), 105–17.

Chapter 2

Beyond New York:
The Challenge to Local History

MARC LEE RAPHAEL

Introduction

Marc Lee Raphael, a third-generation westerner and native of Los Angeles, opens his essay with a spirited vindication of local Jewish history as the essential foundation upon which to construct a balanced history of American Jewry. It is Raphael's contention that an American Jewish history true to the diversity and complexity of the Jewish experience in the United States can only be fashioned once we know how succeeding generations of Jews in all regions of the country and the products of different religious and secular experiences have led their lives in a wide variety of American and Jewish communal contexts. Generalizations about America's Jews heedless of local differences, insists Raphael, are bound to be inadequate and misleading.

Raphael's advocacy of Jewish history grounded in local settings does not ignore the fact, however, that local Jewish history all too often has been parochial in the worst rather than in the best sense and that practitioners have been interested primarily in lauding communal leaders and memorializing the institutions that they built. The local and community histories that Raphael commends place a given locality within the larger context of American Jewish history and have been undertaken by "scholars who bring general ideas, which alone can bring meaning, to the study of numerous large and medium-sized Jewish communities that are yet unstudied."

Although it is a truism to state that a general history of America's Jews must derive from the histories of local Jewish communities, Raphael is critical of the way in which this has been done. For too long, he argues, there has been an exclusive reliance on the New York Jewish experience as the model of what was "typical" for all Jews; as a consequence, American Jewish history has been distorted. To correct this skewed perspective serious attention must be given to what Jews achieved and endured beyond New York and its environs. In this way, research in western Jewish history and the history of Jews in other regions may restore balance and precision to American Jewish history.

In surveying the literature, especially for the period after 1880, Raphael notes one striking feature that may distinguish western Jewish history from the Jewish experience farther east. Based on Mordecai M. Kaplan's perceptions and confirmed by his own life experience as a westerner and historian, Raphael argues that "Jews came West in the first place . . . to start a new life, not to repeat the patterns of the past." Expanding on this observation, he contends that the history of the Jews of the West has been marked by a radical discontinuity with Jewish life in the Old World that contrasts with the notable continuities in the history of the Jewish communities of the East.

What is less debatable is that the demography of western Jewry differs markedly from what scholars have described for the East. As several essays in this collection point out, first-generation East European Jews migrated west in large numbers only under special circumstances, such as the health seekers who came to Denver or the agrarian idealists who founded Clarion, Utah. Compared to the East, therefore, the West was without that first generation of East European Jews whose presence transformed Jewish life in the cities of the Northeast. By the time East Europeans did arrive in large numbers in the West, especially after World War II, they were primarily second- and third-generation Americans divorced from the Jewish culture of the immigrant generation and well acculturated into the American mainstream. Before 1940, therefore, the relatively small western Jewish communities were marked by far less diversity than was to be found in the East where East Europeans developed the culture of Yiddishkeit and its supporting institutional network. For example, the established Yiddish theater, which catered to the tastes and traditions of the Jews of New York for a full theatrical season, was represented by road companies in the larger western communities in which audiences were too small to sustain anything longer than brief appearances.

Another important aspect of western Jewish history touched on by Raphael is the fate of religious orthodoxy. In recent years, he points out, the Orthodox in the West, like their brethren in the Midwest and East, have become more visible and vocal within the Jewish community. Curiously (according to Raphael), as the public presence of the Orthodox has increased, the percentage of Jews who identify themselves as Orthodox has decreased. How to explain this feature of American Jewish history remains unresolved, but Raphael urges that it be studied in its western dimensions, where the factors contributing to the Orthodox revival may be somewhat different or appear in different

forms than elsewhere. He speculates that the new position of Orthodoxy in the West may reflect the presence of a larger number of Jews
from less religious backgrounds who have newly turned to Orthodoxy
than are to be found among the older communities of the Midwest
and Northeast. This hypothesis fits the fact that first- and second-
generation East European Jews, among whom one would expect to find
the majority of the Orthodox, did not move west in great numbers.

What Professor Raphael's brief discussion of contemporary Orthodoxy in the West sharply underscores is that, practically, the religious
history of the Jews in the West has not been studied at all. We do not
know what were the prevailing religious practices among Jews in the
West in the nineteenth century no less than in the twentieth century.
We do not know to what extent and for how long western Jews in
small towns struggled to retain Orthodox dietary practices such as
kashrut in the home. We do not know whether rabbis in the West, in
accommodating to their western environment, defined their roles differently than did their colleagues in the other regions of the country.
The questions about Judaism in the West to which we cannot respond
are manifold. But, to return to the point made by Raphael at the beginning of his essay, the answers to our inquiries about western Judaism
will be forthcoming only as historians undertake investigations based
on local sources that trace and document the history of synagogues
and synagogue ritual, the development of religious educational institutions, and the careers of rabbis who have held western pulpits. In
the absence of such studies, the history of Jews in the West remains
incomplete, as does the history of Judaism in America.

BEYOND NEW YORK

The Jewish "community" is a composite of subgroups
differentiated by region, religiosity, gender and class.
There is no "typical" Jewish family, Jewish institution,
etc.

—Gary A. Tobin and Alvin Chenkin
American Jewish Year Book, 1885

The litany of accusations against local history is exhaustive and is
repeated nearly every time someone publishes a book on a Jewish community. There is no need to rehearse the list again, for by this time
these criticisms are not to be taken seriously or at least no more seriously than those criticisms leveled against any work of historical
scholarship. I have defended local history before, arguing that it is
valuable for the insights it offers into particular societal processes, for
the information it offers about a society, for the questions it raises about
other similar cases, and for the opportunity it provides to the historian
to craft a study built upon numerous case studies.[1]

What I have not ever done is to justify a local study by pointing
to its representativeness. Such a defense would imply that a broad
general history of, say, American Judaism, is representative, whereas
a study of Atlanta, Cleveland, Indianapolis, or Portland must prove
to be so. This is patent nonsense and tells us something about the
growth of the field of American Jewish history, a field that began, to
a large extent, from the top down.

First, let me draw an analogy. Let us imagine that we took the
Republican party analyses of federal, state, and local budgets during
the 1970s and 1980s seriously. Republican presidential candidates have
articulated numerous generalizations about the pattern of federal, state,
and local government spending as well as the impact of changes in

government policy on the scope, structure, and revenues of the private, nonprofit sector. They include such statements as "local governments considerably outspend the nonprofit organizations and government" and the "charitable sector serves primarily the poor" as well as the term *welfare state*, which has become little more than a buzz word.

If people wanted to test some of these hypotheses, of course, they would immerse themselves in federal, state, and local budgets, and then carefully survey hundreds (perhaps thousands) of nonprofit organizations in local field sites (day-care centers, programs for the elderly, museums, YMCAs, job-training programs, and hospitals come immediately to mind), taking care to provide a reasonable representative cross-section of the nation in terms of region, size, socioeconomic condition, and philanthropic tradition. The results, needless to say, would be of immense interest to communities of all sizes and in every region of the United States. Shedding much-needed empirical light on a set of institutions and relationships that are vital to American society, but that have largely escaped serious scrutiny up to now, they would undoubtedly challenge some long-standing misconceptions about the character and role of nonprofit institutions and about the operation of the American version of the modern welfare state.

The writing of American Jewish history did not proceed logically; for quite some time, misconceptions and inaccuracies graced the standard works of interpretation. This occurred because historians and sociologists—and some individuals with no training in either the humanities or social sciences—rather than building a network of empirical local studies, simply began with broad generalized interpretations. It would be as if someone wrote the history of Italian Jewry in the early modern period without consulting the studies of Cecil Roth on Venice and Florence,[2] Shelomo Simonsohn on Milan and Mantua,[3] David Ruderman on Ferrara,[4] and Ariel Toaff on Rome.[5]

What could one do if the goal was a study of American Jewry or American Judaism, and Moses Rischin's study of New York Jewry,[6] Arthur A. Goren's work on a part of that Jewry,[7] Max Vorspan and Lloyd P. Gartner's history of Los Angeles Jewry, [8] and all the carefully documented local histories of the 1960s and especially the 1970s had not yet been written? One option, of course, would be to write impressionistically, basing sweeping generalizations about American Jewry on one's own experiences. Some, in fact, did precisely this. Chapter 7 ("The Jewish Revival, 1940–1956") of Nathan Glazer's 1957 book *American Judaism*—long the most widely used text in the field—is, according to Glazer himself, "most[ly] based on personal observation," whereas Chapter 6 ("Judaism and Jewishness, 1920–45"), on the decades of the

1920s and 1930s, is crafted, again, according to Glazer, "as much, or more, from novels as from any other written source." This may help to explain why many of Glazer's conclusions, especially those of a sociological nature, are not only invalid today but were invalid at the time of publication.[9]

Another common method was to use the New York Jewish experience, about which much had been written before Rischin's work—albeit by poorly trained or even untrained students of American Jewry—as a general model for the entirety of American Jewish life. After all, nearly all of America's Jews lived there—or so it seemed—so why not generalize about the rest of American Jewry on the basis of the experience of a large majority. Many New Yorkers have written memoirs about their parochial conception of Jewish life in the United States. They knew there were bustling Jewish communities in Chicago, Philadelphia, and Baltimore; they knew about the Jews of Hollywood; and they knew that Jews vacationed in, and retired to, Miami Beach; but they had only the vaguest awareness of Jews scattered across the rest of the United States. That Boston, for example, was not only the home of the Yankees and the Irish but nurtured Jews who contributed as much significant thought about the relationship of Jews to American society as has any community in the country, this was not only unknown to Jews growing up in New York in the 1940s and 1950s but, more important, virtually ignored in works on American Jewry before the 1960s. In short, studies of American Jewry frequently informed us, at best, of New York Jewry, but purported to tell us something about Jews or Judaism in America.

Although it may be an exaggeration to claim, as has one Jewish scholar, that "universal history is local history writ large," there is no doubt that American Jewish history is precisely that.[10] Anyone teaching about Jews and Judaism in the United States obviously must discuss a wide variety of subjects. These range from patterns of settlement, socioeconomic mobility, and organizational development to Zionism, culture, philanthropy, anti-Semitism and religious life. In every area, it is necessary to generalize; but one must always take care to do so on the basis of local experiences.

The development of a clearly defined Conservative Judaism, for example, emerges not only from the records, published and unpublished, of the rabbinical and synagogal organizations, the Rabbinical Assembly of America, and the United Synagogue of America, but from discussions of this branch of American Judaism in the histories of the Jews in Birmingham,[11] Cleveland,[12] Columbus,[13] Indianapolis,[14] Los Angeles,[15] Milwaukee,[16] Minneapolis/St. Paul,[17] New York,[18] Richmond,[19] and Rochester[20] as well as from the numerous detailed and highly useful histories of Conservative Jewish synagogues, primarily produced by anonymous local authors rarely trained as historians.[21] Although congregational histories are generally quite limited in breadth and usually oblivious to larger historical developments, their often rich descriptions of synagogue practices make them valuable data bases. It is by drawing on these communal histories and congregational studies that one can generalize about mixed seating, mixed choirs, Jewish Theological Seminary versus Yeshiva University graduates as rabbis, the move against the selling of honors, dignity, decorum, organs and English in the services, travel on the Sabbath, late Friday evening services, level of *kashrut*, and much more that helps define a self-conscious Conservative Judaism. Alas, most studies of Conservative Judism as a national movement have simply ignored the local experiences.

Or, similarly, take the long-term existence of a vibrant Yiddish culture. Even before Kenneth Libo and Irving Howe's glorious account of this world in New York, everyone knew that the Lower East Side, and other parts of the city as well, fostered such a milieu. But was there a vibrant, dynamic, creative Yiddish culture or Zionism or Jewish socialism anywhere else—or even a Jewish criminal or two to rival Louis Lepke and other New York City Jewish hoodlums? We now know the answer, thanks to two decades of research into the pastiche of Jewish immigrant life in early twentieth-century Jewish communities outside New York. Here Columbus, Ohio, may be typical. Although only 1 percent of the city's population in the first decade of this century, and but a small minority on even the most "Jewish" street, East European Jews created socialist, Zionist, and religious organizations and institutions— qualitatively much like those back East—to attain the security and identity that flow from a structured system of the family, the organization, and the synagogue. This community frequently caught the attention of non-Jewish reporters. Noted one newspaperman in 1904, "stores and shops and clubs bear signs in Yiddish and all sorts of goods are being offered for sale, from prayer books to suits."[22]

Everywhere in this country, from Washington State to Georgia and from New England to El Paso, Yiddish-speaking Jewish immigrants created communities to which they belonged and in which they were surrounded by men and women who noted with pride the individual's every success and offered assistance when success was not achieved. In every region of the land, rabbis and petty criminals, peddlers and teachers, religious functionaries and artisans, meat markets and baker-

Celebration of Passover Seder by Rabbi Robert Gan and members of Temple Isaiah, Los Angeles, in the high desert at Saddleback-Butte State Park, near Lancaster, eighty miles from Los Angeles, 1977. (Courtesy of Barry Levine.)

ies, synagogues and bathhouses (perhaps, as in Columbus, even Jewish houses of ill-fame) coexisted, and the size of the community only determined the number, not the texture, of immigrant institutions.[23]

In recent years, with the abundance of local studies available to sociologists and historians, our picture of all, or at least much of American Jewry, has greatly expanded. Serious works of the 1970s and 1980s have carefully utilized this material. Although numerous scholars still ignore much of it, others have not only greatly expanded our grasp of the American Jewish experience but have fleshed out the history of national organizations and institutions by studying the effect of national decisions at the local level as well as the pressures local chapters exerted on national leaders. Their studies have also corrected generalizations and even inaccuracies by broadening their research, and they have included the experiences of Jews and Jewries previously unknown or ignored. Even so, there is so much more we would like to know.

The greatest and most obvious need in American Jewish scholarship is for histories by trained scholars who bring general ideas, which alone can bring meaning, to the study of numerous large and medium-sized Jewish communities that are yet unstudied. Four communities with more than 150,000 Jews are without written histories (Philadelphia in the twentieth century, Greater Washington, and Boston and Miami); a fifth, Chicago, has not been the subject of a serious history since 1933—for more than half a century. Three Jewish communities with populations over 50,000 (Detroit, St. Louis, and San Francisco) and at least nine cities with more than 25,000 Jews (Cincinnati, Dallas, Denver, Houston, New Haven, Phoenix, Pittsburgh, Providence, and San Diego) are lacking published histories.

This has not always been for lack of historians wishing to study local experiences. One historian has tried for years to write the history of Boston Jewry, but no major Jewish organizations seem interested in cooperating; another has confronted similar indifference in Cincinnati. In other cases, historians have simply been unable to find the requisite sources to investigate certain themes. Jeffrey S. Gurock, for example, in preparing his history of Yeshiva University[24] discovered that hundreds of students entering Yeshiva College in the 1920s and 1930s had been active in Mizrahi in Brooklyn. Unfortunately, two years of sleuthing did not uncover any Mizrahi records; such stories could be repeated over and over. Although Marshall Sklare is probably wrong when he notes that the challenge of comprehending the twentieth-century Jewish experience has "hardly begun," the synthesis Professor Henry Feingold has suggested and nurtured—a multivolumed history of Jews and Judaism in the United States—still demands a plethora of communal histories.

Of course, many such studies do now exist. The recent emergence of local histories is due to a revival of the genre, a mature sense of rediscovering the past as many communities celebrate such milestones as a hundredth anniversary, and the arrival of a new generation of Jewish historians trained in the field. Many of these studies have used sophisticated historical tools to ask new and important questions, especially about social and religious life, family relations, class divisions, mobility, and communal organization among those Jews who are not the community elite.[25]

At the same time, the filiopietistic, apologetic, and hagiographic focus of many of the older communal histories can still be found in the New Social History. The amateurs who wrote most American Jewish communal history before 1970 or so were unaware of the larger historical questions that might have moved their books from antiquarian, elite, institutional, and biographical description to works of rich archival and demographic research, critical investigation, and historical analysis.[26]

We might be willing to grant the need for a sophisticated history of Boston, Cincinnati, Detroit, Philadelphia, Pittsburgh, St. Louis, and Washington, DC—but what about the West? Why should anyone care about the Jews of Albuquerque, Denver, El Paso, Oakland, Phoenix, San Diego, Seattle, and Tucson? Aside from a few Jewish cowboys (and their gals), a Jewish Indian chief or two, and Big Mike Goldwater (who alternated between Arizona, where he founded his fortune, and San Francisco, where he was an eight-time synagogue vice-president), what need is there to chronicle more of the same? I think there are several reasons—beyond those I have already discussed—that apply to all communal histories.

In the late 1950s, or perhaps in 1960, Mordecai M. Kaplan delivered a lecture at the Wilshire Boulevard Temple in Los Angeles. Although the lecture dealt with Judaism in America, Kaplan did respond to one listener's question about the primary difference between the Jews of Los Angeles, which he had visited many times, and the East Coast by noting that the western metropolis lacked a European tradition. The Jews came west in the first place, he argued, to start a new life, not to repeat the patterns of the past. Kaplan's distinction seems no less persuasive three decades later. Abe Cahan described the Lower East Side as a seething human sea fed by streams, streamlets, and rills of immigration flowing from all the Yiddish-speaking centers of Europe and "made up of representatives of every country on the face of the globe." But the "voice, language, nuance and especially situation of a tumultuously varied ethnic, religious and human milieu" were much less in evidence in the West, if, indeed, there were even Jewish communities in some of these western cities around 1900 when Cahan wrote of the "peddler's cry and the urchin's bawl."[27]

In the East and even the Mideast (Ohio), the degree of continuity with Old World life is everywhere still discernible. You can, of course, see this still in the East: The New York knish peddler and street musician of the 1980s had their brothers both in the Warsaw of the 1930s and the Lower East Side of the 1890s. In the West, however, elderly women today are much more likely to be pictured sunbathing than schmoozing, elderly Jewish men lawn bowling or golfing than kibitzing. (The suntan, of course, is a Jewish legacy, or at least half-Jewish legacy on the male side. Douglas Fairbanks, Sr., who established a new American image of realized upper-middle-class American manhood that to this day pervades southern California Jewry, made the suntan an American preoccupation.) This has been no less true of ritual, another strong common bond between Old and New Worlds in the East, notwithstanding an occasional picture in *Moment* or elsewhere of young Jews in Venice or San Francisco observing the Rosh Hashanah ceremony of *tashlich* at the edge of the Pacific or a Klezmer wedding band serenading in Malibu, California.

This tight connection between Old and New Worlds in the East also meant that these Jewish communities were far more diverse than those of the West. Cleveland, in the 1930s, contained a Jewry almost as variegated as that of Poland at that time. There one could see every shade of political activism represented, from ultra-Orthodox and Orthodox Zionism to vigorous rivalries on the far-left. Those communities in the West known to me strike this observer as far more homogeneous, even bland. Perhaps this is partially the result of their size (or lack thereof); neighborhoods were predominantly middle class and almost never Jewish. One wonders, then, what forces help to maintain the Jewishness of the community in the absence of rich Jewish cultures or Old World habits? Or, as one author queried in a recent issue of the *Jewish Journal of Greater Los Angeles*, "Can Jewish culture survive the hot tub?" Are these perhaps the most AMERICAN of American Jewish communities?

A few years ago, this historian undertook a study of Orthodox Jewish life in several southern and western cities, namely, Atlanta, Los Angeles, and Phoenix, and noted a strange phenomenon. At the same time that Orthodoxy is undergoing dramatic institutional proliferation and raising the level of its public voice by several decibels, it is declining numerically. This development seems to parallel patterns in midwestern and eastern cities where Orthodox Jews are becoming a much more strident part of the community but, at the same time, declining in their number and proportion of the population.[28]

In Boston in 1965, to illustrate this rapid decline, 14 percent of the adults considered themselves Orthodox;[29] in 1975 only 5 percent of the adults considered themselves Orthodox;[30] and a 1981–1982 study by Steven M. Cohen indicated that only 6 percent of Boston Jews considered themselves Orthodox.[31] The apparent resurgence of Orthodox Jewry in Atlanta, Boston, Cleveland, Columbus, St. Louis, and elsewhere is not due to increased numbers of persons, but to increased numbers of institutions (day schools, kosher food establishments and facilities, ritualariums) as well as social and professional organizations. These institutions have become geographically widespread, increasing the visibility and influence of the Orthodox community. Is this true in the West, however? None of the most recent studies of this subject—I think

Rabbi Robert Gan of Temple Isaiah leads the Seder service in the high desert, 1977. (Courtesy of Barry Levine.)

of those by Heilman,[32] Helmreich,[33] Cohen,[34] and Waxman[35] — explore the Orthodox communities of the West. One thus wonders: What factors in the development of these Jewish communities have been most important? Have there, perhaps, been significant numbers of individuals from less religious homes who have become Orthodox?

Several Jewish sociologists who recently wrote general surveys of American Jewry have noted how little information is available to them about western Jewry. The theme that most interests them, and about which studies of western Jewry would contribute much, is that of the nuclear family. There is much talk that Jewish families in the West are without nuclear components, that they are the most dramatically American of American middle-class families in their freedom of mobility. Some, of course, dispute this, but the answer will only emerge after we have careful studies of western Jewry over a period of time.

The most striking distinction every sociologist discovers who investigates the contemporary Jewries of the West is the high intermarriage rate. Witness the available material on Denver: In a recent study, a demographer notes that "marriages between Jews and non-Jews outnumber marriages between two Jews."[36] But Denver is not alone; the

Rabbi Jonathan Krause leads campers in an outdoor Kabbalat Shabbat at UAHC Camp Swig, Sarasota, California, summer 1985. (Courtesy of Camp Swig.)

same phenomenon has been described in Phoenix, Seattle, and elsewhere.[37] Related to this are other items about western Jewry that would flesh out our portrait of American Jews, including studies of single and divorced Jews (42 percent of Denver Jewish households are not married!), gay congregations, levels of secular education and mobility, and, as William Toll has so sensitively done for Portland, attachments to institutions.[38]

Would this information of a sociological nature shatter some of the well-established conclusions about older Jewries (Cleveland, Columbus, Milwaukee, Minneapolis, and New York) such as: that substantial differences in Jewish identification exist between urban and suburban Jews; that Jews in smaller communities are much more likely to have joined and participated in synagogues and voluntary organizations; that Jewish identification has increased when Jews have been attacked anywhere (the Holocaust, wars in Israel, etc.); and that non-Jewish spouses have had a substantial impact on adult Jewish identification.

Are contrasts between East and West as extreme as some contemporaries seem to think? Recently the federation director in Phoenix insisted that eastern Jews affiliate with religious institutions and give to Jewish philanthropies in spite of rabbis and executives, whereas western Jews, meaning Phoenix Jews, affiliate with congregations and write checks only if they like the rabbi and director and have lived in the community for several years. He also insisted that the West "releases energy and gives one courage to struggle against the conformity of spirit [his term] which strangles New York Jewry." Imagine how different the portraits of two American Jewries, Worcester, Massachusetts (10,000) and Phoenix, Arizona (35,000), would be—one reputedly the most affiliated Jewish community in the nation, the other the least so—and how hard it would be to make one or the other a "typical" Jewish community.

What is needed, then, as historians begin to unravel the histories of the Jews of the West, is careful attention to the demographic characteristics of the "waves" or "trickles" of Jewish immigration to western cities. We have massive information about such patterns for eastern cities in the period of mass migration, but we know little about its characteristics in the West during any period. Where did the Jews who settled Berkeley, Fremont, Riverside, and San Diego, for example, come from? What about their ages, sex, occupational backgrounds, family size, and Jewish cultural baggage? What type of environment did they find? What interesting comparisons might be drawn from their interaction with other ethnic and racial groups in the West that might add to our knowledge of interethnic urban history?

Were these Jews of a later generation than those who came to New York? If so, their profile will be substantially different from the Jews of Baltimore or Philadelphia, too. For example, between the first and second generations in Baltimore, Cleveland, New York, and Philadelphia, there were enormous declines in Orthodox denominational identification and generous increases in Reform denominational identification; between the second and third generations there were substantial defections from the Orthodox and Conservative denominations into the Reform ranks; and by the fourth generation defections from Orthodoxy virtually terminate and Orthodoxy holds its own and the other denominations lose some people. What happens, then, when a whole generation is missing, when Orthodoxy emerges for the first

time in the third or fourth generation, and when we actually find—
unlike in the East—that Reform Jews not only outnumber Conservative
Jews but are increasing more dramatically than Conservative or Orthodox Jews?

Nearly everyone who visits a Jewish community in the West comments on the obsession with self-fulfillment and the informality of
Jewish life. The dream surely lives on among western Jewry, the dream
that promises so much in the matter of American living. Or is it the
dream that threatens to become an antidream, an American nightmare?
At Sabbath morning services at a traditional congregation in the desert
near Los Angeles not a single one of the more than 100 males present
wore a tie. The sixty-year-old rabbi, a graduate of the Jewish Theological Seminary, does much of his premarital counseling beside his pool.
A Jewish urologist, sixty years of age and prominent in organized Jewish life, wore jeans, an open-necked shirt, and a gold chain tight around
his neck during his very busy office hours. Now, surely, Judaism does
not stand or fall on a dress code; nevertheless, what is the direction
of Jewish life in such places?

People from Los Angeles always say that things happen first in
California, that there is a wider sense of the possible there, more
space—physical as well as psychic—and should anyone want to know
what the Jews are doing about anything, the best place to find out is
in California. Actually, they say, in southern California, the megasuburb
that now extends from Mexico to Kern County is not just a forerunner, but a microcosm of the country as a whole. It is, of course, not
just one state but several regions, and Jewish communities, with distinctive contours, cling to the coastal, desert, mountain, and fertile valley
landscapes. Few American regions have experienced accelerations and
quantum leaps comparable to those experienced by southern California in the years since 1920. And now, just as eastern Jewries imitated
New York, other western Jewries are surely imitating southern California patterns, even while they are breaking away from them. One
Phoenix Jewish leader has insisted that Los Angeles is their Old World;
and Phoenix is typical of those western Jewries searching for their own
identity, just as Columbus and Indianapolis and Atlanta both imitated
the Lower East Side and reacted against it. Where will it all lead? The
swimming pool counselor rabbi insisted that "southern California Jewry
is where the rest of the American Jewry will eventually be," whereas
a Los Angeles Jewish sociologist prophesied that if "American Jewry
everywhere follows the trend of several western Jewish communities
that I have studied, the direst predictions about American Jewish
decline will come true." The answer, of course, lies in the future, but

serious historical and sociological studies of western Jewish communities will help us understand how and why the patterns that will unfold before us are to be explained and understood. This is an exciting prospect, indeed.

Notes

1. Marc Lee Raphael, "American Jewish Local Histories: Deficiencies and Possibilities," *CCAR Journal*, 20 (Autumn 1973), 59–68; and idem. "The Genesis of a Communal History: The Columbus Jewish History Project," *American Jewish Archives*, 29 (April 1977), 53–69.

2. Cecil Roth, *History of Jews in Venice* (Philadelphia, 1930); and *The Last Florentine Republic* (London, 1925).

3. Shelomo Simonsohn, *History of the Jews in the Duchy of Mantua* (New York, 1977); and Shelmo Simonsohn, ed., *The Jews of the Duchy of Milan*, 2 vols. (Jerusalem, 1982).

4. David Ruderman, *The World of a Renaissance Jew: The Life and Thought of Abraham ben Mordecai Farisol* (New York, 1981).

5. Ariel Toaff, *The Ghetto of Rome in the Sixteenth Century*, in Hebrew (Ramat Gan, Isr., 1974).

6. Moses Rischin, *The Promised City: New York's Jews, 1870–1914* (Cambridge, MA., 1962).

7. Arthur A. Goren, *New York Jews and the Quest for Community: The Kehillah Experiment, 1908–1922* (New York, 1970).

8. Max Vorspan and Lloyd P. Gartner, *History of the Jews of Los Angeles* (San Marino, CA, 1970).

9. Nathan Glazer, *American Judaism* (Chicago, 1957). For extensive comments on Glazer's methodology, see *American Jewish History*, 78 (December 1987), 207–84.

10. Moshe Davis, foreword, in Vorspan and Gartner, *The Jews of Los Angeles*, viii.

11. Mark Elovitz, *A Century of Jewish Life in Dixie: The Birmingham Experience* (Tuscaloosa, AL, 1974), 89–97.

12. Lloyd P. Gartner, *The History of the Jews of Cleveland* (Cleveland, 1978), 166–72, 278–79.

13. Marc Lee Raphael, *Jews and Judaism in a Midwestern Community: Columbus, Ohio, 1840–1975* (Columbus, 1979), 182–86.

14. Judith Endelman, *The Jewish Community of Indianapolis, 1849 to the Present* (Bloomington, IN, 1984), 140–47.

15. Vorspan and Gartner, *The Jews of Los Angeles*, 162–63.

16. Louis J. Swichkow and Lloyd P. Gartner, *The History of the Jews of Milwaukee* (Philadelphia, 1963), 213–14.

17. W. Gunther Plaut, *The Jews in Minnesota: The First Seventy-five Years* (New York, 1959), 192–201, 205–9.

18. Deborah Dash Moore, *At Home in America: Second Generation New York Jews* (New York, 1981), 128–47.

19. Myron Berman, *Richmond Jewry, 1769–1976: Shabbat in Shockoe* (Charlottesville, VA,1979), 214, 293–95.

20. Stuart E. Rosenberg, *The Jewish Community in Rochester, 1843–1925* (New York, 1954), 175–80.

21. These include *Adath Israel of Trenton, New Jersey: Fortieth Anniversary* (Trenton, 1963); *After 100 Years: A Sparse History of Temple B'nai Israel of Toledo, Ohio* (Toledo,

1970); *A Century of Dedication: The Story of Beth Shalom of Kansas City, 1878–1978* (Kansas City, MO, 1978); *A History of Congregation Beth El* (Richmond, VA, n.d.); *The History of Temple Adath Yeshurun* (Syracuse, NY, 1973); *Temple Beth El: A Condensed History* (Rochester, NY, n.d.); *Temple Beth Shalom of Wilmington, Delaware: Fifty-Year Historical Record, 1922–1972* (Wilmington, 1972); *Temple B'nai Israel of Elizabeth, New Jersey: A History of the Temple* (Elizabeth, 1947); *Temple Emanu-El of Providence, Rhode Island: The First Fifty Years, 1924–1974* (Providence, 1974).

22. Quoted in Raphael, *Jews and Judaism*, 109.

23. The most recent work on East European Jews in the West (Arizona, New Mexico, and Texas) is Floyd S. Fierman, *Roots and Boots: From Crypto-Jew in New Spain to Community Leader in the American Southwest* (Hoboken, NJ, 1987). It, like so many other studies, demonstrates the difficulties of following an identifiable Jewish life in areas where there are too few Jews to establish any of the secular or religious institutions that constitute a community.

24. Jeffrey S. Gurock, *The Men and Women of Yeshiva* (New York, 1988).

25. William Toll, "The 'New Social History' and Recent Jewish Historical Writing," *American Jewish History*, 69 (March 1980), 325–41.

26. Oscar Handlin, "A Twenty Year Retrospect on American Jewish Historiography," *American Jewish Historical Quarterly*, 65 (June 1976), 295–309.

27. Moses Rischin, ed., *Grandma Never Lived in America: The New Journalism of Abraham Cahan*, (Bloomington, IN, 1985), xxvi, 97.

28. A recent study of St. Louis Jewry pointed to this concomitant phenomenon of increased vitality coupled with decreased numbers of Orthodox Jews; Gary A. Tobin, "A Demographic and Attitudinal Study of the Jewish Community of St. Louis" (St. Louis, 1982).

29. Morris Axelrod et al., *A Community Survey for Long Range Planning: A Study of the Jewish Population of Greater Boston* (Boston, 1967), 120.

30. Floyd J. Fowler, *1975 Community Survey: A Study of the Jewish Population of Greater Boston* (Boston, 1977), 77.

31. Steven M. Cohen cited in Sherry Israel, *Boston's Jewish Community: The 1985 Combined Jewish Philanthropies Demographic Study* (Boston, 1987), 52.

32. Samuel C. Heilman, *The People of the Book: Drama, Fellowship and Religion* (Chicago, 1983).

33. William B. Helmreich, *The World of the Yeshiva: An Intimate Portrait of Orthodox Jewry* (New York, 1982).

34. Steven M. Cohen, *American Modernity and Jewish Identity* (New York, 1983).

35. Chaim I. Waxman, *America's Jews in Transition* (Philadelphia, 1983).

36. Bruce A. Phillips, "Factors Associated with Intermarriage: A Preliminary Investigation." Paper delivered at the World Congress of Jewish Studies, 1985, in author's possession.

37. Phillips, "Intermarriage"; and Bruce A. Phillips and William S. Aron, *The Greater Phoenix Jewish Population Study* (Phoenix, 1984).

38. William Toll, *The Making of an Ethnic Middle Class: Portland Jewry over Four Generations* (Albany, NY, 1982).

Chapter 3

Zion in Utah:
The Clarion Colony and Jewish Agrarianism

ROBERT A. GOLDBERG

Introduction

The history of the Jewish agricultural colony at Clarion, Utah, presented by Robert A. Goldberg is somewhat special, for western Jewish history has been notably small town and urban. In painstakingly reconstructing the story of those who organized, settled, and finally failed at Clarion, Goldberg places the Clarion experiment within the larger framework of the Jewish Back to the Soil Movement and attempts to isolate those factors that explain the failure of a long train of Jewish efforts to settle on the land in the United States and elsewhere.

Goldberg's analysis of Clarion and comparison of its fate with that of other Jewish agricultural colonies leads him to the conclusion that the positive interaction of five elements was crucial to eventual success: farming experience, favorable environmental conditions, sufficient capital availability, morale, and the availability of alternatives. The colonists of Clarion, unfortunately, lacked these in the right combination, although Goldberg concedes that their farming experience increased and the environmental conditions did improve.

Placing the history of the Clarion colony within a general explanatory model rooted in the American Jewish agricultural experience, Goldberg concludes that Clarion reflected no patterns distinctive to the West. If the myth of the West as a Garden of Eden—in Henry Nash Smith's classic conception in *The Virgin Land*—played any role in Jewish colonization in the region, it was peripheral. If the Clarion story is not emblematic of the western Jewish experience, Goldberg's account demonstrates once again that the history of Jews in the region is inseparable from the total Jewish experience. Like other Eastern European immigrants, the colonists were eager to escape the constraints of the New York and Philadelphia ghettos; they professed various and conflicting ideologies that they brought with them from the Old World to the New World; they remained financially dependent on the support of their well-wishers in the East; and they turned for aid on occasion to the established Jewish community of Salt Lake City.

Despite Goldberg's virtual rejection of the idea that the West had any impact on Clarion, its short history and its eventual failure—and the failure of others like it—may serve as a reminder that it has been almost impossible to reverse long-term patterns that have resulted in the decline of the American farm population to a very small minority. Yet, despite its failure, the utopian dreams that informed many of the pioneers who invested their lives in Clarion and other agricultural colonies are a tribute to the social idealism that has illumined many phases of American Jewish history and that has made its most pronounced contribution to the labor and socialist movements.

ZION IN UTAH

More so than most Americans, even of the last century, America's Jews have been a predominantly urban people. Leaving the *shtetls* and cities of Eastern Europe, they migrated to the urban centers of industrializing America where they attempted to rebuild their lives and to renew their sense of community. On the Lower East Side of America, in the tenements, factories, and streets, immigrant Jews adjusted to the rigors of life on America's urban frontier. For them and their descendants, greater metropolitan America remained their natural habitat and gained immeasurably from their presence.

Only occasionally is the modern Jew reminded of his agrarian biblical roots. On Succoth, the Feast of Tabernacles, Jews still construct booths to commemorate the final gathering of the harvest in ancient Israel; and, of course, the Five Books of Moses, the words of the Prophets, and the Psalms abound with agricultural allegories and allusions. American Jews look with pride upon Israeli farmers and boast of their ability to make the desert bloom. Few American Jews realize, however, that they need not look back thousands of years to their biblical ancestors nor across thousands of miles to the Israeli *kibbutz* to come face to face with their Jewish agrarian heritage, for no group in modern America was more obsessed with the agrarian idea in their fashion than their forefathers who between 1881 and 1915 founded over forty agricultural colonies across the length and breadth of the

American continent. This collective effort in America was ideologically inseparable from an international Jewish Back to the Soil Movement that saw Jews establish dozens of farming settlements that extended from Argentina to Palestine, from Russia to Canada as well as in America and elsewhere.

The back-to-the-soil call attracted support across the whole spectrum of American Jewish opinion. German and Eastern European Jews, rich and poor, conservatives and radicals, Yiddishists and Zionists, the religious and the apolitical saw settlement on the land as a remedy to Jewish problems. To end urban overcrowding, to restructure Jewish economic life, to "productivize" the Jew immigrants were encouraged to take up the plow. Farming would decrease the oversupply of labor and congestion in the cities, create a proper environment for child rearing, and accelerate Americanization. Furthermore, the farm would inhibit anti-Semitism by countering the stereotype of the Jew as a commercial parasite. A return to agriculture would, moreover, bring about a Jewish spiritual and physical revival, restore a sense of dignity, free Jews from the economic uncertainties of the sweatshop, and demonstrate to Christians the Jewish stake in America. Finally, philanthropists were attracted to the agrarian solution because it emphasized self-help and work rather than charity or perpetual dependency for the Jewish poor. The agrarian impulse, then, cannot be understood except as a product of the European past, the American present, and the spiritual heritage of world Jewry. It was a current of energy—moral, intellectual, emotional, and material—that flowed back and forth between Jews wherever they lived.[1]

To explore this neglected chapter in American Jewish history in depth, let us look at Clarion Colony. Founded in 1911, some 135 miles southwest of Salt Lake City, Utah, it was the last major effort to settle Jews on the land in the United States before the Great Depression. Largest both in population and in land area, this colony proved to be the most long-lived Jewish settlement west of the Appalachians. Thanks to a unique data base, consisting of journals, diaries, organizational records, and interviews, it has been possible to reconstruct the Clarion experiment in remarkable detail. The values and ideals of the colonists, their daily rhythm of life, their struggle for survival, and the causes of their failure are open to examination. From the Clarion experience can be discerned the factors that determined the life cycles not only of western Jewish colonies but of Jewish settlements throughout the country.

The Clarion Colony arose first in the mind of Benjamin Brown. Born in Russia in 1885, Brown migrated to America at the age of fif-

teen, and following a short stint as a peddler, obtained a job as a farm
laborer near Philadelphia where he acquired a passion for agriculture
that would inform his entire life. Believing that the farm offered Jews
an escape from the ghetto and the prospect of prosperity, in 1909, he
began agitating for the organization of a nonreligious Jewish farming
colony that he was certain would serve as a model for a wave of Jewish
farm settlements throughout the United States.[2]

In an effort to mobilize men and money for his Jewish Agricultural and Colonial Association, Brown addressed large and small gath-
erings in Philadelphia and New York City. In his speeches, the out-
lines of the future colony grew more distinct. What Brown sought
was 150 to 200 young married men with approximately three hundred
dollars each whose savings would generate an operating capital of between forty-five thousand and sixty thousand dollars for the purchase
of land, equipment, livestock, and building equipment—a substantial
outlay for the time that would prove insufficient. Initially, the colonists were to work the land communally and be paid wages. At a
later date, the colony was to resemble the Israeli *moshav* with privately owned land and equipment and cooperative buying and selling. Politics and religion would be "private things" in the colony.[3]

Benjamin Brown suggested a western location for the colony because land was cheaper; the temptation to return to the city, less; and
the likelihood of the settlement becoming a boarder-resort, as had occurred to Jewish farms in upstate New York, remote. His message was
always multifaceted, extoling the good life on the farm but reminding
his listeners of the impelling need to ameliorate the Jewish condition
in the eastern cities.[4]

Brown's message obviously touched a wide range of people. The
colony's idealistic and cooperative features drew socialists like Esther
and Joseph Radding, for whom this was an opportunity to "work out
our special Jewish problems. To devote our entire life by becoming
farmers, by working with the soil."[5] Although Zionist David Boyarsky
hoped to train himself in the colony for eventual migration to Palestine and anarchist Isaac Isgur saw the colony as a working model of
a society without laws, government, or violence, the majority of re-
cruits put more practical considerations first. For them, the project
promised freedom from sweatshop and slum and a life of good health,
clean air, and economic security. Carpenter Barnet Slobodin joined
because "it was hard to make a living. We were working for practically
nothing."[6] The Mastrow family feared for their future in the city: "How
could we ever acquire anything? How could we ever hope to raise our
life standards? This was our chance."[7] Thus, a combination of ideals

71

and practical needs drew together a heterogeneous coalition of social-ists, Zionists, the religious Orthodox, and those who perceived no higher loyalty than to family or circle. With each group conceiving a colony in their own image, the weed of dissension was well fertilized.[8]

On April 17, 1911, Brown and civil engineer Isaac Herbst boarded a westbound train to inspect land for the proposed colony. After view-ing property in New Mexico and Colorado, where land prices were too high and transportation facilities inadequate, the men traveled to Utah where Jewish friends in Salt Lake City had informed Brown that the state had opened a prime tract of land that would be irrigated with water from a canal under construction. State officials boasted the canal would provide abundant water and eliminate the caprice of weather.[9] The more than eight thousand acres offered for sale, de-scribed by Utah's governor William Spry as "among the very choicest agricultural lands in the state,"[10] were located in south-central Utah, three miles from the small town of Gunnison.

Brown and Herbst were quite impressed, for the land, sufficiently large for their colony, was in the midst of a valley turning green with cultivated crops and near a railroad depot that put Salt Lake City within marketable range. Both men believed that the Mormons would be receptive to the project because they, too, had experienced the rigors of colonization and suffered religious persecution. The association agreed to purchase more than six thousand acres with 10 percent of the price due immediately and the rest, with interest, payable in equal installments over ten years. Unfortunately, the initial bank draft did not clear because of insufficient funds in the association's account. This served as a premonition of things to come.[11]

The key to the colony's future was the state canal. Begun in 1908, by 1911 it had reached the southern one-third of the eight-mile-long tract of Jewish colony land. Although it was predicted that all Jewish land would be irrigated by the canal by 1913, construction had only passed the middle one-third by 1914 and was not completed until 1918, more than two years after the settlement's demise. The newly built canal, with sides and bottom of dirt, lacked the gates and weirs necessary to regulate the water received by each farmer. Moreover, because there was no past data concerning canal capacity, state en-gineers could only estimate the extent of water seepage and the water quantity available for delivery.[12]

The first twelve colonists, chosen for their mechanical skills, ex-perience with horses, and "seriousness," arrived at the settlement on September 10, 1911; they erected four large white tents to serve that winter as communal living and dining shelters. Although lacking in

The original settlement in the southern part of Clarion: a frame structure and tents, 1911. (Courtesy of Sarah Sack Bober.)

farming experience, the men became concerned. The land, remarked Barney Silverman, sloped steeply, "resembling the sides of a saucer."[13] The "raw earth," as Isaac Friedlander described it, was covered by sagebrush, tall grasses, and weeds.[14] Large patches of ground were bare of any vegetation. Closer inspection of the soil revealed a sandy, gravelly consistency underlain by a hardpan subsoil. The state of canal construction had fixed the initial area of cultivation in the southern section of the colony on some of the worst land in the tract. Although the colonists were unaware of it at the time, the area had a short growing season, with a late spring, an early fall, and minimal rainfall. There was not a single well. Water had to be hauled in a large tank from Gunnison twice a week, a six-mile round-trip that consumed most of a day.[15]

Despite their initial concerns and lack of experience, the colonists began the very next day, September 11, to clear the land for cultivation. Working collectively for fifteen dollars in weekly wages, that fall the men prepared fifteen hundred acres for the coming spring's planting and laid out and dug irrigation channels from the canal to the fields. They eagerly accepted the advice of local Mormon farmers and followed the instructions of a professor sent at the governor's insistence from the state agricultural school at Logan.[16]

Any trepidation the colonists might have had about the Mormons quickly disappeared. Mormons welcomed Jews as neighbors, tendering advice, food, friendship, tools, hired and voluntary labor, and moral support. "They acted to us," recalled Nathan Ayeroff, "not as strangers but as brothers."[17] The Mormons saw the Jews as biblical brethren descended from Joseph, their mutual ancestor. Their own recent history of midwestern pogroms, an exodus across the Mississippi River into the wilderness, and the settlement in a promised land with its own Dead Sea confirmed in Mormon minds a similar chosen destiny. Mormons respected Jewish beliefs and attempted no proselytizing; the economic stimulus the Jews brought to the area facilitated their reception. Still, the sense of common identity, past and present, religious and pioneering, united the two peoples. Difficulties that arose resulted primarily from mutual ignorance and personality conflicts rather than from anti-Semitism.[18]

When winter's cold made farm work impossible, the colonists retired to their tents and hammered out the principles and purposes of their experiment. They anticipated that their colony would be the first of a multitude of similar Jewish settlements throughout the United States. Initially, the colony would engage solely in the cultivation and marketing of agricultural produce. Later, the settlers would diversify and establish a canning factory to process their crops. From these beginnings, a town would grow where every branch of agriculture, commerce, manufacturing, and mining could be undertaken. A new society rooted in all of these economic endeavors would revitalize the Jew in his as well as in others' eyes. Perceiving themselves as the harbingers of the economic and social future of Jewish America, they appropriately named their colony Clarion.[19]

That winter the colony was struck by the first of many economic crises. Payments for land, tools, wages, and livestock had drained the association of its financial resources. It owed the state of Utah the initial 1912 installment for land and water, and material bought on credit required additional sums. To raise money Ben Brown returned East to recruit new members and reinforce in old members the need to fulfill their financial obligations. The appeal was successful, the money raised, and the colony's economic health restored, briefly.[20]

Work began again in earnest at the end of February 1912. By late March, the plowing and planting of wheat, oats, and alfalfa was com-

Riding a disk harrow: Samuel Sack, in Russian worker's cap and peasant blouse, prepares the land for planting, c. 1913. (Courtesy of Sarah Sack Bober.)

pleted; by May, green sprouts had broken through the soil. The happiness produced, however, proved short-lived. Strong winds, dust storms, heat, flies, and mosquitoes plagued the colonists. The colony's tractor broke down, leaving only continued payments in its wake. Water still had to be transported from Gunnison. With the arrival of additional families, water trips had become more frequent and, thus, more burdensome, and the effort to alleviate the shortage by the digging of wells proved unsuccessful.[21]

Worst of all were the problems infesting the colony's lifeline, the state canal, for the canal engineers had proven unduly optimistic about the quantity of water that could be delivered and even about the quality of the canal itself. In the summer of 1912, the canal's banks burst six times and left the colony without water for thirty-five days. When the canal was in repair, less than one-fifth of Clarion's water needs could be met. For only two days during that summer was the water flow sufficient to irrigate all the colony's fifteen hundred acres.[22]

In any case, an additional water supply would not have solved all of the colony's troubles. The area initially cultivated consisted of marginal land, used even today for grazing only. The combination of poor soil, scarce water, and inexperience doomed the first year's harvest. Half the crop was lost, and six hundred acres produced only half the expected yield. The loss in costs and labor stunned the colonists.[23]

Again, the colony was in financial straits. This time, assistance arrived from members of the Salt Lake City Jewish community. From the colony's creation, Salt Lake City Jews had acted as intermediaries with machine and tool suppliers to insure that the settlers received the most favorable terms and the fastest delivery of goods. They had also donated money and material to aid in colony development. To help Clarion over its latest financial hurdle local Jews organized the Utah Colonization Fund, which issued bonds in support of Clarion and thus facilitated Ben Brown's efforts to solicit support from wealthy eastern Jews. Clarion's Jews craved the moral and finanacial support of the Jews in Salt Lake City and the East, brethren who linked them to the centers of American Jewry and the fabric of international Jewish life, thus bolstering their sense of mission and purpose.[24]

The only crop brought forth in abundance that first harvest was dissension. With the colony's turn in fortune, Brown's judgment and qualifications came under attack. He was accused of mismanagment and dictatorial practices; in addition inaccurate bookkeeping by the colony's secretary generated charges of chicanery. Further exacerbating group tensions was the factionalism inherent in the heterogeneous membership. Anarchists, international socialists, Jewish socialists, and Zionists quarreled with one another, and the religious Orthodox minority, with its requests for a ritual slaughterer and a *Sefer Torah*, added to the turmoil.[25]

With dissension simmering and the poor harvest a major setback, the settlers moved as planned into the colony's next phase, with individual land ownership replacing collective work and control. On October 15, 1912, each of the association's members drew lots to select his own forty-acre farm. This produced further bickering over the comparative quality of the land of each farm. Unfortunately, the forty-acre plots proved far too small to support a family. Even worse, rocky soil cut by dry washes made sections of each plot unsuitable for farming.[26]

The farming cycle began again in spring 1913. The farmers performed the usual chores on their individual plots, and the colony as a whole worked to complete two long-delayed tasks. First, the settlers had to locate a source of water in the colony and end the practice of transporting it from Gunnison. In May, the association bought a well-drilling rig and began searching for water. After several failures, water was found two hundred feet below the surface. The water was welcome, even though it was always covered by an oily blue film. This proved, however, to be the colony's only successful well.[27]

Also related to Clarion's future was the colony's second task, the construction of a school. The local school board, in light of the colony's growing population, created a Clarion district and appointed a teacher, with the provision that the settlers were to erect a building. The Mormon board also allowed the colonists the option of hiring a second teacher to provide a religious education for the children. In a common effort and with great hope, a one-room school, housing grades one through five, was built to accommodate the colony's twenty-eight children. What began in harmony and cooperation degenerated into bitter feuding when the program of Jewish education was considered. Again, the dissension and debate can only be understood in the context of the ideological diversity that pervaded the whole Jewish immigrant world. Nationalists wanted to hire a teacher who would support Jewish identity through instruction in the Yiddish language, literature, and folklore. Radicals felt than an emphasis on "Jewish" subjects would distract students from the international struggle for socialism. The religious minority sought instruction in the Hebrew liturgy. Finally, some were content to employ only the Mormon teacher selected by the school board. A compromise was eventually reached: It called for a teacher who would support Jewish identity through Yiddish language, literature, and folklore and at the same time interpret Jewish history from an international socialist perspective. Hardly anyone was satisfied. Colonist Abe Wernick wrote, "Long after these meetings there was tension in the air and the opposing factions did not look at each other when they met." After just eighteen months, the ideological cracks had grown wider and more exposed.[28]

Yet, for the colonists, the schoolhouse and the well symbolized an increasing permanence. There were other signs in 1913 that the colony might survive the dangerous period and achieve some stability. By the spring, Clarion's population had grown to 156 persons living on thirty-six farms. Almost twenty-four hundred acres had been planted in alfalfa, wheat, and hay, and the canal finally appeared to be functioning. Between October 1912 and June 1913 only 5 colonists left, and they were promptly replaced by settlers with sufficient funds to establish themselves without association aid.[29]

Still, life in the colony was hard. Each colonist family lived in a one-room shack, twenty-five-feet square and set on a concrete foundation. The wood-burning stove served all heating and cooking functions, for coal was too expensive. The builders left the walls unfinished, with upright two-by-fours exposed. Heat and cold cracked and shrank the lumber, allowing the wind to whistle through the chinks in the walls. Many of the children still remember the high-pitched wail of the wind and the blankets covered with snow that fell through the warped wallboards. In Clarion, where "a piece of string became a treasure," money was scarce, and eggs, milk, and cheese were bartered in town for needed commodities.[30]

The optimism born of struggle received a series of crushing blows during the summer and fall. Heavy rains in the mountains sent torrents of water into the dry washes and toward the colony. The water blocked the conduits under the canal, flowed over its walls, and flooded the hay, wheat, and alfalfa fields. Rocks, sand, and gravel covered the land, and gullies cut some farms in two. "The place," wrote Isaac Friedlander, "looked like the aftermath of an earthquake."[31] Another storm in the fall followed by an early frost further devastated crops. The colony's greatest tragedy occurred that August when one of the original twelve colonists was killed in a logging accident.[32]

The succession of catastrophes led to soul-searching meetings, planned and spontaneous, in which the settlers asked: Is Clarion worth more work and hardship? Should we give in? With only a few dissenters, the group decided to continue on the land and not to return in defeat to the city. Colonist Nathan Ayeroff spoke for the group: "To be on the land, to be free, to work for yourself . . . to breathe fresh air all the time, how could you leave[?]"[33] The colonists gathered up the rocks and again cleared their fields. But the optimism of the first years vanished, to be replaced by a fatalistic determination to survive. In order to continue on the land, the colonists were forced to market all their grain, leaving nothing for seed. Anything of value was sold to raise money for food and clothing; funds from eastern relatives tided some over the difficult months. To stave off hunger the Ayeroff family remembers eating cats.[34]

The colony's future again rested upon Ben Brown who returned to the East to sell Clarion's bonds and succeeded in raising six thousand dollars, sufficient to purchase seed, to forestall the repossession of wagons and tools, and to buy time. Yet everyone agreed with colonist Moshe Malamed that "the knife [is] at our throats."[35]

The water appeared in the canal on schedule in the spring of 1914. But again, as in the first year, the flow was insufficient and ir-

Isaac Herbst and a surveyor team affix the farm boundaries and mark off Clarion's main road, c. 1913. (Courtesy of Sarah Sack Bober.)

regular: The soil cracked under the sun and the crops withered. The problem this time was unrelated to construction. Rather, the colonists experienced a water shortage because of the greed of neighboring farmers, living just below them, who took advantage of the absence of locks on the canal gates and used more than their allotted share of water. After repeated appeals to state officials brought no redress, thirty frustrated and angry colonists led by Brown marched along the canal, seized control of the water gates, and closed off those belonging to the Mormon farmers. Order was eventually restored, but no one had benefited. It was clear long before threshing time that the harvest would not carry the colony into the next year.[36]

Fifty-two families remained on the land during the colony's last spring. Incredibly, association members still were arriving from the East as late as January to replace those who had departed. What happened in the last year is not entirely clear. Ben Brown resigned as president in reaction to popular dissatisfaction and his own sense of personal failure. Owing to a late frost, a hay crop planted in March proved sparse when cut in June. Creditors demanded their money and more repossessions of equipment and livestock occurred. A poor harvest in the fall forced approximately thirty of the families to accept funds raised by Salt Lake Jews to buy railroad tickets to Los Angeles, Chicago, Philadelphia, and New York City.[37]

Seventeen families remained, but on November 25, 1915, a state order terminated the colony's title for nonpayment of monies owed. Chosen to represent the remnant, Brown cajoled the state into a last concession that allowed those who remained to retain ownership if they made a token payment immediately and met the prescribed financial schedule in the future.[38]

In January 1916, the state auctioned the colony's land and managed to sell just over one-tenth of the tract. All houses and barns were sold to satisfy creditors. Most of the remaining colonists left after three or four years, although some of them continued to farm nearby. Others took up land in New York, Michigan, California, and Pennsylvania. The last Jews left the Clarion area in the mid-1920s because they feared for the loss of their children's religious identities through assimilation.[39]

How are we to account for this dismal failure? It appears that five interrelated variables were crucial in determining Clarion's fate: farming experience, environmental conditions, capital availability, colonists' morale, and the existence of alternatives. Clarion's people were urbanites familiar with the sweatshop, store, or pushcart. Even the few with farming experience were unprepared for the semiarid conditions of Utah. Added to the heavy toil attendant on colony groundbreaking, their inexperience ill-fitted them for pioneering. A poor site choice exacerbated the problems generated by inexperience. Water scarcity, an undependable irrigation canal, marginal soil, and capricious weather drained the colony of enthusiasm and of its meager supply of monetary resources.

Yet neither the lack of experience nor the environment are sufficient explanations for Clarion's fall. Each day on the land increased the colonists' store of agricultural knowledge. Hard work, trial and error, and the aid and advice of the Mormon farmers strengthened the colonists in their physical, emotional, and mental ability to stay on the land. The success of those colonists who remained in the Clarion area for a decade after the colony's demise or who took to the land elsewhere is evidence of their will to adapt to farming. Moreover, those who persisted were adapting to an environment that had begun to shed its harshness and was becoming more predictable. The most difficult tasks had been accomplished. The land had been cleared and fields created. Fences and outbuildings had been erected. The canal had become increasingly dependable.

Clarion's life could have been extended if it had had the capital and esprit to sustain it through the difficult years. Adequate financial resources would have bought the settlers time to survive the early colonization period, allowing them to gain the required experience to control their environment. The patronage of a generous outside benefactor alone would not have assured the colony's future, for to root the colonists to a harsh land also required a morale that was intense and cohesive. The harship, denial, and self-doubt that accompany any colonization project can be held at bay, if not dispelled, when men and women are passionately bound to a common goal. The colony's avowed purpose was to rebuild the Jewish people through agriculture, but the colonists lost sight of this mission when personal animosities, ideological conflicts, and cultural disagreements caused diverse factions to direct their energies against one another and thus to dissipate trust, goodwill, and strength. Further eroding morale was the indifference of the outside world. The Mormons did not threaten the colony and so offered no common ground to the quarreling groups. When Clarion's call was ignored and financial contributions failed to materialize, their greatest fears were realized; their mission had no meaning. This sense of meaninglessness cannot be overemphasized. The moral and financial threads that tied Clarion to the East and beyond to their brethren in Europe strengthened resolve and fired the cause. When cut, there was little in reserve to cushion the fall. Finally, for the Clarion majority, idealism had always exerted less influence upon thought and action than had self-interest. When conditions worsened, they could find few things to justify continued allegiance.

Directly related, yet separate, was the existence of alternatives. New York City, Philadelphia, and Los Angeles called to the Jews as they did to Gentiles, offering rescue and release from farm life. The familiar urban world, even with its drawbacks, promised relief from economic uncertainty, deteriorating relations with fellow colonists, and idealism gone sour. Without the bulwarks of high morale, financial security, and agricultural achievements, the siren of alternatives could not be silenced. Clarion's obstacles to economic self-reliance and ethnic viability had proven too formidable to conquer.

With Clarion as a model and the five variables as a framework, let us briefly review the Jewish colonization experience in America historically, for regardless of region, the factors influencing the success and failure of the American Jewish colonies were similar.

The first attempts to settle groups of Jews on the land go back to

81

the 1820s when colonization was undertaken in Florida, but unfavorable environmental conditions led to its discontinuance. In 1825, Mordecai M. Noah's purchase of over two thousand acres of land on Grand Island in the Niagara River near Buffalo, New York, as an agricultural refuge for Jews proved chimerical. A decade later, marginal soil and poor harvests drove thirteen Jewish families to abandon the Sholem Colony in New York state.[40]

Large-scale colonization began only in the 1880s, with the onset of the great Jewish migration, when the Hebrew Emigrant Aid Society, the Russian Emigrant Relief Committee, the Hebrew Colonization Society, and the Montefiore Agricultural Aid Society in New York City and Philadelphia prepared to direct and fund the colonization movement aided by the Alliance Israélite Universelle and the Baron de Hirsch Fund. In addition, philanthropic agencies appeared in Cincinnati, Boston, New Orleans, St. Paul, and St. Louis. The work of these organizations combined with the desires of individual immigrants and more organized groups of settlers activated the Back to the Soil Movement in America.[41]

The first colony of Russian Jews was planted on Sicily Island, Louisiana, in 1881, when the Alliance Israélite Universelle and the New Orleans Agricultural Society aided sixty families to establish themselves on twenty-eight hundred acres of land. Despite adequate supplies, a forbidding environment of swamps, oppressive heat, floods, snakes, and malaria-carrying mosquitoes proved devastating. Most of the colonists returned to the city. Others journeyed to South Dakota in 1882 to participate in the formation of Cremieux, which grew to include two hundred people and to encompass five thousand acres. Yet by 1885 it, too, had disappeared, succumbing to drought, prairie fire, hailstorm, and insufficient funds. In the same year, the nearby settlement of Bethlehem Yehudah also perished after an eighteen-month existence, the victim of crop failure and factionalism.[42]

Of the six North Dakota colonies, Painted Woods established in 1882 was the most substantial. Initially, the colony consisted of twenty-two families, each homesteading a 160-acre tract. At its height, 232 colonists plowed and planted wheat, their operations subsidized by the Baron de Hirsch Fund and the Montefiore Agricultural Aid Society. This support, however, proved insufficient. Fire, drought, crop failure, and severe winters ravaged the colony. After four years, nearly all the colonists had surrendered to the elements.[43]

Second to the Dakotas, Kansas, with seven settlements, was the most active western site for Jewish colonization. In 1882, the Hebrew Union Agricultural Society placed sixty Russian Jews on 160-acre farms in the Beersheba Colony. The society maintained strict supervision of the project by appointing a manager and placing the settlers on a weekly ration. The *American Israelite*, a newspaper, boasted, "The Superintendant of the colony at Beersheba has the people completely under control, and they obey the word of command as soldiers; they were at first unruly and self-willed, but by a systematic course they now are tractable and docile."[44] To the chagrin of its patron Beersheba had ceased to exist by 1886. A poor location, marginal soil, parsimonious support, and friction between the colonists and their overseer all contributed to its decline. Even less was accomplished in the Hebron, Montefiore, and Lasker colonies, all organized and funded by the Montefiore Agricultural Aid Society and all suffering from undercapitalization because of the overextension of their sponsor. None of these efforts lasted more than four years. Touro Colony died within a year of its birth. Little information has survived concerning the two other Jewish colonies in Kansas.[45]

A similar tale is to be told for the Cotopaxi Colony of Colorado. With support from the Hebrew Emigrant Aid Society, thirteen immigrant families, only one with prior farming experience, settled on government land in the central part of the state. "It was," said an observer, "the poorest place in the world for farming, poor land, lots of rocks and no water."[46] The colony vanished in a year, its members returning to the East or relocating in Denver.[47]

A decade after the colonization surge of the early 1880s, settlement was attempted in Michigan where a group of peddlers sought financial security in farming by purchasing sixteen farms on marginal land that lumber companies had cut and burned over. Begun in 1891, the Palestine Colony experienced difficult times, suffering crop failures in 1893, 1894, and 1897. Yet the colonists refused to give up, supplementing their meager incomes by peddling and by securing emergency grants from the Baron de Hirsch Fund and the Detroit Jewish community. Only in 1899, unable to maintain themselves and their families on the soil, did they cease their struggle.[48]

The Arpin Colony in Wisconsin also was situated unwisely on cutover land, with blackened tree stumps offering an additional obstacle to successful farming. In 1904, the Milwaukee Jewish Agricultural Society obtained 720 acres and installed eight families on farms. By 1906, three more families had joined the project, all receiving five dollars per week from the society. Little favorable news, however, was received from the colony where inexperience, loneliness, and low morale sapped energy from the effort: "The Russian and Roumanian immigrants who settled in the colony did not care about farming at

Communal mealtime for the original colonists, c. 1913. (Courtesy of Sarah Sack Bober.)

all and accepted the chance to get on farms only because there was nothing else for them to do."[49] By 1909, just three families continued to till Arpin's soil.[50]

Clearly this brief overview of the Jewish American colonization effort offers a litany of idiosyncratic causes for failure. Despite much sacrifice, marginal soil, malaria, hailstorms, floods, prairie fires, inadequate water and fuel supplies, factionalism, high interest rates, inexperience, and meager capital resources prevented the colonies from taking root in American soil. Agricultural societies acted too hastily and with too little foresight when choosing site and settler and in estimating project costs.

Concentration on the particular or specific, however, conceals as much as it reveals, for patterns that highlight the common features of events can easily be observed. Moreover, without a broad context, we are no closer to an understanding of why Gentile settlements in the United States or Jewish colonies elsewhere that operated under similar conditions were able to survive. The capsule histories pre-

sented reveal that lack of farm experience, environment, capital availability, the existence of options, and morale all played a role in the
destinies of the colonies, and varied one from another. Thus, Sicily
Island's failure, although certainly tied to environment, must also be
understood in terms of decaying morale and the existence of urban
or other colonial options. Capital was available to the Sicily Island Colony and, although important, was less critical in determining its fate
than that of less favorably endowed settlements. The negative interaction of all the variables is apparent in the Beersheba Colony, although
internal friction and factionalism clearly give greatest significance to
the morale factor. Arpin's history, too, should emphasize a lack of will
without overlooking the other problems that the colonists confronted.
Simple explanations of failure, such as inexperience, the absence of
water, or prairie fire, will not suffice. Farming ability and environment, although necessary variables, are insufficient as explanations
without the factors of capital, morale, and alternatives.

Finally, mention must be made of successful Jewish farm colonies
in New Jersey that have led some scholars to single out the East as
more conducive to colonization. Yet the relative success of the Jewish
effort in New Jersey was less a function of region than the interplay
of the variables. Of twenty Jewish colonies dotting the New Jersey
landscape, half surmounted the obstacles of the intial settlement stage.
Among the largest and most significant of these colonies were Alliance,
Woodbine, Carmel, and Rosenhayn. Like most Jewish colonists, these
farmers were immigrants who came to the soil with little or no agricultural expertise. Often their small farms were situated on marginal
soil that other farmers had avoided as unsuitable for cultivation. Many
New Jersey colonists, however, overcame their limitations because
they received large infusions of financial aid that enabled them to
build capital resources and to acquire the knowledge to surmount
crises and gain stability. Philanthrophic societies approached their
New Jersey colonization projects as "privately subsidized social experiment[s]"[51] whose "model" farms required patient cultivation, careful weeding, and continuous care: "Those who wished to do things
differently lacked the power; a few were expelled as troublemakers.
Policy decisions usually came from above."[52] Later, when philanthropic aid and direction decreased, farmers and their families supplemented their income with local factory employment. Success, however, cannot be measured solely with a ledger book. The New Jersey
colonies did not remain Jewish endeavors, for within two generations
the colonies had begun to lose their distinctive religious identities. New
Jersey's Jewish farmers could not look beyond their own families and

farms for a rationale to keep them on the land. The neighboring markets of Philadelphia and New York, previously an advantage, now became economic and social magnets strongly attracting Jewish farmers and their children back to the urban world. Self-interest and private need spurred their departure and, thus, the loss of group solidarity.[53]

The Alliance settlement was representative of these trends. In 1882, the Hebrew Emigrant Aid Society, with the support of the Alliance Israélite Universelle, purchased twelve-hundred acres near Philadelphia and placed twenty-five families on fifteen-acre plots. The area was linked to a large urban market by railroad and was spared both flood and drought dangers. To ease the immigrants' transition to agriculture, the society hired a farming instructor, gave each family a monthly stipend, dug wells, built homes, and financed the acquisition of tools and equipment. The following year, cigar and shirt factories were opened to provide additional employment opportunities and income. By 1887, the colony had begun to record good harvests and show a yearly profit, and it numbered 529 people. In the depressed nineties, when farm prices and profits dropped and foreclosure threatened, the Alliance Colony suffered along with the rest of the nation's farmers. In this crisis, the Baron de Hirsch Fund salvaged the colony by refinancing mortgage debt and offering farmers longer payment schedules at lower interest. The opening of another local factory further bolstered the colony, which by 1905 counted 891 inhabitants. Yet three years later, Alliance disposed of its colony and cooperative features and became a community of factories and shops surrounded by private farmers.[54]

Financial security did not ensure ethnic stability. As early as 1919, non-Jewish families comprised one-third of the Alliance population, a demographic shift also apparent in Rosenhayn where eighty-seven Jewish and seventy-eight Gentile families lived, and in Carmel with sixty-nine Jewish and twenty Gentile families. The original Jewish settlers had been supplemented by Italians and Poles. Between 1901 and 1919, the Jewish population in the colonies had become relatively static, with few seeing themselves as permanent settlers. By 1919, only 219 persons of the region's total Jewish population of 2,739 had lived on the land more than fifteen years. With nothing able to slow it down the tide had turned. There was no holding America's Jewish farmers to the farm.[55]

The struggles of the Clarion colonists and their brothers and sisters in the other Jewish settlements suggest an explanation for their success and failure. It does not call for a regional or cultural interpretation, for the histories of the American Jewish colonies were written in the interplay of five factors—experience, environment, capital, morale, and alternatives. In the negative or positive interaction of these variables can be discerned the course of colonization. They also reveal why Jews in America failed to achieve economic stability or a secure ethnicity on the land. Further research of Jewish agricultural settlements in Canada, Argentina, Russia, and Palestine may highlight the centrality of these variables for the colonization process in these countries. Perhaps, the Clarions of America and the *kibbutzim* of Israel differ in degree rather than in kind and, thus, represent different stages along the same continuum.

Clarion and the Jewish colonies of America are now forgotten or, at most, command attention as quaint historical sites. Jewish immigrants in the United States, like most of their contemporaries, took to the city, and their descendants have had little incentive to stray from that path. The small minority who dared to farm are lost or misunderstood. Yet the road taken to Clarion and the other doomed colonies needs to be resurveyed and delineated, for it is an essential part of the Jewish American experience. These Jewish farmers, defying stereotypes and risking their all to bring about a restructuring of Jewish society, acted out of a sense of loyalty to their coreligionists who remained in the eastern ghettos. The casualties of Jewish agrarian failure were not confined to the farm. Jews in the cities or Eastern Europe and in America who supported the Back to the Soil Movement with heart and soul as well as with words and funds were deeply affected. They followed developments in the American, Canadian, Russian, and Argentine colonies as they did those in Palestine with pride and joy. Long before the term *global village* gained currency, Jews throughout the world have lived lives interconnected religiously, culturally, socially, and economically. Thus, the farms did not die in silence. In a Jewish world of the spirit, undivided by national boundaries, their deaths were mourned.

Intrinsically valuable as models of courage, determination, and discipline and against all odds, the Clarions of America speak not merely of achievements by Jews, but of Jewish achievements. That these men and women failed is their history. That they dreamed and struggled and were greater than themselves is their legacy.

Robert A. Goldberg

Notes

1. *Jewish Exponent*, July 5, 1889; Gabriel Davidson, "The Jew in Agriculture in the United States," *American Jewish Year Book*, 37 (Philadelphia, 1935–1936), 134; Rabbi Joseph Krauskopf, "What to Do with the Russian Refugee," *Sunday Discourses Before the Reform Congregation Keneseth Israel, 1905–1906* (Philadelphia, 1906), v. 19, 52; Uri D. Herscher, *Jewish Agricultural Utopias in America: 1880–1910* (Detroit, 1981), 23–24, 37–48.

2. Interview with Sarah Brown, Phoenix, by Michael Walton and Patricia Walton, November 6, 1982; interview with Lillian Brown Vogel, Los Angeles, June 17, 1983; Benjamin Brown, "Memoir," trans. by Sarah Brown (n.p., n.d.), in the author's possession, 1–2.

3. B. Brown, "Memoirs," 1–2; Barney Silverman, "A Short History of Clarion" (unpublished, 1967), in the author's possession, 3–5.

4. Interview with Barney Silverman by Ben Kristol, Philadelphia, September 1965; Silverman, "Short History," 7.

5. Esther Radding, "Journal" (unpublished, 1962), in the author's possession, 157.

6. Interview with Barnet Slobodin by Joseph Slobodin, New York, August 25, 1974.

7. Interview with Beckie Mastrow Pullman, Glendale, CA, June 17, 1982.

8. E. Radding, "Journal," 118–129, 138, 158; interview with Al, Joseph, and Samuel Ayeroff, Los Angeles, March 23, 1982; interview with Sivan Hamburger, Los Angeles, March 23, 1982; interview with Dr. Albert Isgur, Los Angeles, February 7, 1982; interview with Mina Boyarsky Michaelson, Los Angeles, March 26, 1982; Abraham Wernick, "The Clarion Colony: Its Beginnings, Its Life, Its Demise," trans. by Max Rosenfeld (Los Angeles, n.d.), in the author's possession, 6–8.

9. B. Brown, "Memoirs," 6; Silverman, "Short History," 21; *Jewish Exponent*, September 15, 1911; "In re Clarion Colony, Utah," 2, Ben Roe Papers, Special Collections, Marriott Library, University of Utah.

10. *First Successful Jewish Colony in the United States* (Salt Lake City, 1912), 3.

11. Silverman, "Short History," 34–36; *First Successful Jewish Colony*, 5.

12. Everett L. Cooley, "Clarion, Utah—Jewish Colony in Zion," *Gunnison Valley News*, March 12 and 19, 1970; Conrad Frischknecht to Everett L. Cooley, October 3, 1960, Everett L. Cooley Papers, Special Collections, Marriott Library, University of Utah; C. J. Ullrich, "Report on the Water Supply—Piute Project," (Salt Lake City, 1917[?]), in the author's possession; *Gunnison Gazette*, October 14, 1910; interview with Carl Carpenter, Clarion, May 15, 1982; interview with Lamont Nielsen, Clarion, June 26, 1982.

13. Silverman, "Short History," 40.

14. Isaac Friedlander, *Virgin Soil*, trans. by Louis C. Zucker (Los Angeles, 1949).

15. Silverman, "Short History," 42–44; interview with Samuel Chatsky by Ronald N. Goldberg, Miami, FL, May 18, 1982; interview with Allen Frandsen, Clarion, September 20, 1983; interview with Harry Kimura, Clarion, September 20, 1983; U.S. Department of Agriculture, *Soil Survey of Sanpete Valley Area, Utah, 1981*, 76–77, 80–81; Friedlander, *Virgin Soil*, 14.

16. B. Brown, "Memoir," 9–10; Wernick, "Clarion Colony," 17–19, 26; Silverman, "Short History," 41, 45–46; Rabbi Charles J. Freund, "Significance of the Jewish Farm Colony at Clarion, Utah," *Improvement Era*, 16 (December 1912), 250.

17. Interview with Nathan Ayeroff by Edward Eisen, Los Angeles, 1972.

18. Michael Walton, "The House of Israel in Mormon Theology" (unpublished paper, 1984), in the author's possession, 1–3; Ezra Taft Benson, *A Message to Judah from*

Joseph (Salt Lake City, 1978), 6–15; LeGrand Richards, *The Mormons and the Jewish People* (Salt Lake City, n.d.), 2, 7–9; Friedlander, *Virgin Soil*, 19–20; *Gunnison Gazette*, February 16, 1912; Chatsky interview; Silverman interview. See also, Rudolf Glanz, *Jew and Mormon: Historic Group Relations and Religious Outlook* (New York, 1963).

19. Silverman, "Short History," 50, 53; *First Successful Jewish Colony*, 16; Friedlander, *Virgin Soil*, 11, 14; Moshe Malamed, "Diary, 1910–1913," trans. by Adah B. Fogel (Philadelphia, n.d.) in the author's possession, 5–7; Jewish Agricultural and Colonial Association, "Articles of Incorporation," November 28, 1911, Incorporation Record, Sanpete County, Utah, bk. 2, 431–39.

20. Silverman, "Short History," 56–56A; Malamed, "Diary," 6–8; Wernick, "Clarion Colony," 32, 36, 38.

21. Wernick, "Clarion Colony," 43, 52–55, 72.

22. Utah State Board of Land Commissioners, "Minute Book," 12, May 12, 1912:522 and June 18, 1912:577–78; *Gunnison Gazette*, July 5, 1912; Silverman, "Short History," 58.

23. Frandsen interview; Nielsen interview; Silverman interview; Silverman, "Short History," 58; Utah State Board of Land Commissioners, "Minute Book," 12, August 6, 1912:678; Silverman, "Short History," 60; Isaac Landman to Rabbi Joseph Krauskopf, August 1912, 1, Box 15, Rabbi Joseph Krauskopf Papers, Urban Archives Center, Temple University, PA.

24. Silverman, "Short History," 83–85; Utah Colonization Fund, "Articles of Incorporation," June 11, 1912, Salt Lake County, no. 9620; Wernick, "Clarion County," 34–35, 47–48, 63–65.

25. Wernick, "Clarion Colony," 40–41, 44–46, 86, 106–7; B. Brown, "Memoir," 10–15; Malamed, "Dairy," 11; Ayeroff interview; Chatsky interview; Hamburger interview; Isgur interview; Michaelson interview; Vogel interview.

26. Chatsky interview; David Friedman to Issaac Landman, September 23, 1912, Box 9, Krauskopf Papers; Silverman, "Short History," 69–70; Wernick, "Clarion Colony," 56–58, 59.

27. Wernick, "Clarion Colony," 87–88; interview with Joseph Brownstein by Ben Kristol, Philadelphia, June 1965; *Gunnison Gazette*, May 9 and November 14, 1913; Silverman, "Short History," 74–76.

28. Wernick, "Clarion Colony," 100–105; *Gunnison Gazette*, September 5, 1913; Malamed, "Diary," 14–15; Chatsky interview; Friedlander, *Virgin Soil*, 31–32.

29. Wernick, "Clarion Colony," 78–79, 83–84, 88, 93–94.

30. Interview with Michael Bernstein, New York, July 28, 1982; interview with William Brownie and Edith Horowitz, Philadelphia, October 30, 1983; Isgur interview; Pullman interview.

31. Friedlander, *Virgin Soil*, 38.

32. Ibid., 37–38, 42–45; Silverman, "Short History," 93, Wernick, "Clarion Colony," 91–93.

33. N. Ayeroff interview.

34. Wernick, "Clarion Colony," 85–86, 95–97; N. Ayeroff interview; Ayeroff brothers interview; Friedlander, *Virgin Soil*, 39, 41; Silverman, "Short History," 95.

35. Wernick, "Clarion Colony," 108; Malamed, "Diary," 20.

36. Chatsky interview; Friedlander, *Virgin Soil*, 46–47; Wernick, "Clarion Colony," 133.

37. Wernick, "Clarion Colony," 1, 141, 146, 151–156, 167; *Gunnison Gazette*, January 29, June 18, July 2, September 17, and November 19, 1915; Pullman interview; Silverman, "Short History," 102–4; B. Brown, "Memoirs," 20.

38. Wernick, "Clarion Colony," 164; Utah State Board of Land Commissioners,

"Minute Book," 14, November 5, 1915:166–169, January 4, 1916:224–225, January 5, 1916:228, and December 6, 1916:578; Gunnison Gazette, January 7 and 21, 1916.

39. Brownstein interview; interview with Herman Lieberman, Los Angeles, June 17, 1983; interview with Lena Brown Marinoff, Los Angeles, March 24, 1982; B. Slobodin interview; letter, Ben Kristol to author, February 12, 1982; letters, Benjamin Paul to author, February 11 and 28, 1982.

40. Leo Shpall, "Jewish Agricultural Colonies in the United States," Agricultural History, 24 (July 1950), 120–21; Jews in American Agriculture (New York, 1954), 16; Darwin S. Levine, "A Brief Survey of the Activities of Jews in American Agriculture" (M.A. thesis, Columbia University, 1928), 26–33; Richard Singer, "The American Jew in Agriculture: Past History and Present Condition: (unpublished prize essay, Hebrew Union College, 1941), 28–30; Herscher, Jewish Agricultural Utopias, 29–30; Jonathan D. Sarna, Jacksonian Jew: The Two Worlds of Mordecai Noah (New York and London, 1981), 61–76.

41. Levine, "Brief Survey," 40–41; Singer, "American Jew," 96–105.

42. Herscher, Jewish Agricultural Utopias, 32–37, 48–52; Levine, "Brief Survey," 42–48, 60–61; Singer, "American Jew," 439–41; Shpall, "Jewish Agricultural Colonies," 129–33; Violet Goering and Orlando Goering, "Jewish Farmers in South Dakota—the Am Olam," South Dakota History, 12 (Winter 1982), 232–46.

43. Singer, "American Jew," 409–19; W. Gunther Plaut, "Jewish Colonies at Painted Woods and Devils Lake," North Dakota History, 32 (January 1965), 61–64; Lois Schwartz, "Early Jewish Agricultural Colonies in North Dakota," North Dakota History, 32 (January 1965), 61–64 and 32 (October 1965), 229–31.

44. American Israelite, January 19, 1883.

45. Elbert L. Sapinsley, "Jewish Agricultural Colonies in the West: The Kansas Example," Western States Jewish Historical Quarterly, 3 (April 1971), 159; Singer, "American Jew," 453–70, 473–86; Levine, "Brief Survey," 48–51, 56–59; Lipman G. Feld, "New Light on the Lost Jewish Colony of Beersheba, Kansas, 1882–1886," American Jewish Historical Quarterly, 60 (December 1970), 159–63; A. James Rudin, "Beersheba, Kansas," Kansas Historical Quarterly, 34 (Autumn 1968), 296–97.

46. Quoted in Dorothy Roberts, "The Jewish Colony at Cotopaxi," Colorado Magazine, 18 (July 1941), 127.

47. Levine, "Brief Survey," 64; Herscher, Jewish Agricultural Utopias, 55–60; Roberts, "Cotopaxi," 124–29.

48. Herscher, Jewish Agricultural Utopias, 61–70; Gabriel Davidson, "The Palestine Colony in Michigan: An Adventure in Colonization," Publications of the American Jewish Historical Society, 29 (1925), 61–74; A. James Rudin, "Bad Axe, Michigan: An Experiment in Jewish Agricultural Settlement," Michigan History, 56 (Summer 1972), 120–24, 127, 130.

49. Singer, "American Jew," 391.

50. Nora Levin, While Messiah Tarried: Jewish Socialist Movements, 1871–1917 (New York, 1977), 73–75; Singer, "American Jew," 379–94; Louis J. Swichkow, "The Jewish Agricultural Colony of Arpin, Wisconsin," American Jewish Historical Quarterly, 54 (September 1964), 84–90.

51. Joseph Brandes, Immigrants to Freedom: Jewish Communities in Rural New Jersey Since 1882 (Philadelphia, 1971), 7.

52. Ibid., 8.

53. Herscher, Jewish Agricultural Utopias, 31, 109–12; Shpall, "Jewish Agricultural Colonies," 146; Brandes, Immigrants to Freedom, 49, 60–68; Singer, "American Jew," 283–310.

54. Levine, "Brief Survey," 82–83; Shpall, "Jewish Agricultural Colonies," 141–43; Herscher, *Jewish Agricultural Utopias*, 73–83; Brandes, *Immigrants to Freedom*, 55–58; Philip R. Goldstein, *Social Aspects of the Jewish Colonies of South Jersey* (New York, 1921), 13–16; Singer, "American Jew," 261–79.
55. Goldstein, *Social Aspects*, 29–31; Brandes, *Immigrants to Freedom*, 93.

Chapter 4

Chasing the Cure in Colorado:

The Jewish Consumptives' Relief Society

JEANNE ABRAMS

Introduction

Jeanne Abrams, in her study of the Jewish Consumptives' Relief Society of Denver (JCRS), offers a perspective on western history that is frequently overlooked and often forgotten. If most of those who trekked west came to seek their fortunes, a goodly number came to recover their health. Early in its history, Colorado earned a reputation for offering a dry climate and clear mountain air that could perform medical miracles. "One traveler . . . wrote," reports Robert Athearn, "'I was told that in some sections [of Colorado] it was so healthy that a man had to be killed to start a burying ground.'" (*Coloradans* [Albuquerque, 1976], 93) By the opening years of the twentieth century, an ever-growing number of Eastern European Jews afflicted with tuberculosis were journeying to Colorado and other western sites in search of sun, fresh air, and a moderate climate. Denver, with an already-established Jewish community, attracted those wracked by the ill health that accompanied life in the sweatshops and crowded tenements of the East Coast ghettos.

As Abrams documents in some detail, the Jews of Denver reacted to the arrival of Jewish health seekers by establishing two hospitals for the treatment of tuberculars, the National Jewish Hospital (NJH) sponsored by the Americanized Reform community and the JCRS organized by more recent immigrants from Eastern Europe who tended to be traditional in their religious practices. With the formation of these two national Jewish centers for the treatment of consumptives, the history of the Denver Jewish community took a unique turn. Indeed, the demographic development of the Denver Jewish community in the first two decades of the twentieth century can be attributed to the presence of the two hospitals. The growth of the total Jewish population and, more particularly, the increase in the Eastern European segment of that population would probably not have occurred had the hospitals not existed. Furthermore, the presence of Eastern European

Jewish patients and their families compelled the local Jewish leadership to establish such additional institutions as The Sheltering Home and the Ex-Patients Home, which otherwise would have been unnecessary, Abrams' essay reminds us that however similar the history of Jewish communities in the West may be, however useful the search for patterns and generalizations, each community has elements that are unique.

The history of the JCRS also illustrates the fact that writing the history of Jews in the West, even the history of Jews in one western community, cannot be done successfully without paying proper attention to developments elsewhere. It was the conditions of poverty, poor housing, and inadequate sanitation in East Coast cities that contributed to the incidence of tuberculosis among Eastern European Jews and that led to the establishment of two national hospitals in Denver. It was an Eastern European tradition of *tzedakah*, brought from Russia and Poland, that motivated the JCRS leadership and that was embedded in the concept of proper treatment implemented at the JCRS. Dr. Charles Spivak's commitment to socialism, nurtured in youth in Russia, impelled him to rely on a large following of Jewish working people to provide the financial base upon which to erect the hospital rather than turn to the Americanized Jewish middle class for support. Furthermore, Abrams' discussion of the fund-raising apparatus established by JCRS sets the institution within a national framework. Fund-raisers for the hospital fanned out across the country and contacted those persons and organizations likely to respond to urgent pleas for contributions. Students of local Jewish history must be sensitive to forces that lie outside local community control and to which all Jewish communities are obliged to respond.

CHASING THE CURE IN COLORADO

In nineteenth-century Europe and America, tuberculosis held the dubious distinction of being the leading cause of death. The advent of the Industrial Revolution and the rise of massive cities with their congestion and poor sanitation, ventilation, and nutrition, all contributed to a high incidence of the disease. Although tuberculosis afflicted members of all classes, slum dwellers seemed especially susceptible to the debilitating, often fatal, disease.

There was no one accepted standard for tuberculosis treatment at the turn of the century. Various medications, surgical treatments, and folk remedies still competed with the open-air method of treatment, which, after the opening in 1884 of the first American tuberculosis sanitorium by Dr. Edward Trudeau at Saranac Lake in upstate New York, was widely accepted by contemporary medical opinion. By the mid-1880s, some two decades before Denver's two Jewish sanatoria were opened, a sanatorium movement had been established and sanatoria began to spring up in various parts of the United States. According to Dr. Arthur Myers, a pioneer and leader in the medical treatment of tuberculosis, sanatoria were "considered the best place for tuberculosis patients, not only because of their therapeutic facilities but also because isolation in them prevented the spread of tubercule bacilli."[1]

Colorado, with its dry sunny climate, proved to be a magnet for tuberculosis victims. It has been demonstrated that through publicity, by word of mouth, and through various publications, Denver in particular became a center of hope for persons afflicted with tuberculosis or consumption, as it was also commonly known.[2] In 1887, the Denver Chamber of Commerce proudly proclaimed: "Colorado is the mecca of consumptives, and rightfully; for dry air, equitable temperature and continuous sunshine are as yet the most reliable factors in the care of that disease."[3] Moreover, as historian Billy Jones has pointed out, "No portion of the health frontier, with the possible exception of southern California, received greater nationwide publicity after the Civil War than Colorado."[4] As early as 1896, the state was being flatteringly referred to as The World's Sanitorium.[5]

Although a handful of cities in the United States established specifically Jewish sanatoria, Denver was the *only* city in the country to boast two *national* Jewish sanatoria: the National Jewish Hospital (NJH), which opened in 1899, and the Jewish Consumptives' Relief Society (JCRS), which followed in 1904. A few major cities in America with large Jewish populations, most notably New York and Philadelphia, established nearby sanatoria, but for the most part these institutions were open only to local residents. Outside of Denver the largest Jewish sanatorium was probably the Bedford Sanatorium, which was located at "the highest point in Westchester County." Although Bedford, an outgrowth of New York's Montefiore Hospital, had a large bed capacity, even some of its patients were encouraged to go to Denver because of the city's climate and the reputation of the two Jewish tuberculosis hospitals there.[6] In the case of tuberculosis, at least, western geography and climate were destiny. The growth of Denver's Jewish population after 1900 was stimulated by an influx of predominately Eastern European Jews who joined other Americans to "chase the cure" in Colorado's benevolent environment.[7]

If the Jewish population in the West stagnated or even declined between 1900 and 1940, the special situation produced by the attraction of two Jewish tuberculosis hospitals led to a significant increase in Denver's Jewish population. As Rabbi William Friedman, a founder of the NJH later recalled:

> The fame of Colorado's capitol [sic] city, nestling in a valley flooded with sunshine, protected from the extreme heat and cold, attracted not only the ambitious searcher for wealth, but the enfeebled seeker of health. ... No wonder Colorado was a land of promise towards which tens of thousands turned their faces. ... In this hegira journeyed hundreds

of penniless Jewish sufferers whose emaciated faces and hollow cheeks and hacking cough were sadly eloquent of close confinement in crowded tenements.[8]

Although thousands of people of diverse ethnic origin migrated west in search of a cure, the migration of Jewish consumptives was disproportionately high, and their destination clearly was Denver:

Almost from the earliest days of the opening up of the western country a constant stream of health-seekers has been pouring over the arid lands of Colorado, Arizona, New Mexcio and California. Many of these migrants made Denver their objective, and among them a goodly proportion were of Jewish extraction. These Jewish health-seekers going to Denver almost since the days of the first settlers, early forced themselves upon the attention of the more fortunate members of the growing Jewish community there, and efforts were commenced in the late 80's which culminated at the end of that decade in a well-defined movement for aid and succor.

. . . . .

Among Jews, the migration of consumptives is largely due to the cities of the west and southwest, the goal of most of them being Denver. This is due to Denver's reputation as a health resort, its location, its relative size among western cities, and the location in Denver of two Jewish hospitals for consumptives.[9]

When the JCRS—founded by a group of twenty Jewish immigrant tradesmen to aid Jewish victims in all stages of the disease—formally opened on September 4, 1904, tuberculosis still reigned supreme as the leading cause of death in the United States.[10] The JCRS estimated that around the turn of the century approximately 154,000 persons died annually from tuberculosis and more than ten times that number were afflicted with the disease.[11] For the next fifty years, the JCRS sanitorium on West Colfax Avenue would admit patients free of charge and serve as a haven for thousands afflicted with the White Plague. Although the institution was to be formally nonsectarian, it is clear that initially the JCRS was organized primarily to serve Jewish patients in need of a distinctively Jewish environment.

The migration of these health seekers to Denver from cities throughout America placed a severe economic and social burden on the city's established but small Jewish community. Even those who had no chance of being admitted into either of the two already overcrowded hospitals came to Denver in the hope that somehow Colorado's climate alone would magically cure their ailment. Ultimately, an organizational structure was created to meet the needs of the many newcomers that included the Denver Jewish Sheltering Home, founded in 1907 to care for the needs of the children of the sick, and the Ex-Patients Association, which was incorporated a few years later to assist discharged patients in need of employment and housing.

In 1899, in order to cope with the the numerous, generally indigent, Jewish victims of tuberculosis who began to descend on Denver in the late 1880s, prosperous members of the local Reform German Jewish community banded together to found the NJH.[12] This hospital extended its services free of charge, but unlike the JCRS, imposed a rigid set of rules that governed admissions. Abiding by the predominant medical opinion of the era, NJH in its early years generally admitted only patients with incipient tuberculosis. In addition to a formal application and a formal medical examination, prospective patients at NJH were required to have sufficient means of support to remain in Denver after their stay or sufficient funds to return to their hometowns to discourage long-term residence by poor patients who might become a serious financial drain on local Jewish charity. Although no time limit was generally set on JCRS patients, at NJH all patients were allowed to remain at the hospital for a limit of six months only.[13] Finally, there was also a feeling on the part of many Eastern European Jews, who comprised the vast majority of the early JCRS patients, that the NJH acted in a patronizing and condescending manner toward them, making it particularly difficult for religious Jews to observe the laws of *kashrut* and Jewish festivals and rituals.[14] At one point Dr. Moses Collins, the first manager of NJH, maintained that following Jewish dietary laws was "pronounced inadvisable for medical reasons" and urged that milk be served at all meals for tuberculosis patients, even when meat appeared on the menu.[15] It is interesting to note that at New York's Bedford Sanatorium and other German Jewish institutions, the Eastern European Jews often confronted similar difficulties. A medical director there considered the customary usage of Yiddish by many of his patients somewhat backward and referred to the language derogatorily as jargon.[16]

If the West made claim to a more open social and class structure, it was not evident in the relationship between Denver's Eastern European and German Jewish communities who rivaled New York City's uptown and downtown Jews in their social tensions. Little love was lost between NJH, largely supported by Denver's German Jews, and the Eastern European-based JCRS. As a leading social worker, Boris

Bogen, later remarked, "At the turn of the century condescending attitudes and superiority feelings on the part of the givers of service aroused wide resentment and led to immigrant self-organization."[17] In Denver, the JCRS was established to provide an alternative to the NJH for destitute Eastern European Jewish tuberculosis victims seeking a more Jewish environment as well as to help initiate a pioneering medical effort to assist patients with more severe cases of the disease who were not admitted elsewhere. Of the twenty-one sanatoria in Colorado listed in 1911 by the National Association for the Study and Prevention of Tuberculosis, only nine admitted consumptives in all stages of the disease. In Colorado, the JCRS alone admitted all consumptives, regardless of race or creed, in all stages of the disease— and at no charge.[18] Of the four other sanatoria in Colorado that treated patients free of charge, three admitted their own members only and the fourth, the NJH, although free, generally admitted only patients with incipient cases of tuberculosis.[19]

The leaders of NJH and the JCRS clashed not only along ethnic, religious, and medical lines but perhaps even more importantly along philosophical lines. The Denver German Jewish community undoubtedly feared the radical orientation of the JCRS leaders, and not without reason. The three major JCRS leaders in the early years, Dr. Philip Hillkowitz, Dr. Adolph Zederbaum, and Dr. Charles Spivak, were all of Eastern European origin. These three physicians, particularly Dr. Spivak, not only monitored the daily needs of the JCRS but were also responsible for the philosophy that guided the institution at every step of the way. Spivak, probably the single most important force behind the JCRS, had emigrated from Russia to the United States as a young man in the 1880s. In Russia, after receiving a thorough Jewish as well as secular education, he became a socialist as a teenager and subsequently maintained a lifelong friendship with Abraham Cahan, the well-known editor of the socialist *Jewish Daily Forward*. Like so many other Eastern European immigrants who helped swell Denver's Jewish population at the turn of the century, Spivak migrated west for health reasons in 1896 along with his wife Jenny, who had probably contracted incipient tuberculosis in Philadelphia.[20]

In his position as executive secretary of the JCRS, Spivak supervised fund-raising operations, and his personal philosophy, informed by a unique blend of Yiddishkeit, secularism, and socialism, undoubtedly strongly influenced JCRS policies. Although Spivak's professed socialism was apparently tempered over the years, to a great extent his outlook, no doubt, was responsible for the emphasis the early JCRS placed on appealing to the working class for the bulk of its income, as is evident in a letter that he wrote in 1906 to one of his traveling fund raisers: "Abandon entirely the idea of making any strenuous efforts to meet our rich brethren. If our Institution is to be a people's institution, it should be supported by the people only. Let us collect our moneys in dollars and quarters."[21] His views were seconded by Dr. Philip Hillkowitz, JCRS president from 1904 to 1948, when he made an obvious allusion to the differences between the NJH and the JCRS support in his first presidential address, "We are proud of the humble and lowly origin of our Society. We rejoice in the fact that our beginning was distinctly a movement from below, not initiated by men of high economic or social standing."[22]

Because patients were treated free of charge at the JCRS, it is understandable that fund-raising would become a pivotal and perennial task. Although the JCRS was, indeed, basically organized by Eastern European immigrants, it soon developed one of the most sophisticated and successful fund-raising campaigns in the United States. Recognizing that the major sources of support would come from modest contributions from the Jewish working and lower middle classes, the JCRS leaders consciously set about building a network of contacts throughout the United States that would ultimately attract large numbers of supporters from all segments of the American Jewish community. Although the JCRS hospital was located in the West, its financial ties connected the institution with Jewish communities throughout the country. In 1914, Spivak observed of the JCRS patients, "We have in our institution chasidim and agnostics, Jews and Christians, republicans and progressives, socialists and anarchists, men of all kinds of religious, political and economic opinions."[23] What insured the financial success of the institution was that this wide spectrum that made up the JCRS patient population also described those who comprised the institution's financial supporters.

It is interesting to note that although the JCRS Sanatorium came to resemble the modern, sprawling Progressive Era-type of hospital in outward appearance, in its sources of financial backing it differed radically. Most hospitals before the turn of the century depended largely on various combinations of philanthropic contributions and interest dividends, but as early as 1905, paying patients increasingly became the major source of hospital funding.[24] In his study on the transformation of American medicine, Paul Starr has pointed out that this was especially true in the southern and western areas of the United States where less capital was available for philanthropy.[25] In Denver almost all sanatoria charged patients for medical care.[26] Thomas Galbreath, a young easterner who came to Denver for his health in 1905, observed that the cost of care, even in an inadequate boardinghouse or sanatorium, ran from ten to twenty-five dollars per week.[27] In the light of these figures, it is even more significant that in Denver at the time only the JCRS and NJH treated all patients without charge.

The primary reason for the general shift from charity to paying patients was that the financial needs of the growing American hospital had exceeded the ability of the traditional donors to meet them.[28] Because the JCRS continued to admit all patients free of charge, its ongoing success depended almost entirely on private contributions. Financial depressions and inflationary cycles in the American economy had generally resulted in significantly decreased contributions to charitable institutions including hospitals,[29] yet both the JCRS and NJH continued to attract private support in the Jewish community.

The dedicated efforts of the leaders and volunteers, the high standards set by the staff, and the quality of medical care at the sanatorium were all vital components in the achievements of the JCRS over the years. As necessary as these elements were, however, the success of the JCRS was ultimately dependent on the ability of the organization to tap contributors in all parts of the United States at all socioeconomic levels. The strong Eastern European tradition of *tzedakah*, which viewed charity as a clear obligation rather than as a mere commendable act, helped to insure the financial success of the JCRS. Obligations to care for the sick and indigent would stretch beyond western boundaries. An editorial appearing in a 1909 issue of the *Sanatorium* offered an effusive but perceptive description of the financial underpinnings of the JCRS organization:

> The phenomenal rise and rapid growth of the Jewish Consumptives' Relief Society has been the marvel of all students of philanthropy. Starting with an initial fund of $1.10, it has within the short space of five years evolved into one of the foremost national organizations counting close to 20,000 members and contributors. Without depending on wealthy endowments or rich bequests, it has appealed directly to the masses of Jewish people native as well as immigrant, and by virtue of mere strength of numbers has become the most popular and widely known institution in American Jewry.[30]

An impressionistic survey of the JCRS financial records does, indeed, confirm the notion that a large portion of the contributions came from men and women of modest means with small donations, sometimes as little as twenty-five cents, recorded over and over again.[31] As Milton Goldin has observed in *Why They Give*, poor immigrants felt an obligation to aid those who were even less fortunate and Eastern European immigrants in particular, so large a portion of the JCRS pa-

Patients dropping by the JCRS cooperative store, 1916. (Courtesy of the Ira M. Beck Archives of Rocky Mountain Jewish History, Center for Judaic Studies, University of Denver.)

tients and contributors, gave because turning to each other for aid did not offend their dignity.[32] Moreover, to support immigrant organizations like the JCRS, Eastern European Jews throughout America supported a combination of fund-raising activities that included paying dues, buying tickets to annual dinners, giving donations to collectors in the street, and filling charity boxes.[33] Although small donations were the norm, the JCRS certainly did not discourage occasional large contributions, even when they came from German Jewish leaders like New York's well-known Maecenas, Jacob Schiff, who contributed one thousand dollars in 1904.[34]

For the decade following 1910, the *Teller Report* on tuberculosis among Jews in Denver gives us valuable insight into the makeup of the JCRS contributors. The major source of funding came from mem-

bership dues collected from individuals, auxiliary societies, and organizations throughout the country, with the majority of memberships
falling in the three- and five-dollar category. The balance of yearly
funds came from donations by individuals and societies, bequests
and legacies, special fund-raising entertainment programs, interest
on bank balances, and sales of products grown or manufactured at
the JCRS.[35]

In a conscious effort to raise money and gain support from all
over the country, the JCRS initiated and supported local auxiliaries
in almost all major cities in the United States; this resulted in a nationwide network that provided financial and moral support to the
organization. In addition, and perhaps more important, field secretaries, or financial solicitors, either were hired locally or were sent
out on the road from Denver to publicize the needs of the JCRS and
collect funds for the sanatorium. Philip Hillkowitz's sister, Anna Hillkowitz, served as one of the first JCRS field secretaries and traveled
all over the United States, stopping in New York City, Philadelphia,
Kansas City, Cincinnati, and Wichita as well as in such smaller towns
as Huntington, West Virginia.[36] Some of Anna Hillkowitz's letters reflect the continuing battle between the NJH and the JCRS. Writing
from Cincinnati on May 1, 1906, Anna complained that she was prevented from raising much money in that city because of interference
by the "Muller gang,"[37] led by Muller, a trustee of the NJH and executive secretary of the institution at that time. A little over a week later,
Anna again reported conflict with the representatives of the NJH at
a convention she was attending in Philadelphia:[38] "If you had seen how
Pisko[39] . . . and Muller cornered everybody. . . . Mr. Grabfelder[40] got
up and told a big *lie* that the NJH took patients not only in the incipient stages, but in the second, aye and even the advanced stages of
consumption."[41] The bitterness and ill feeling between the NJH and
the JCRS persisted outside the Denver community. Competition for
funding from many of the same sources was a frequent point of irritation between the two organizations for many years to come. The
strength of the JCRS was its ability to tap resources from a multitude of small contributors. When the sources for funding were larger
organizations such as national fraternal orders or citywide Jewish
federations, the competition between NJH and the JCRS intensified,
and as Anna Hillkowitz's letters demonstrate, feelings ran high.

Jacob Marinoff, who had served for a short time as the first superintendent of the JCRS, was another interesting representative of the
group that made up the first JCRS field secretaries. An article appearing in the November 1907 issue of the *Sanatorium* described a ban-

quet held to honor Marinoff—who was shortly to become the editor of the great Yiddish humor weekly, the *Big Stick*—for a strenuous and successful year as a field secretary in the New York area,[42] a key source of fund raising—thus illustrating the financial links that ran from Denver to the East and West coasts. In the same issue, Marinoff was commended for placing charity boxes in New York City workshops, on the recommendation of various fraternal orders, in order to solicit working people to deposit nickels and dimes to aid consumptives at the JCRS. The article then proceeded to list the contributions received from the first fifty-three boxes, some with less than ten cents,[43] for a grand total of $18.25, thus indicating the poverty of the contributors themselves. For nearly fifty years, the JCRS charity boxes could be found in homes, stores, synagogues, and factories throughout the United States.

A discussion of JCRS fund-raising would be incomplete without emphasizing the support the organization received from various national fraternal organizations and the numerous JCRS ladies' auxiliaries throughout the country. Indeed, ladies' auxiliaries founded in countless cities—Chicago, St. Louis, New York, Baltimore—made possible the erection of a number of essential buildings on the JCRS grounds and even helped to keep the organization afloat during the Great Depression. These groups also testify to the national character of the JCRS organization.

Paralleling the support of the ladies' auxiliaries was the aid of fraternal orders and labor unions throughout the country. According to a 1907 issue of the *Sanatorium,*

> The workingmen of the populous East Side of New York have from the first been staunch supportes of the JCRS. These fraternal orders, lodges, and societies are strong pillars of support to our cause and many a wage-worker scrapes and skimps from his meager earnings to send us his annual membership dues.[44]

Support from unions and fraternal orders were particularly significant in New York City and on the East Coast where these organizations were especially strong. One of the early fraternal groups that came to the aid of the JCRS was the Independent Order B'rith Abraham (IOBA). The IOBA, a national fraternal order, had been founded as an alternative to the largely German, Reform-based B'nai B'rith, which had discriminated against admitting Eastern European Jews in its early days. In 1913, the IOBA claimed 182,000 members.[45] Many fraternal organizations and unions such as the IOBA and the Arbeiter Ring (Workmen's Circle) supported the JCRS by imposing a tax on their members. Even before the JCRS had officially opened its doors in the fall of 1904, eight hundred dollars had been collected on the floor of the IOBA National Convention held in May of that year. At the same convention, the IOBA members agreed to place a two-and-one-half cents per-capita-per-annum tax on all its members.[46]

The support of these fraternal organizations and the trade unions, composed as they were primarily of Eastern European Jews, once again demonstrates the networks of mutual aid of the Eastern European community and the links between Jews in the West and their fellow Jews in the East, South, and on the West Coast. Although tuberculosis was no respecter of social status, the laboring classes were most susceptible to the disease because they were subject to the unhealthy working conditions associated with sweatshops and congested urban living. By banding together, individuals in lodges and unions could pool their limited resources and contribute to an organization like the JCRS to insure that their members would receive proper medical care. With its patently Jewish atmosphere and flavor, the JCRS appealed particularly to the Eastern European Jews who comprised the membership of such organizations. Not surprisingly, the success of the Eastern-European-based JCRS instilled a feeling of pride in working-class contributors, who doubtless viewed the JCRS sanatorium as a symbol of their independence from German Reform domination. Again, Boris Bogen offered a perceptive analysis of the situation: "The phase these two institutions represent [NJH and the JCRS] in the United States is interesting to note. They represent the rivalry in the sphere of charity between the older American Jewry (the Reform element) and the newer (and Orthodox element) which arrived in our country during the last thirty years."[47]

Lastly, financial support was also received from a multitude of small synagogues and in some instances from federated Jewish charities that were beginning to spring up all over the country by 1910.[48] It was common for field secretaries to visit local synagogues to secure donations from their congregants as well as for synagogues to conduct appeals on various Jewish holidays for the JCRS cause.

The history of the JCRS was once described as "a ceaseless struggle to keep pace with the constantly increasing numbers of patients knocking at its gates."[49] Although the nickels and dimes of the poor did, indeed, provide the major funding for the JCRS at the beginning, as the years passed, more sophisticated campaigning resulted in the extension of the geographical and economic groups that contributed to the institution. As the American Jewish community grew and traditional Jewish observance declined, the JCRS increasingly began to depend on what

Daniel Elazar has termed the "Contributors and Consumers" group of American Jews, those whose affiliation with Judaism consists primarily of giving money to Jewish causes and the periodic utilization of the services of Jewish institutions, such as synagogues, for wedding or burial services.[50] The increasing frequency of checkbook Judaism in America brought financial support to the JCRS from men and women in all economic strata throughout the United States.

Yet, it is apparent, at least until Spivak's death in 1927, that the primary financial support for the JCRS came from contributors whose incomes were modest. Because these supporters had little money to give, of necessity their contributions needed to be marshaled en masse. At the turn of the century, most Jewish philanthropy in the United States was controlled and directed by German Reform Jews. At one level, the organization of the JCRS was, undoubtedly, an attempt to democratize Jewish philanthropy in the United States. As Bogen later observed, the JCRS demonstrated that the Eastern European Jews were capable of successfully initiating, managing, and directing their own agencies.[51]

If the JCRS effected major changes in the fund-raising sphere of the American Jewish community, it had a significant, if more subtle, effect in the realm of tuberculosis treatment as well. As already noted, in admitting terminally ill tuberculosis patients, the JCRS departed radically from then-contemporary standard medical practice. Although doctors in most hospitals in the United States at the turn of the century were developing a more professional and distant relationship with their patients and hospitals during the Progressive Era were becoming increasingly impersonal,[52] at the JCRS this was not the case. At least for the first twenty-five years of its existence, the institution remained more closely patterned after the typical nineteenth-century hospital, functioning (according to historian David Rosner) simultaneously as a health care facility and social service agency[53] akin to the strong Eastern European tradition of *tzedakah* and the manner in which charity and social services were dispensed.

Aside from treating tuberculosis patients in all stages of the disease, the JCRS did not differ substantially from other sanatoria in specific medical treatment on a day-to-day basis. At New York's Bedford Sanatorium, for instance, the medical routines seem remarkably similar to practices in Denver. Like the JCRS, Bedford stressed good nutrition along with plenty of rest and fresh air. Patients who broke rules were frequently dismissed.[54]

The first known example of an institution featuring open-air treatment of tuberculosis was the Royal Sea Bathing Infirmary established in 1791 in Margate, England, by a Quaker physician.[55] However, most American sanatoria of the late nineteenth and early twentieth centuries were patterned after the German open-air treatment model. A tuberculosis open-air sanatorium founded in 1854 in Silesia emphasized constant fresh air and forced feeding for all tuberculosis patients. This method was adopted at Colorado's first open-air sanatorium, the Nordrach Ranch, which opened in Colorado Springs in 1901. At Nordrach, the director, Dr. John White, insisted on a full open-air treatment for all his patients, who were required to live in canvas tents day and night in all season of the year. Also, following the German model, patients were (in historiam Douglas R. McKay's words) subject to "disciplined gluttony."[56] In order to gain the desired twenty-five pounds required by White, patients were literally forced to stuff themselves at meals and were "not allowed to leave the table until every morsel was eaten and every drop consumed."[57] In addition, strict rest periods at Nordrach required total silence one hour before and one hour after meals. Nordrach was known for its "firm and unrelenting" discipline and was, not surprisingly, termed a prison by some of the patients.[58]

In contrast, although a general open-air treatment was followed at the JCRS, it was certainly not as extreme as the program at Nordrach Ranch. In actuality, treatment at the JCRS more closely resembled the description of a more modern and moderate method of tuberculosis treatment described by Dr. Philip Jacobs, a leading tuberculosis expert, in 1932: "A regimen of simple living consisting of rest, fresh air, good food and freedom from worry, together with proper medical supervision, will bring about a natural process of healing."[59]

As at Nordrach, early patients at the JCRS also lived in "tent" cottages, but they were constructed of lumber as well as canvas. Even so, Dr. Hillkowitz may have been exaggerating somewhat when he claimed, "Even during one of the cold spells when the temperature dropped to 10 degrees below zero, additional blankets made the patients fairly comfortable."[60] However, the JCRS adminstration was not as intractable as Nordrach's Dr. White, as early as 1905 supplementing the tents with indoor wards for the more seriously ill patients. It must be emphasized that reliance on fresh air was a common feature of most tuberculosis treatment at the turn of the century, and application of the theory ranged from moderate to extreme. According to Golda Meir's sister, Shana Korngold, who was a patient at the NJH in 1908, "Even on the coldest night did the sick ones, well wrapped up, sleep outside."[61]

As far as diet was concerned, although nutrition and generous portions of food were encouraged at the JCRS, at no time were patients subject to near forced feeding as was one unfortunate woman

"The Tents": Spivak, Colorado, c. 1933. (Courtesy of the Ira M. Beck Archives of Rocky Mountain Jewish History, Center for Judaic Studies, University of Denver.)

at the Cragmore Sanatorium in Colorado Springs who was required to consume twenty-eight raw eggs—considered especially healthful for tuberculosis patients—before she left the table.[62] In matters of diet the JCRS tried to cater to the patient's ethnic background, which in the early years was predominately Eastern European. For example, the JCRS was diametrically opposed to the early NJH policy that did not provide for a kosher kitchen. In a 1908 article, Dr. Aldolph Zederbaum argued that maintaining kosher dietary laws was in no way detrimental to the health of the tuberculosis patients: "It is mere nonsense to claim that a sick person cannot thrive on Jewish meat and delicacies." And he continued, "At the Sanatorium of the JCRS dairy articles never appear with meat." Zederbaum further argued that the patients' mental as well as physical health was at risk and that by forcing patients to forsake the dietary laws they held dear, more damage would be done to their health than any positive nutritional value that could possibly result from their violating the laws.[63]

Although the JCRS adhered fairly closely to the norm in the open-air treatment of tuberculosis, it departed radically from prevalent medical and social attitudes by attempting to cater to the *total* patient and his or her needs. Progressive Era models of efficiency had often resulted in hospitals that seemed dehumanized and mechanical. Eastern European Jews were not accustomed to the complicated, organized, and frequently impersonal bureaucratic methods for dispensing charity at Reform Jewish institutions at the turn of the century. The rules and regulations maintained by the Reform charities were in line with the efficient and rational new methods of progressive reformers and were seen by some as a way to Americanize Eastern European Jews.[64] Charity was often administered by scientific formula, so that by studying forms and questionnaires, the "proper" amount of charity could be distributed to the worthy poor. An early editorial appearing in the JCRS's *Sanatorium* disdained the scientific and sociological devices for dispensing charity at American hospitals in the Progressive Era. Claiming that personal and human elements were entirely lacking in such a method, the author of the editorial, doubtless Dr. Spivak, urged instead that charity be "dispensed in the spirit of the good, old charity . . . let it be 'Charity of the Heart' and not of the head."[65]

Spivak's views clashed with the goals of progressivism that sought to apply efficient, profitable business techniques to all aspects of American society. Jewish societies in Eastern Europe to aid the sick, the aged, and orphans as well as burial societies and the various gradations of the poor dispensed *tzedakah shtetl*-style in response to need and without "red tape."[66] Spivak would have disagreed strongly, for instance, with Abraham Abraham, a wealthy German Jewish Reform businessman, who in 1903, as president of the Jewish Hospital of Brooklyn, declared, "Even charitable institutions, however laudable and worthy, should be conducted on sound business principles."[67] Spivak apparently took an opposite view, "We may not be able to return him [the patient] to his family as a useful working unit, we may actually waste money without any hope for any return, nevertheless, we feel that he or she must receive our care and attention, that whole-souled and whole-hearted charity is, after all, the only true, pure and unalloyed charity."[68]

In addition, although the "modern" Progressive Era hospital was often insensitive to patient needs that were not strictly medical,[69] at the early JCRS, the staff and board of trustees members seemingly involved themselves in all aspects of patients' lives. On arrival at the JCRS, the patients were welcomed with open arms, if with a somewhat paternalistic attitude. In this, the JCRS resembled the late-nineteenth-century and early-twentieth-century hospitals that had not yet begun to develop into modern medical complexes. As Rosner notes of these earlier hospitals, "Often the trustees of these small facilities would act as personal guardians or patrons of particular patients to the extent of visiting them regularly to check their medical and moral progress."[70] Spivak's daughter, Deena Spivak Strauss, recalled that all new patients received a bouquet of flowers and a basket of fruit on their arrival at the JCRS sanatorium and that her father often would shop for patients in his free time because they were generally not allowed off the JCRS grounds.[71] As was true of many nineteenth century community hospitals, the JCRS more closely resembled a private home or small hotel than the modern hospital as we know it.[72] It is interesting to note that a return to a homey, personal setting is increasingly becoming the norm in our postmodern hospitals, which have begun to offer many amenities to attract patients.

Although a benevolent spirit seemed to pervade the JCRS, life for the patients was well regulated, to say the least. A directive, entitled "Rules for the Conduct of Patients," was issued to each patient on arrival. The earlist JCRS memo, dated November 1, 1904, attempted to win support and goodwill and encouraged each patient to view the rules as supportive of "the spontaneous good conduct of every member of a well-regulated household."[73] The use of the word *household* is significant, for the JCRS seemed to be regarded as a home by both the patients and administration. Dr. Spivak in particular was regarded as a father figure and nicknamed Papa Spivak by many of the patients.[74] Dr. Hillkowitz observed of Spivak, "The patients were his children and they affectionately considered him as a father. He always took time to listen to their personal woes. He took a deep interest in their work and in their play."[75] There seems little doubt that Spivak's strong personality was responsible, in part, for the rather homelike setting that characterized life at the JCRS during his lifetime. Social worker Chester Teller, a more disinterested observer than Hillkowitz, was also impressed by the atmosphere and observed in his report on the JCRS that was published in 1916, "The relations between officers and patients is informal and sympathetic. The patients, or guests as they are sometimes spoken of, constitute a kind of big family . . . a spirit of comaraderie and fellowship pervades the place."[76]

The continuing commitment at the JCRS to a homelike setting and free medical services were perhaps the most significant features that distinguished the JCRS from the typical Progressive Era hospital. Although the early JCRS leaders and patients were by no means all observant Jews, they were bound together by strong cultural and ethnic ties that included a specific manner in which charity and hospital care were to be dispensed. In the *First Annual Report of the JCRS, 1905,* Spivak outlined the basic premise that was to govern the institution, "The Society wishes to inaugurate a radical departure from similar organizations, by eliminating from the conduct and management of its Sanatorium, anything and everything that would tend to remind the inmates of the fact that they are public charges."[77] On another occasion, Dr. Hillkowitz pointed out that as a matter of principle the JCRS sanatorium endeavored to strike a "distinctly Jewish tone."[78] The JCRS free-service policy and its Jewish environment guaranteed that, unlike many modern hospitals, at the JCRS patients from lower social and economic classes were not forced into inferior and separate medical institutions. The success of the JCRS was a tribute to the dedication and perseverance of Spivak, Philip Hillkowitz, and countless others among the JCRS leaders as well as to the poor but numerically dominant Jews of Eastern European origins throughout the United States who marshaled their resources to insure that the JCRS sanatorium would provide an environment that would meet the religious and cultural as well as the medical needs of their coreligionists.

Of the thousands of patients who passed through the JCRS gates, many became permanent Denver residents. The vast majority of the early JCRS patients were of Eastern European origins and part of a larger migration to the West of health seekers from various immigrant groups. According to Billy Jones, health seekers who came to the southwest before the turn of the century accounted for at least 20 percent of the region's population and were second numerically only to those who migrated west seeking land.[79]

In some cases, perhaps, the goals of health seeker and land seeker combined, for the image of the mythic American West proved extremely attractive to many Eastern European Jewish immigrants. Spivak, himself a stauch proponent of Jewish agrarianization, viewed the West as the last frontier where an abundance of land could ultimately support great numbers of immigrants.[80] Surely, many patients at the JCRS and the NJH were also drawn to an idealized Denver wherein New York's crowded slums gave way to a dream of open spaces and new opportunities.

In Denver, owing to the attraction of the two national Jewish hospitals, the percentage of Jewish health seekers who augmented the city's Jewish population, either temporarily or on a long-term basis, was probably significantly higher than Billy Jones's estimate and lasted well into the twentieth century. This was not true in the small number of other cities in America where Jewish sanatoria were established. In New York and Philadelphia, for example, local residents afflicted with tuberculosis were treated at nearby sanatoria and then, on being discharged, would return to their homes nearby. The number of Jews who remained in Denver after being discharged from the two hospitals appears, particularly after 1910, to have been substantial. In 1916, social worker Chester Teller estimated that over 2,000 Jewish consumptives had resided in Denver during the previous year.[81] My examination of patient records from 1905 to 1907 reveals that for the first 100 patients admitted to the JCRS 32 died in the sanatorium. Of the remaining 68 patients, 27 (40 percent) were listed in the *Denver City Directory* for at least one year following their hospital discharge.[82]

As in the case of other ethnic groups, the Eastern European Jewish health seekers brought their own set of cultural values to the West, and those who remained often became influential and vital members of their adopted communities. If most Eastern European Jews came West seeking economic opportunity, many of those arriving in Denver came to seek renewed health. In this respect, the emigration to Denver was different.

Notes

1. Arthur Myers, *Tuberculosis: A Half Century of Study and Conquest* (St. Louis, 1970), 21–22.
2. James Giese, "Tuberculosis and the Growth of Denver's Eastern European Community: The Accommodation of an Immigrant Group to a Medium-Sized Western City. 1900–1920" (Ph.D. diss., University of Colorado, 1979).
3. *Fourth Annual Report of the Denver Chamber of Commerce*, Denver, 1887.
4. Billy Jones, *Health Seekers in the Southwest, 1817–1900* (Norman, 1967), 89.
5. Ibid., 93.
6. Dorothy Levenson, *Montefiore* (New York, 1984), 72.
7. Giese, "Tuberculosis and the Growth of Denver's Eastern European Jewish Community," 130–34. Giese estimates, based on admittedly informal and crude information, that as many as 60 percent of the NJH and JCRS ex-patients remained in Denver after discharge and were thereafter joined by their families. However, the length and permanence of their residence is not indicated.
8. Adress by Rabbi William Friedman, 1923, Pisko File, NJH Archives, Denver.
9. Chester Jacob Teller, *Report on the Problem of Combined Poverty and Tuberculosis Among Jews in Denver, CO* (New York, 1916), 2, 20, copy in Beck Archives of Rocky Mountain Jewish History, Denver.
10. Dr. Charles Spivak, "The Genesis and Growth of the JCRS," *Sanatorium*, 1 (January 1907), 6; JCRS Archives, Denver, Box 170.
11. *Thirty Years of Saving Lives, the Sanatorium of the Jewish Consumptives' Relief Society, 1904–34*; JCRS Archives, Denver, Box 170, 7.
12. Giese, "Tuberculosis and the Growth of Denver's Eastern European Jewish Community," 11.
13. Rosslyn Stewart and Laurie Simmons, "A Small Gathering of Men: The Origins of Denver's Jewish Consumptives' Relief Society," unpublished essay in the Beck Archives of Rocky Mountain Jewish History, Denver, 1981.
14. Dr. Philip Hillkowitz, "Dr. C. D. Spivak and the JCRS," *Sanatorium*, 12 (October–December 1927), 4; JCRS Archives, Denver, Box 170.

15. *Denver Jewish Outlook* (October 7, 1904), 6.

16. Levenson, *Montefiore*, 72.

17. Boris Bogen, *Jewish Philanthropy* (New York, 1907), x.

18. Philip Jacobs, *A Tuberculosis Directory* (New York, 1911), 16–18.

19. Ibid. The Modern Workmen of America Sanatorium and the Union Printer's Home admitted only union members. The U.S. Naval Hospital at Las Animas, Colorado, admitted only naval personnel.

20. For a more complete version of Spivak's life, see Marjorie Hornbein, "Dr. Charles Spivak of Denver: Physician, Social Worker, Yiddish Author," *Western States Jewish Historical Quarterly*, 11 (April 1979), 195–211; and Jeanne Abrams, "Chasing an Elusive Dream: Charles Spivak and the Jewish Agricultural Movement in America," *Western States Jewish History*, 18 (April 1986), 204–11.

21. Charles Spivak to Anna Hillkowitz, 14 May 1906, Hillkowitz Correspondence Folder, JCRS Archives, Denver, Box 223.

22. Jewish Consumptives' Relief Society, *First Annual Report of the JCRS, 1905*, JCRS Archives, Denver, Box 170, 12.

23. "Tenth Annual Report of the JCRS," *Sanatorium*, 13 (September–December 1914), 96; JCRS Archives, Denver, Box 170.

24. David Rosner, *A Once Charitable Enterprise* (New York, 1982), 42.

25. Paul Starr, *The Social Tranformation of Medicine* (New York, 1982), 171.

26. For example, in Denver according to Philip Jacobs, *Tuberculosis Directory*, 116–18, in 1911 the Agnes Memorial Sanatorium charged patients nine to twelve dollars per week; the Denver Episcopal Church Home from twenty-five dollars per month to twenty-five dollars per week, based on the amount of nursing care required; Mrs. Lare's Tent Sanatorium, one dollar per day and up, according to care required; the Sunlight Sanatorium, ten to twenty-five dollars per week; the Swedish National Sanatorium in Denver six dollars per week, although about one quarter of its patients were treated free of charge.

27. Thomas Galbreath, *Playing the Lone Game Consumption* (New York, 1915), 19.

28. Morris J. Vogel, "The Transformation of the American Hospital, 1850–1920," in Susan Reverby and David Rosner, eds., *Health Care in America* (Philadelphia, 1977), 114.

29. Rosner, *A Once Charitable Enterprise*, 36.

30. *Sanatorium*, 3 (January 1909), 1; JCRS Archives, Denver, Box 170. The ability of the JCRS to recruit supporters from across the nation is set in perspective by the observation of Charles Rosenberg that "ethnic and religious groups saw their [medical] institutions as symbols of community identity and responsibility." Charles Rosenberg, *The Care of Strangers: The Rise of America's Hospital System* (New York, 1987), 8.

31. The many record boxes in the JCRS Archives contain countless receipts that acknowledge small contributions, in particular, Boxes 233–35; the JCRS "Book of Life," Boxes 269–93, literally records thousands of modest contributions.

32. Milton Goldin, *Why They Give: American Jews and Their Philanthropy* (New York, 1976), 237.

33. Ibid, 63.

34. Dr. Philip Hillkowitz, "President's Report," *First Annual Report of the JCRS, 1905*, JCRS Archives, Denver, Box 170, 14.

35. Teller, *Report on the Problem of Combined Poverty and Tuberculosis*, 93.

36. Anna Hillkowitz Correspondence Folder, Correspondence of the JCRS Fieldworkers, JCRS Archives, Box 223, Denver.

37. Anna Hillkowitz to Charles Spivak, May 1, 1906, Anna Hillkowitz Correspondence Folder, JCRS Archives, Denver, Box 223.

38. The convention attended by Anna Hillkowitz is not specified in the letter, but it seems likely that this, too, was either the national convention of the IOBA or of the Arbeiter Ring.

39. Mrs. Seraphine Pisko was the financial secretary of the NJH at the time.

40. Samuel Grabfelder was national president of the NJH when the letter was written.

41. Anna Hillkowitz to Charles Spivak, May 9, 1906, Anna Hillkowitz Correspondence Folder, JCRS Archives, Denver, Box 223.

42. *Sanatorium*, 1 (November 1907), 202; JCRS Archives, Denver, Box 170.

43. Ibid., 203.

44. *Sanatorium*, 1 (November 1907), 202; JCRS Archives, Denver, Box 170. The truth of this statement is borne out by the fact that contributions from 50 New York City workingmen in 1907 ranged from three cents to one dollar.

45. Arthur Goren, *The American Jews* (Cambridge, MA, 1982), 46.

46. *Eighth Annual Report of the JCRS, 1911*, 196; JCRS Archives, Denver, Box 170.

47. Bogen, *Philanthropy*, 34.

48. *Eighth Annual Report*, 197; JCRS Archives, Denver.

49. *Thirty Years of Saving Lives*, 13.

50. Daniel Elazar, *Community and Policy: The Organizational Dynamics of American Jewry* (Philadelphia, 1980), 73.

51. Boris Bogen, "Dr. Spivak, as a Social Worker," *Sanatorium*, 22 (October–December 1927); 6, JCRS Archives, Denver, Box 170.

52. Rosner, *A Once Charitable Enterprise*, 34.

53. Ibid., 18.

54. Levenson, *Montefiore*, 65–72.

55. Renee Dubois and Leah Dubois, *The White Plague, Man and Society* (Boston, 1952), 173.

56. Douglas R. McKay, "A History of the Nordrach Ranch: Colorado's First Sanatorium of the Open Air," 56, *Colorado Magazine* (Summer/Fall 1979), 184.

57. Ibid., 185.

58. Ibid., 186.

59. Philip Jacobs, *The Control of Tuberculosis* (New York, 1932), 29.

60. Dr. Philip Hillkowitz, "President's Report," *First Annual Report of the JCRS, 1905*, JCRS Archives, Denver, Box 170.

61. Shana Korngold, *Zikhroynes* (Memories), from an excerpt reprinted in *Rocky Mountain Jewish Historical Notes*, 2 (March 1979), 3.

62. McKay, "History of Nordrach Ranch," 187.

63. Dr. Adolph Zederbaum, "Kosher Meat in Jewish Hospitals and Sanatoria," *Sanatorium*, 2 (November 1908), 275.

64. Bella E. Schultz, "The Highest Degree of *Tzedakah*: Jewish Philanthropy in Kansas City, 1870–1933," in Joseph Schultz, ed., *Mid-America's Promise: A Profile of Kansas City Jewry* (Kansas City, 1982), 202.

65. Editorial, *Sanatorium*, 1 (May 1907), 41; JCRS Archives, Denver, Box 170.

66. Paul Weinberger and Dorothy Weinberger, "The Jewish Religious Tradition and Social Services," in Paul Weinberger, ed., *Perspectives in Social Welfare* (New York, 1974), 402–3.

67. Quoted in Rosner, *A Once Charitable Enterprise*, 49.

68. *First Annual Report of the JCRS, 1905*, 61.

69. Rosner, *A Once Charitable Enterprise*, 1.

70. Ibid.

71. Interview with Deena Spivak Strauss, March 1982. Beck Memorial Archives, University of Denver, Tape No. 90.

72. Rosner, *A Once Charitable Enterprise,* 19.

73. Scrapbook No. 1, Box 197, JCRS Archives, Denver.

74. Ida Uchill, *Pioneers, Peddlers, and Tzadikim,* (Denver, 1959), 249.

75. P. Hillkowitz, "Dr. C. D. Spivak and the JCRS," 4.

76. Teller, *Report on the Problem of Combined Poverty and Tuberculosis,* 107.

77. *First Annual Report of the JCRS, 1905,* 60.

78. Dr. Philip Hillkowitz, "President's Report," *Sanatorium,* 3 (March 1909), 53; JCRS Archives, Denver, Box 170.

79. Billy Jones, *Health Seekers in the Southwest,* 200.

80. For Spivak's views on Jewish agricultural settlements, see Jeanne Abrams, "Chasing an Elusive Dream: Charles Spivak and the Jewish Agricultural Settlement Movement in America," *Western Jewish History,* 18 (April 1986), 204–17.

81. Teller, *Report on the Problem of Combined Poverty and Tuberculosis,* 46.

82. JCRS Patient Records, Boxes 98 and 99, JCRS Archives, Denver, and the *Denver City Directory* for the years 1905 to 1907.

Chapter 5

Zionism versus Anti-Zionism:

The State of Israel Comes to San Francisco

FRED ROSENBAUM

Introduction

The study by Fred Rosenbuam of the San Francisco chapter of the anti-Zionist American Council for Judaism (ACJ) returns us to the city from which Moses Rischin surveyed all of western Jewish history. Rosenbaum's study offers a glimpse into the attitudes and activities of some of the grandsons and granddaughters of the pioneers as the third generation confronted a traumatic moment in western, American, and world Jewish history. As consciousness of a supreme catastrophe began to grip American Jewry, Zionism seemed the appropriate and necessary response in every sector of American Jewish opinion. As Rosenbaum indicates, a small minority of America's Jews, opposed to Jewish nationalism and fearful that anti-Semites would charge American Jews with dual loyalty, organized the ACJ.

Although the council was national in scope, with local chapters throughout the country, the San Francisco branch was especially successful in attracting an elite leadership, enlisting a large membership and raising a substantial percentage of the total funds collected by the organization nationally. If one cannot ascribe a distinctive western dimension to the history of the ACJ, Rosenbaum's research does raise the question of precisely why the council should have received so much support in San Francisco. Was San Franciscan Jewry unique or was this particular episode reflective of the broader sweep of western Jewish history? Rosenbaum's analysis hints at certain factors that were general to the history of Jews in the West that may have been especially pronounced in San Francisco in the decade of the 1940s.

The very status and position of those attracted to the ACJ in San Franciso argues for the continued hospitality of the West to a population diverse in its national, ethnic, and religious origins. Those Jews who wished to disassociate themselves from Zionism and thereby proclaim their loyalty to America were well established both in the Jewish and in the larger San Franciscan community. They were men and

117

women who had achieved recognition measured by the American standards of wealth and professional accomplishment, and they had been "fully integrated"—or so their club memberships and prominence in civic and cultural life would indicate. Their opposition to Zionism was motivated, at least in part, by their desire to preserve their standing as patriotic Americans in a western milieu that traditionally had been open to Jews and that remained largely undisfigured by anti-Semitism. Perhaps the council appealed to elite San Franciscans precisely because the West had given them so much that they feared to lose.

But the popularity of the council in San Francisco rested also on the weakness of the Zionist opposition. This aspect of the history of the council may well reflect the fact, noted in several of the essays in this volume, that first- and second-generation Eastern European Jews did not emigrate in large numbers to the West until World War II. Consequently, that segment of the Jewish population most responsive to Zionism was especially underrepresented in San Francisco in the 1940s.

Although no other western or, indeed, American Jewish community developed a local chapter of the ACJ comparable to the one in San Francisco, in the context of the western Jewish experience, the success of the ACJ in San Francisco may not seem anomalous at all.

ZIONISM VERSUS ANTI-ZIONISM

If there is a single issue on which American Jews approach a consensus, it is the necessity for a Jewish state. Jews may be critical of Israel for a host of reasons, ranging from its foreign policy to its internal social and economic maladies, but the need for the state itself is rarely questioned.

Yet in the tumultuous decade of the 1940s, a bitter debate over the merits of statehood for the Jews of Palestine constituted the most divisive episode in the entire history of San Franciscan Jewry. It was a struggle that pitted a small group of wealthy influential families of German origin and of pioneer antecedents who were members of the city's Classical Reform "cathedral synagogue," Temple Emanu-El, against San Francisco's other Jews, most of whom were of East European origin, traditionally observant and of modest means. It was a debate over the nature of Judaism and the Jewish people and, ultimately, on the most appropriate response to the persecution and the destruction of most of Europe's Jews. But in this battle, the pronounced social and cultural differences between the two sides were as important as the momentous issues themselves.

The central figure in the anti-Zionist camp was Irving F. Reichert, who in 1930, at the age of thirty-six, had become the rabbi of Temple Emanu-El, the largest and most prestigious synagogue in the West.[1]

Ordained at Hebrew Union College nine years earlier and a member of the last class under the presidency of Kaufmann Kohler, Reichert was nationally known as one of the most articulate and forceful exponents of Classical Reform Judaism. Much like the scholarly Jacob Voorsanger, who had held the Emanu-El pulpit at the turn of the century, Reichert aimed at integrating the Jews into American society. "The fundamental fact that Judaism is a religion, *and a religion only*," was axiomatic for him.[2] Reichert made light of the ethnic culture of the large Jewish immigrant community in America, "dependent on kitchen recipes, musicians, painters and story-tellers but not on God."[3] And although he would define a Jew solely according to religion, he opposed as "medieval nostrums" such practices as the wearing of a *kippah* or *tallit* or the introduction of Hebrew into the school curriculum or the liturgy. His emphasis, instead, was on the present-day relevance of the ethical message of the prophets, a fraternity in which he included Jesus.[4]

The highest priority of his career, though, was the fight against Jewish nationalism. For him, Zionism was "a retreat from the highway of Jewish destiny and achievement in America to the dead end street of medieval ghettoism."[5] In this regard, he articulated what was becoming a minority position within American Reform Judaism, but one that had been propounded by its founder, Isaac Mayer Wise, and accepted by an overwhelming majority of the movement's adherents from the time of its inception in the mid-nineteenth century through the early 1920s.[6]

Reichert's best-known critique of Jewish nationalism appeared in a widely reprinted sermon delivered in January 1936. Rebutting an article in the *Atlantic Monthly* by the Zionist Ludwig Lewisohn, the rabbi pronounced Zionism "alien to the historic traditions of Israel [that] took upon itself the yoke of the Law not in Palestine but in the wilderness at Mount Sinai."[7] Beyond this theological consideration, though, the response to Lewisohn enunciated the main political position Reichert and his allies would reiterate for the next two decades: the creation of a Jewish state would threaten the status of the Jews in America and even lead to an upsurge of anti-Semitism. Often designated the dual-loyalty argument, it was phrased as follows by Reichert:

> One wonders what the Gentile world makes of all this [Zionism]. It is notorious that anti-Semites, when other arguments fail, sometimes succeed in prejudicing even friendly Christians against the Jew by quoting this type of nationalistic propaganda to convict us out of our own mouths

for being a nationality imbedded within a nation. There is too dangerous a parallel between the insistence of Zionist spokesmen upon nationality and race and blood, and sinister pronouncements by Fascist leaders in European dictatorships. . . . We may live to regret it.[8]

Finally, the rabbi compared the "provocative language" employed by the Zionists to the posturing of a "swashbuckling, saber-rattling Nazi."[9]

Yet, for the next six years, Reichert held his anti-Zionist sentiments in check. He grudgingly accepted the position of neutrality of the Reform movement's Central Conference of American Rabbis (CCAR), framed in 1935, which took "no official stand on the subject of Zionism," a marked retreat from the vehement opposition to Jewish nationalism of its founding fathers.[10] In 1942, however, Reichert and many of his like-minded colleagues came to the conclusion that the majority of the CCAR—now convinced that the need for a refuge in Palestine outweighed all other considerations—was no longer neutral but actually pro-Zionist. When, at its annual conference in the spring, a resolution supporting the creation of a Jewish army was upheld, Reichert and ninety-one other dissenting rabbis vowed to hold their own gathering in Atlantic City. Even before they assembled, in June 1942, however, the battle lines had been drawn irrevocably when David Ben Gurion in his historic speech a month earlier at the Biltmore Hotel in New York had declared statehood as the official policy of the Zionist movement and the Biltmore Declaration of Independence had received the unanimous endorsement of all those assembled. With the growing awareness in early 1942 of the full extent of Hitler's plans to exterminate the Jews, a new spirit of gravity came to permeate the Zionist leadership and the Biltmore program, which emerged from the five-day conference at the New York hotel, reflected a movement more unified and determined than ever before.[11]

Reichert and his ninety-one fellow rabbis in Atlantic City, the "goy nineties," as the Zionists called them, after countering with a pronouncement that "dual citizenship in America is more than we can accept,"[12] formed the American Council for Judaism, (ACJ) an organization of Reform rabbis and laypersons dedicated to combating Jewish nationalism. The leading rabbis of the council tended to be elderly men who had begun their careers in the early years of the century, ministering to large wealthy temples dominated by congregants of German origin. They included Morris Lazaron of Baltimore, Edward Nathan Calisch of Richmond, Samuel Goldenson of New York, and Louis Wolsey (dubbed Cardinal Wolsey by his enemies) and William Fineshriber, both of Philadelphia. A much younger man, the fiery Elmer

Berger gave up his pulpit in Flint, Michigan, to become the executive director, a post he would hold until his ouster in 1968. At a meeting in April 1943, held in his Jenkintown, Pennsylvania, mansion, the philanthropist Lessing Rosenwald, chairman of the board of Sears Roebuck and Company, agreed to assume the presidency of the council. Rosenwald also provided the initial funding for the organization and, in the years to come, proved to be its leading financial backer.[13]

A national vice-president and the official spokesperson for the council in the West, Reichert went about organizing the San Francisco section, the most successful by far of the thirty-five chapters eventually established throughout the country. His impressive lay leadership came almost exclusively from the board of directors of Temple Emanu-El, where he had served for almost a decade and a half. Monroe Deutsch, the first president of the local section, was provost and vice-president of the University of California, Berkeley, and the president of San Francisco's prestigious Commonwealth Club. The two vice-presidents of the ACJ were Reichert and Hattie Hecht Sloss—the wife of former California State Supreme Court Justice Marcus Sloss—who was widely admired for her philanthropic work for both Jewish and non-Jewish causes. The wealthy clothier Grover Magnin served as treasurer, and Daniel Hone, a well-known attorney, held the office of secretary. Other executive board members included Daniel Koshland, one of the owners of the Levi Strauss Company—who because of his support for a broad range of Jewish institutions was arguably the most respected lay leader in the city—and Mrs. Joseph Ehrman, Jr., the socialite daughter of a former governor of Oregon, who Reichert would marry after the death of his first wife, Madeleine. The board of directors included both J. D. and Harold Zellerbach, among the leading manufacturers of paper products in America; Mrs. I. W. Hellman, widow of one of the West's leading bankers; as well as prominent attorneys, insurance executives, and real estate developers.[14]

More cohesive and better organized than their counterparts in other cities and facing weaker Zionist opposition than elsewhere, each member of the board personally solicited a hundred memberships from a list of his or her friends and acquaintances and also sent out a packet of information on the council's aims along with a membership application to three thousand others.[15] Meanwhile, Reichert shocked the Jewish community by using the occasion of his Kol Nidre sermon to unveil the ACJ program publicly and to solicit members. Entitled "Where Do You Stand?" his exhortation stressed the dishonesty of the

Zionists and demanded that his congregants "make a decision . . . and take a place on one side or the other."[16]

By early 1944 the council had recruited over 1,000 members, employed a part-time secretary, and opened a new office on Market Street.[17] The chapter's correspondence with the national office in Philadelphia reveals that by the time the San Francisco membership peaked the following year, at somewhere between 1,150 and 1,400, it constituted almost one-third of the ACJ's national enrollment.[18] The San Francisco chapter also produced enough revenue to send the hard-pressed main office about twenty thousand dollars annually in the mid-1940s, nearly 30 percent of the national operating budget, and, leaving aside Lessing Rosenwald's large personal contribution, almost one-half the funds raised by all of the chapters combined.[19]

Clearly, the basic tenets of the ACJ had touched a responsive chord among the members of San Francisco's Jewish elite, who in the midst of World War II joined the council almost to a man. Not only had anti-Zionism been an important component of Classical Reform Judaism for three generations, but it had been expounded in the pulpit of Temple Emanu-El with special vigor by one of the giants of the American rabbinate, Jacob Voorsanger.[20] During the years 1886 to 1908, which coincided with the youth of many of those who would join the council in the mid-1940s, this incisive historian, linguist, and publicist thundered against Jewish nationalism as "the wildest of all wild dreams."[21] Drawing on ancient texts, he argued that "our holy land, our promised land" is not "Turkridden" Palestine, but rather golden California with "its hills and dales."[22]

In benevolent San Francisco, as nowhere else, ideas such as these remained intact even in the face of the Holocaust. It was not that the pioneer families were insensitive to the harrowing cries of their brethren in Nazi-occupied Europe, but rather that they interpreted Hitlerism as an aberration and believed in the integration of the Jews into the host country as the natural order of things. Just as Voorsanger in 1900 predicted that the Jewish Question in Russia would eventually be solved with the overthrow of the Czar and the establishment of a democratic government in his place, so Reichert argued in 1944 that Jewish life would one day be resurrected in Germany.[23] No Jewish community in America was more removed geographically, of course, from Europe and its horrors; and the Pacific rather than the Atlantic orientation of the West Coast, in the most general political and cultural terms, certainly tended to diminish the impact of modern European Jewish history. But even more important in this regard was the gulf created by historical experience. Nearly a century of virtually unprecedented

freedom, toleration, and prosperity in the San Francisco Bay Area
had rendered the leaders of that Jewish community incapable of ade-
quately assessing the needs and desires of the rest of world Jewry.[24]

The activities of the San Francisco section, which included a number of well-attended events, usually held at the Jewish Community
Center projected the distinctive outlook of its members. In addition
to Berger and Rosenwald, each of whom spoke on several occasions,
in the fall of 1945, the consul-general of France was honored by the
council at an evening commemorating the emancipation of French
Jewry a century and a half earlier. A program devoted to the contributions of Jews to California featured both distinguished speakers in the
areas of agriculture, law, medicine, social welfare, and music as well as
young ushers dressed in cowboy costumes. In explaining the strength
of California Jewry from the Gold Rush to the present day, one of the
lecturers quoted Temple Emanu-El's pioneer rabbi, Elkan Cohn, Voorsanger's predecessor and mentor, who had written that "while Israelite, it had known no other nationality than that of American."[25]

Although many San Franciscan Jews were infuriated by the council in the mid-forties—including the Russian-born Zionist cantor of
Temple Emanu-El, Reuben Rinder, and his wife Rose—there was little
organized opposition until the end of the decade. The local Zionist
Organization of America (ZOA), which had fought an uphill struggle
of its own in the twenties and thirties, felt that it had little to gain and
much to lose from an all-out public feud with the city's most prestigious Jewish leaders. When, immediately following World War II, their
great moment of opportunity finally arrived, the Zionists held rallies,
disseminated literature, and took much pride in the fact that donations to the Jewish National Welfare Fund, much of which went to
Palestine, doubled in the year 1946 alone to almost one and one-half
million dollars.[26] Young Saul White, rabbi of the fast-growing Congregation Beth Shalom, and soon to join the Conservative movement,
reprimanded the ACJ by name in March of 1946 at a Zionist rally attended by five hundred people.[27] But this was the exception, not the
rule, until well after Israeli statehood. More typical was the silence
on the council issue of Morris Goldstein, rabbi of the city's second-
largest and somewhat traditional Reform synagogue, Shearith Israel,
whose brother, Israel, rabbi of New York's B'nai Jeshurun, was one of
the leading Zionist spokespersons in the country.

Beginning in mid-1948, Rabbi Reichert became executive director
of the ACJ's Western Region, a full-time position for which he was paid
ten thousand dollars annually plus expenses, about two-thirds of the
salary he had received in his last year as spiritual leader of Emanu-El,[28]

where his contract had not been renewed as a result less of his anti-Zionism than of his shortcomings as a pastor, educator, and administrator.[29] By the late forties, most of the rabbis associated with the council at the time of its formation had a change of heart and were no longer affiliated with it. Some, like Lazaron, who continued to be active in the ACJ, were forced out of their pulpits by their congregations for ideological reasons. Many others—Calisch is the best example—were elderly and, in any case, ready for retirement.[30]

Reichert, still in his mid-fifties and one of the handful of rabbis still on the council rolls, was a dynamic speaker and powerful writer who joined the ACJ's professional staff at the most critical moment in the organization's history—the creation of the State of Israel. Daily newspaper reports and radio broadcasts brought home not only the fact of the Jewish state but also the heroism exhibited in the War of Independence and the waves of emotion associated with the dramatic absorption of hundreds of thousands of new immigrants, many of them Holocaust survivors. A number of key supporters of the council—such as Lloyd Dinkelspiel, Dan Koshland, and his business partner and brother-in-law Walter Haas—now raised doubts about whether the ACJ should continue to exist at all.[31]

But for almost four years following independence, Reichert fought vigorously to hold the organization intact, echoing Berger's line that now that Ben Gurion had won a beachhead in Palestine, it was imperative to prevent him from "Zionizing" the American Jew, that is, raising money for the Jewish state, propagating the Hebrew language and notions of a Jewish peoplehood, and, most pernicious of all, in his view, encouraging *aliyah*. Moses Lasky, a brilliant San Franciscan attorney who became active both in the local and national ACJ in the early fifties, indulging in a bit of rhetorical rodomontade, metaphorically compared the influence of Israel in America with that of the Communist Chinese in Korea, south of its Yalu border, "Zionism uses the state [of Israel] as a sort of haven north of a Yalu River to subvert our American view of Judaism and to herd us into a new ghetto. We shall not bomb north of this Yalu, but we must keep watch along the river line."[32]

This was also the theme put forward by Reichert. In an ambitious advertising campaign in the *San Francisco Jewish Community Bulletin* in the fall of 1949, the rabbi, aided by a public relations consultant, designed hard-hitting verbal and visual messages, such as the one on October 7, showing a Boy Scout playing a bugle in front of an American flag. Under the heading "ZIONISM SAYS" appeared the statement, "Our next task . . . consists of bringing all Jews to Israel . . . [and] we appeal

ZIONISM SAYS

David Ben-Gurion,
Israeli Prime Minister,

(in address to American Histadrut delegation, as reported by Jewish Telegraphic Agency, Aug. 31, 1949)

"Although we realized our dream of establishing a Jewish state, we are still at the beginning . . . Our next task will not be easier than the creation of the Jewish state. It consists of bringing all Jews to Israel . . .

"We appeal chiefly to the youth in the United States and in other countries to help us achieve this big mission. We appeal to the parents to help us bring their children here. Even if they decline to help, we will bring the youth to Israel, but I hope that this will not be necessary."

Daniel Frisch, President,
Zionist Organization of America,

(in "The New Palestine", Jan. 13, 1949)

"Certainly the contribution of American Jewry should be measurable not in dollars alone, not even in political acumen alone. We ought to be able to send to Israel American-bred young people who want to live as Jews — minus the hyphen — under the smiling skies of the reborn Israel."

WE SAY:
This land is YOUR land — this flag is YOUR flag

Son, that thrill you feel when you salute the Stars and Stripes, when you sing "The Star-Spangled Banner," is shared by all of your 149,000,000 fellow-Americans.

YOU have the grandest birthright on earth

Freedom of speech, freedom of worship, freedom of thought, the right to work at the job of your choice—to travel or live where you please in this miracle-land of 48 states of breathless beauty and boundless opportunity.

WAKE UP—Count Your Blessings

This is your country, your homeland, your land of promise. Sure, it's not perfect, but it's not finished yet. That's part of your job—our job—all together, Jews, Catholics, Protestants.

Honor your flag! Honor your Faith!

Build your life firmly on these two loyalties—God and Country. Keep them both strong!

THINK IT OVER!

WE ARE FOR:

1. A virile American Judaism, for the fullest realization of our great spiritual heritage.
2. Maximum participation by Americans of Jewish faith in the development of the American democratic way of life.
3. Wholehearted philanthropic aid to our co-religionists and to suffering humanity everywhere.

WE ARE AGAINST:

1. The theory that religious devotion to Judaism must be synonymous with national ties to Israel.
2. Any idea that there is a voice—any voice in America—speaking for all Jews, either as a political, religious, economic or social entity.
3. Domination of American Jewish institutions, philanthropic or otherwise, by zealots for Jewish political nationalism.

If you agree with these principles, join

The American Council for Judaism

593 Market Street, San Francisco 5 · GArfield 1-6536

Be sure to attend the Carroll Binder meeting of the American Council for Judaism at the Jewish Community Center — Monday, October 10, 1949 — 8 p.m. Admission Free!

American Council for Judaism advertisement in San Francisco's *Jewish Community Bulletin*, October 7, 1949.

chiefly to the youth." Under "WE SAY" appeared the copy, "This land is YOUR land—this flag is YOUR flag. Son, that thrill you feel when you salute the Stars and Stripes, when you sing "The Star-Spangled Banner," is shared by all of your 149,000,000 fellow-Americans."[33]

Vociferous objections were voiced by the local ZOA and the Survey Committee, forerunner of the Jewish Community Relations Council, causing the embattled editorial committee of the *Bulletin* to postpone publication of a number of the ads for several weeks, though not to cancel them. The business executive, George Levison, president of the ACJ in 1949 and for many years thereafter, believed that the public controversy over the ad campaign had given the council the boost it needed to overcome the negative news coverage of the past year and a half. "The situation in San Francisco has changed completely," he wrote Berger on October 19, "the problem of the relationship of American Jews to Israel is now a subject of prime consideration in all segments of the . . . community."[34] He also reported favorably on the local reception of Alfred Lilienthal's famous anti-Zionist piece published in *Reader's Digest* one month earlier. But even in the midst of the council's greatest publicity triumph, Levison confided to Berger that "we must not overplay our hand."[35]

Levison knew that even as the national office was launching an ambitious new organizational structure based on four regions, each with its own annual conference, membership in the key San Francisco chapter was slipping rapidly. In the year following the creation of Israel, one-half the members of the local council refused to renew their subscriptions,[36] including Haas, Koshland, and Dinkelspiel, who evidently were unpersuaded by letters from Berger predicting that the Jewish state would soon "drift into the Russian orbit."[37] In addition, a number of younger leaders, such as Frank Sloss (the son of Hattie Sloss and the noted judge), not only left the council but turned their attention to the United Jewish Appeal (UJA) and became active in the annual fund-raising campaign.[38] Reichert's successor at Emanu-El, meanwhile, the young and popular Alvin Fine, a rabbi of Labor Zionist sentiments, attacked the council's ideology from the pulpit beginning in late 1949 and soon thereafter convinced the Religious School Committee to adopt new textbooks that gave proper attention to Israel.[39]

Moreover, the ACJ's hopes of broadening its base beyond the temple set now appeared more remote than ever. "Certainly all of our members belong to the Reform,"[40] wrote Hattie Sloss to Berger early in 1949; later that year, the board had to confront the distressing fact that the council had virtually no members under the age of thirty. Nor could it point to more than a single rabbi on its shrinking rolls. And, despite Reichert's long and strenuous trips throughout the West, he could report no real success anywhere. In Los Angeles, he was shunned by the renowned rabbi of the Wilshire Boulevard Temple, Edgar Magnin, a native of San Francisco and a Classical Reform leader who had been at his post since 1915.[41] The Los Angeles chapter, dormant throughout most of 1948 had to be "reactivated" by Reichert, who complained of "difficulty in maintaining the interest of the members, especially [those on] the Executive Committee."[42] Of Denver, he wrote Berger in August 1949, "the group needs constant stimulation and prodding,"[43] and Portland, he lamented a month later, "appears to be coming apart at the seams."[44]

Yet, far more serious than these setbacks were the inherent contradictions — much more intractable after statehood — in the pro council position of the San Franciscan pioneer families themselves. One issue the local board of directors could not resolve in the late forties was the question of whether members of the council should also contribute to the UJA.[45] Even before independence, the attorney Sidney Ehrman discontinued his one-hundred-thousand-dollar annual gift.[46] A decade later, in 1956, Moses Lasky wrote a seventy-two-page exposé of Zionist fund-raising in America in which he concluded, "The bulk of funds raised by UJA . . . passes to Israel in a manner defeating final accountability. . . . The ends to which the funds are put include governmental purposes of the State of Israel, political purposes in the U.S. and Israel, and indoctrination of American Jews in Zionist philosophy."[47] In the same year, the national ACJ voted to adopt a proposal calling on the U.S. Department of Justice to investigate the UJA.[48]

The vote was denounced as "incredible and outrageous" even by Reichert, who resigned from the council, now (in his words) "a pariah among Jewish organizations." In a lengthy, emotion-laden letter to ACJ President Clarence Coleman, Jr., which the rabbi made available to the national press, Reichert revealed that for years he had had misgivings about the course of the council and expressed his "infinite embarrassment and heartache" with the widening breach between the ACJ and virtually every other Jewish organization in the country.[49] The response of his erstwhile comrades in arms, such as Coleman and Rosenwald, was severe and unforgiving, but Reichert held the council's attack on the UJA to be inexcusable, the last straw in the "the private war" it was waging "against Israel and its people."[50]

Nor was he alone among leaders of the San Francisco chapter who had long admired the philanthropic work accomplished by American Jewry in Palestine and later Israel. Like Hattie Sloss and Mortimer Fleishhacker, he contributed handsomely to the UJA, even while active in the ACJ. Moreover, the Jewish National Welfare Fund, the conduit that channeled money overseas for the UJA, was merged in 1955 with the Federation of Jewish Charities, which had served local needs. The new organization, the Jewish Welfare Federation (JWF) of San Francisco, Marin County and the Peninsula, raised almost two million dollars by the late fifties and was clearly positioning itself to dominate Jewish life in the future.

Council members such as Moses Lasky, Sidney Ehrman, and August Rothschild, who had refused to contribute to the Jewish National Welfare Fund, now continued to boycott the JWF. They had to contend with the reproach of lay leaders, such as the respected attorney Edgar Sinton—himself an early ACJ dropout—who held that they used their council affiliation simply as "an excuse" to avoid making a large donation to the JWF.[51] Be that as it may, the fact remained that the path to leadership in the San Francisco Jewish community increasingly lay through the federation, and those who had no involvement with that organization, regardless of their wealth or professional prominence, relegated themselves to the periphery. Nor could those with such anti-Israel views, of course, hope to play a major role in any respectable national Jewish organization.

Elmer Berger, however, stubbornly opposed ACJ members aiding Israel in any way and even voiced criticism of George Levison, who in 1949 held a local fund-raising campaign for the Hebrew University –Hadassah Medical School.[52] Only in 1955 did the council itself establish a philanthropic fund for overseas needs, including Israel. But this project, of small size and effectiveness, was exposed as mere window dressing by Berger's colleague, Norton Mezvinsky, who resigned from the staff of the ACJ in 1968—after less than a year of service— because of its "reactionary, dogmatic and un-Jewish tendencies."[53]

The divisive role played by Berger—one that especially embittered Mezvinsky—could be detected even in the 1950s when Berger tended more and more to emphasize the "political" as opposed to the "religious" aspects of council concerns, as Berger himself recently put it.[54] In practice, this meant not only working toward the ACJ's stated goal of resisting the Zionist penetration of the American Jewish community but also attacking Israel in the arena of Middle Eastern politics. After being received in five Arab capitals in 1955, Berger wrote glowingly of the treatment of Jews in Egypt, Syria, Lebanon, Morocco, and even Iran.[55] His visit to Jerusalem on the same trip, however, convinced him that "to be a Jew here [in Israel] is to share a nationalism that has ugly overtones of racism and exclusivism."[56] A year later, he publicly broke with the council's two leading laymen, Lessing Rosenwald and Clarence Coleman, Jr., by refusing to moderate his anti-Israel stand in light of the Sinai War.[57] Indeed, he labeled Israel the aggressor in the June War in 1967, and, according to Mezvinsky, assisted several Arab diplomats in preparing the speeches they delivered on the conflict before the United Nations.[58] These and similar actions, however, cost the rabbi the post he had held for a quarter of a century, forcing him to resign from the ACJ in 1968 and impelling him to form a new organization, the much smaller American Jewish Alternatives to Zionism.

Across the country, Berger had the support of a handful of loyal lay leaders both during the storms he weathered in the mid-1950s and even during those he failed to survive a decade later. Most of the San Franciscan leadership, though, downplayed the "political" approach, particularly after the creation of the State of Israel. For people like Hattie Sloss, Monroe Deutsch, and, to a large extent, Reichert, the struggle was primarily over the future of Reform Judaism. In their minds, the Jewish religion, which they based almost solely on prophetic ethics, stood to be corrupted by a state and everything that would inevitably flow from it, from devious politicians to an army bent on conquest. In this sense, Berger's foray into the politics of the Middle East could be just as dangerous as Zionism itself.

The personal style of both Reichert and Berger also posed a major problem for the local chapter of the council. The San Francisco rabbi, engaged by the ACJ immediately following his dismissal from Temple Emanu-El, did not enjoy the confidence of key lay leaders such as Harold Zellerbach, president of the congregation, who had recently been made fully aware of Reichert's failings.[59] Injudicious remarks, such as his thinly veiled comparison—in a speech delivered in Nashville, Tennessee, in 1949—between the Hitler Youth and Zionist programs aimed at college students also served to damage his standing even among council members.[60] Yet Berger, the more dogmatic of the two, used inflammatory rhetoric almost constantly. In the late forties, repeatedly referring to Zionist "smears and bribes," he drew parallels between the methods of ZOA President Daniel Frisch and those of Adolf Hitler, and he declared Jewish nationalism "a totalitarian movement" with "its tentacles in all our personal lives."[61] He also made no attempt to curb his disgust for the Yiddish language, for the culture of the *shtetl*, and for "politically retarded" Eastern Europe, where, in his view, Jews became "prey to the 'nation within a nation' theory."[62]

One enthusiastic supporter of Berger's extremism, even during the rabbi's troubles the year following the Six Day War, was the fanatic anti-Zionist Moshe Menuhin, father of the famed violinist. Raised in

Palestine before World War I, the elder Menuhin immigrated to the United States and in 1918 began working in the Bay Area as a Hebrew schoolteacher and principal. His long lifetime of vehement opposition to Zionism is chronicled in his book *The Decadence of Judaism in Our Time*, whose major theme is the insatiable desire for *Lebensraum* of Israel's "brazen, military junta."[63] Although the work was subsidized by Sidney Ehrman, Moshe Menuhin remained an anomaly and outsider in virtually every respect.

Whereas Menuhin applauded Berger's radical stance, San Francisco's pioneer families, although they had joined the council, often had a very different opinion of its national leader. The businessman Marcel Hirsch, for example, claimed in 1981 that he and others like him had, in effect, been duped by Reichert and "this crazy Elmer Berger, a crackpot."[64] Perhaps more telling, however, is a lengthy letter written to Berger in 1949 by the gracious Hattie Sloss who would remain a member of the council until her death in 1963. "Let us be sure that we do not step over the lines of good taste," she wrote with great concern. "We can be much more effective [if we are] constantly amiable and retain our good manners, than . . . in excitement or anger."[65]

In the end, the local Jewish gentry, long-known for its discretion, was simply not eager for political combat as were Reichert and Berger or even some of their lay counterparts in other American cities. They sought to lead the Jewish community, not hopelessly divide it, as they feared would result from the maximalist goals and belligerent tactics of the council's professional leadership. This circumspect attitude was perhaps best expressed by Alice Haas Lilienthal in explaining the apparent contradiction in her long affiliation both with the ACJ and Hadassah, "First of all, they're both philanthropic. Second of all, I wouldn't want to offend anybody."[66]

A wholehearted commitment to the council was in any case problematic for people whose attachment to Jewish causes of any kind—if anti-Zionism may be called a Jewish cause—was a limited one. These grandchildren of pioneers, fully integrated into San Francisco's high society, had many other interests and concerns in life, from the opera and the symphony to the local museums and universities. Faced with a vicious, public fight over the merits of Jewish nationalism, they opted to turn their attention to other matters. Ironically, their assimilated worldview also served to blunt their anti-Zionism.

In this sense, one can appreciate the failure of the ACJ even in San Francisco, its most promising terrain. Obviously, it was swimming against the tide of history, particularly after the creation of the State of Israel and U.S. recognition in 1948. But even several years earlier, when its membership crested at somewhere between 1,150 and 1,400, one senses that support for the council was "a mile wide and an inch deep."

The large majority of members were two-dollar-a-year subscribers who had simply responded to an appeal with a prestigious letterhead and who would drop out within a few years. Moreover, the wealthy elite, many of whom would remain on the rolls far longer—a membership list of 1969 reveals 117 names[67]—also held back from making a full commitment to the council. Even in the middle and late forties, Berger's desperate fund-raising appeals always fell far short of his needs;[68] given the means of these old families, the twenty thousand dollars raised annually in this period by the San Francisco chapter must be seen as an almost inconsequential sum.

By the decade of the seventies, the San Francisco chapter of the ACJ ceased to exist in any formal sense. A handful of prominent individuals have continued to belong to the national ACJ and one, August Rothschild, regularly attended its annual meetings until ill health precluded cross-country travel.[69] Chance encounters with other council members at cocktail parties, Rothschild explained, was his way of sharing news of council activities. The role of ACJ members today, nationally and locally, he noted, is that of "a watchdog," working within other Jewish organizations in order to counter any Zionist excesses that might arise. But beyond that, neither the council nor its ideology has made inroads in the Jewish community of the Bay Area.[70]

The history of the ACJ in San Francisco reveals the extent to which the Jewish elite of that city could turn its back on world Jewry as a whole. In accordance with their long tradition of Classical Reform Judaism, rooted in a unique, almost philo-Semitic milieu, the pioneer families were persuaded to embrace anti-Zionism even in the midst of the Holocaust. Yet the story of the local council also demonstrates the limits of that position. Even before 1948, unwilling to create a schism over the issue of Zionism and uncomfortable with the abrasive approach of Reichert—even more so of Berger—the ever-cautious San Francisco patriciate withheld its unqualified support of the council. "Ashamed" of themselves, as Daniel Koshland confided, eventually, nearly all the old families would come to accept Zionism and regret their council affiliation.[71] It would take time, but like their fellow American Jews and most Americans, they would not fail to be impressed by the compelling reality of the State of Israel.

Notes

1. Fred Rosenbaum, *Architects of Reform: Congregational and Community Leadership, Emanu-El of San Francisco, 1849–1980* (Berkeley, 1980), 125–46.

2. Irving F. Reichert, "Getting Back to Fundamentals," April 4, 1952, in *Judaism and the American Jew: The Sermons and Addresses of Irving Frederick Reichert* (San Francisco, 1953), 9.

3. Ibid.

4. Reichert, "If I were a Christian Preacher Today," March 28, 1937, in *Sermons*; interview with Louis Freehof, San Francisco, June 1978.

5. Reichert, "Getting Back," in *Sermons*, 15.

6. For a further discussion of the antagonism between nineteenth-century American Reform Judaism and Zionism see Samuel Halperin, *The Political World of American Zionism* (Detroit, 1961), 71–73; and Peter Grose, *Israel in the Mind of America* (New York, 1984), 27–30.

7. Reichert, "One Reform Rabbi Replies to Ludwig Lewisohn," January 11, 1936, in *Sermons*, 133.

8. Ibid.

9. Ibid., 132.

10. Halperin, *Political World*, 78.

11. Ibid., 220–23; Grose, *Israel* 168–72; and Melvin I. Urofsky, *American Zionism from Herzl to the Holocaust* (New York, 1975), 424–29.

12. *Temple Chronicle of Temple Emanu-El*, October 9, 1942.

13. Halperin, *Political World*, 87–88.

14. *American Council for Judaism, San Francisco Records, 1943–49* (ACJ hereafter). The ACJ records are at the University of Wisconsin Library in Madison; transcripts of the San Francisco correspondence are available at the Western Jewish History Center of the Magnes Museum in Berkeley.

15. Draft of a speech by Harry Camp, January 1945, *ACJ*.

16. Reichert, "Where Do You Stand?," October 8, 1943, in *Sermons*, 142.

17. Elinor MacGettigan to Elmer Berger, February 8, 1944, in *ACJ*.

18. *ACJ*. See also Thomas Kolsky, "Jews Against Zionism: The American Council for Judaism, 1942–1948," (Ph.D. diss., George Washington University, 1986), 246.

19. Ibid.

20. Marc Lee Raphael, "Rabbi Jacob Voorsanger of San Francisco on Jews and Judaism: The Implications of the Pittsburg Platform," *American Jewish Historical Quarterly*, 63 (December 1973), 185–203; Rosenbaum, *Architects*, 45–65.

21. *Emanu-El* (San Francisco), June 11, 1897, 5.

22. Ibid., July 10, 1896, 6.

23. Reichert, "The Policy and Program of Reform Judaism," March 3, 1946, in *Sermons*, 34.

24. For a discussion of the conspicuous absence of anti-Semitism in the pioneer West, see Rosenbaum, *Architects*, 17–19; and Earl Raab, "There's No City Like San Francisco," *Commentary*, 10 (October 1950) 371.

25. S. Walter Newman, February 22, 1949, in *ACJ*.

26. Michael Zarchin, *Glimpses of Jewish Life in San Francisco* (Berkeley, 1952), 148.

27. *ACJ*.

28. Ibid.

29. Rosenbaum, *Architects*, 139–43.

30. Halperin, *Political World*, 98–99.

31. Elmer Berger to Lloyd Dinkelspiel, November 16, 1948; and Elmer Berger to Daniel Koshland, November 6, 1948, in *ACJ*.

32. Moses Lasky, "A Statement of the American Council for Judaism," May 10, 1953, in *ACJ*.

33. *San Francisco Jewish Community Bulletin*, Oct. 7, 1949, 3 in *ACJ*.

34. George Levison to Elmer Berger, October 19, 1949, *ACJ*.

35. Ibid.

36. Minutes of the meeting of the Board of Directors, April 11, 1949, in *ACJ*.

37. Berger to Dinkelspiel, November 16, 1948.

38. Interview with Frank Sloss, Menlo Park, CA, March 1986.

39. Rosenbaum, *Architects*, 151–52.

40. Hattie Hecht Sloss to Elmer Berger, February 28, 1948, in *ACJ*.

41. Edgar F. Magnin, *Leader and Personality* (Berkeley, 1975), 148.

42. Irving Reichert to Elmer Berger, November 15, 1948, in *ACJ*.

43. Irving Reichert to Elmer Berger, August 5, 1949, in *ACJ*.

44. Irving Reichert to Elmer Berger, September 2, 1949, in *ACJ*.

45. Minutes, Board of Directors, April 11, 1949.

46. Interview with Louis Weintraub, San Francisco, June 1978.

47. Moses Lasky, *Between Truth and Repose*. (1956), front flyleaf.

48. Irving Reichert to Clarence Coleman, Jr., July 19, 1956, in Western Jewish History Center, Berkeley.

49. Ibid.

50. Ibid.

51. Edgar Sinton, *Jewish and Community Service in San Francisco: A Family Tradition* (Berkeley, 1978), 45.

52. ACJ, Box 67–68.

53. Barry Silverberg, "The American Council for Judaism: Origin, Development and Program," (unpublished paper, April 30, 1973), 22–23, in Western Jewish History Center, Berkeley.

54. Telephone interview with Elmer Berger, February, 1986.

55. Elmer Berger, *Who Knows Better Must Say So!* (Beirut, Leb., 1970).

56. Ibid., 91.

57. Silverberg, "American Council for Judaism," 18.

58. Ibid., 23.

59. Rosenbaum, *Architects*, 141.

60. Ibid., 144.

61. Elmer Berger to Hattie Hecht Sloss, September 16, 1949; Elmer Berger to Irving Reichert, August 23, 1949; Elmer Berger to Amanda Schlessinger, May 3, 1946, in *ACJ*.

62. Elmer Berger to Irving Reichert, August 15, 1949, in *ACJ*.

63. Moshe Menuhin, *The Decadence of Judaism in Our Times* (New York, 1965), 163 and repr., Beirut, Feb., 1969.

64. Marcel Hirsch, *The Responsibilities and Rewards of Involvement* (Berkeley, 1981), 87.

65. Hattie Hecht Sloss to Elmer Berger, November 14, 1949, in *ACJ*.

66. Frances Bransten Rothmann, *The Haas Sisters of Franklin Street*, (Berkeley, 1979), 74; and interview with John F. Rothmann, San Francisco, March 1986, in author's possession.

67. *ACJ*.

68. Elmer Berger to Harry Camp, June 10, 1946, in *ACJ*.

69. Interview with August Rothschild, San Francisco, March 1986, in author's possession.

70. Ibid. To be sure, there are a number of small vocal groups of Jews in Berkeley organized to oppose Israel and her policies; they even question her right to exist. But young Marxists are totally at odds on almost every other issue with the wealthy conservatives who belong to the council.

71. Daniel E. Koshland, *The Principle of Sharing* (Berkeley, 1971), 302.

Chapter 6

From Desert Oasis to the Desert Caucus:

The Jews of Tucson

LEONARD DINNERSTEIN

Introduction

Like so many of the Jews who arrived in Tucson after World War II, Leonard Dinnerstein is a transplanted easterner whose study of the development of the Tucson Jewish community is reflective in many ways of aspects of his own life experience and historical scholarship. His interest in the history of Jews outside the metropolitan Northeast; his concern to document anti-Semitism, particularly in twentieth-century America; and his fascination with the impact of the large Jewish migration to the West in the last half-century are all evident in his survey of Jewish life and communal development in Tucson.

Dinnerstein's discussion of the earliest Jewish arrivals in Tucson demonstrates some patterns that can be replicated in the history of one western town after another. Virtually every Jewish settlement was spearheaded by young men, often related by family ties or marriage, who ventured into developing areas in search of the economic opportunities that the expanding West of the nineteenth century offered those with some capital or credit, some commercial experience, and a willingness to take great risks with the hope of making substantial fortunes in a region given to extreme economic fluctuations. The early merchants in Tucson and elsewhere, a goodly number of whom were Jews, found immediate acceptance, for no one doubted that the exploitation of the West's resources in agriculture, mining, lumbering, ranching, and other pursuits called for mercantile as well as other skills. As business leaders, the early merchants and shopkeepers were frequently among the western town's most active boosters and political spokespersons. In Tucson, as in so many other communities throughout the developing West—as pointed out by Earl Pomeroy—Jews were elected to public office in far greater numbers than in areas of concentrated Jewish settlement in the East. That Jews appeared so prominently reflected their ready acceptance.

One feature of Tucson's history that affected all Tucsonans was the attraction of its climate for persons suffering from arthritis or respiratory diseases. That the small Tucson Jewish community had to make provision for coreligionists seeking health rather than wealth again reminds us that the Jewish presence in the West of the early twentieth century was not always prompted by the American quest for material prosperity. As Jeanne Abrams's essay so clearly demonstrates, the Jews of Denver, to a far greater degree than those in Tucson, had to confront an influx of poor Eastern European Jews who had contracted tuberculosis in the sweatshops and crowded tenements of the East Coast ghettos. Although many Eastern European Jews and their families came West to recover their health, once cured, many stayed introducing their patterns of Jewish life and observance into western towns that otherwise might have remained untouched by the consequences of the massive East European Jewish migration to the United States after 1881. The establishment of a Conservative synagogue (Anshei Israel) in Tucson in 1930 may well reflect the special needs of some of those Eastern European Jewish health seekers or of their children. One senses that more was happening in the Jewish community of Tucson, however small, during this period than we yet know. A more complete analysis of this era in Tucson's Jewish history would be valuable in its own right and might also serve to link the pioneer years with the decades of growth and institutional development after World War II.

In large part, Dinnerstein's essay traces the development of the Tucson Jewish community in the expansionist years after World War II. Once again the story in Tucson parallels trends elsewhere as the growth of population and wealth led to the establishment of institutions to support an ever-more diversified Jewish life and to the defense of Jewish interests wherever threatened. Dinnerstein's discussion of Jewish political activity in Tucson and the formation of the Desert Caucus introduces elements of Jewish history in the latter half of the twentieth century that have been little studied thus far. What his research reveals for Tucson is probably true for western Jewish communities in general: By the 1960s, Jews throughout the West had achieved a degree of maturity and recognition that earned them admission to the highest counsels of American and American Jewish policy-making. Like the region itself, in the post–World War II era western Jewish communities were no longer colonies subservient to a metropolitan East. The ability of the Desert Caucus to exercise influence in Arizona and in the nation's capital on behalf of Jewish interests testifies that the Jews of the West had come of age.

FROM DESERT OASIS TO THE DESERT CAUCUS

The growth of the Jewish community of Tucson has paralleled the expansion of the West. From the late nineteenth century until World War II, the entire region was regarded as an economic appendage of the East. Massive federal spending, begun during the war, however, invigorated the Southwest and "brought the most dramatic changes in the Far West since 1849," contends Earl Pomeroy, leaving "an indelible and distinctive influence on the urban West,"[1] concluded Gerald Nash. Both Tucson and its Jewish population grew accordingly. The training of military personnel, the growth of the aircraft and high-tech industries, and the salubrious climate of the Southwest contributed substantially to the change. Tucson, claiming more sunshine than any other city in the country and long a haven for sufferers from arthritis and respiratory ailments, benefited immeasurably from the transformation. Attracted to the area for the same reasons as others, Jews developed one of the most prosperous communities in the Southwest. How this came about will be the focal point of this essay.

The Pioneers

Philip and Samuel Drachman, Lionel and Barron Jacobs, Joe and Therese Ferrin, Aaron and William Zeckendorf and their nephew Albert Steinfeld, and Jacob S. Mansfeld were among the pioneers who engaged in a variety of economic activities from storekeeping, farming, and ranching to mining and banking. A number of them acquired Indian trading licenses and also served as contractors to the U.S. Army. Some lingered in the Tucson area for a few years and then moved on; others remained and built a life there.

Jews have been in Tucson since the Civil War, yet one would be hard-pressed to find more than a handful of their Jewish descendants left in the city. The names of the pioneers are to be found on streets, businesses, and schools, but their grandchildren and great-grandchildren wear crosses and affiliate with a variety of Christian denominations. Harry Arizona Drachman, allegedly the first white male child born in the Old Pueblo, a favorite nickname for Tucson, was one of ten siblings, all the children of Philip and Rosa Katzenstein Drachman. Only one of them married a Jew and all of their descendants "were to abjure Judaism," observed southwestern historian Floyd Fierman.[2]

How many Jews lived in Tucson in the late nineteenth century is difficult to ascertain. Two different sources set the number at forty-eight for the whole Arizona territory[3] which seems low for reasons one historian, Rudolph Glanz, explained: "To our best knowledge, as late as 1880, no direct report on the territory appeared in the Jewish press of the East or Midwest and there was no subscription to a Jewish newspaper in the region. Apparently no Jew felt the urge, as was the case in other territories, to send to the Jewish press at least a general picture of life in the territory."[4]

In 1882 the *Tucson Citizen* noted the presence of Jews and referred to their "temple," although there is no evidence that a special building for religious worship existed. In 1883, a B'nai B'rith lodge (No. 337) was organized, several more families arrived including ten women of marriageable age, property for a burial ground was purchased, and soon thereafter a Hebrew Ladies' Benevolent Society came into being to help newcomers in distress. The galas of the prestigious Owls Club—formed by a group of "prosperous," "enterprising," and "prestigious" bachelors, including a number of Jews who lived together in a large house along with several servants—soon acquired a reputation for elegance and sophistication as socialites vied for invitations to their events.[5]

The Jewish presence in the political arena was particularly noticeable, with individual Jews serving in Arizona's territorial legislature, on the Pima County Board of Supervisors (Tucson is the county seat), and on the first State Board of Regents. Charles Strauss, who was elected mayor in 1883, presided over the establishment of Tucson's city hall, fire station, and library, initiated a program of street grading, and appointed a Jewish chief of police—in addition, several Jews sat on the city council. In 1886 he also served as the territorial superintendent of public instruction. In addition, Sam Drachman, whose cigar and stationery store served as a gathering place for politicians, won election to the state legislature and the local school board. After his death, he had both a street and an elementary school named for him.[6]

Perhaps the greatest "Jewish" political feat in territorial days was obtaining the University of Arizona for Tucson. Not that it was viewed as much of an accomplishment at the time, for it was bestowed on the community by the territorial legislature after political logrolling kept the state capital in Prescott and the prison in Yuma, whereas Phoenix was awarded the right to build a new insane asylum. In a desperate effort to salvage something for his own community before the legislative session ended, Selim Franklin, a Jew who represented Tucson in the assembly, appealed to his fellow legislators to establish a state university. Because no other county wanted it, Franklin's proposal passed with only one dissenting vote. But his constituents in Tucson were unenthusiastic about Franklin's plum. With the $25,000 sum appropriated by the legislature to begin the university about to revert back to the state because it had not been used in more than a year, Jacob S. Mansfeld—a local book and newspaper dealer as well as a university regent—induced two of the town gamblers and the owner of the "finest saloon in Tucson" to donate forty acres of desert land east of the city, now about a fifteen-minute walk from downtown, to the board of regents. Thus began the University of Arizona, and historians have often pointed to Franklin and Mansfeld as the individuals primarily responsible for that accomplishment. Franklin, moreover, has been dubbed "the Father of the Arizona University."[7]

Tucson's Jewish population declined in the 1890s. William Zeckendorf, after thirty-two years in the Old Pueblo, sold his entire stock and returned to New York City, where he became a renowned real estate developer; the B'nai B'rith Lodge consolidated with the Orange Lodge (No. 334) of Los Angeles, and the Hebrew Ladies' Benevolent Society fell into desuetude[8] and the territory remained without a rabbi. Although for long no Jews served either in the territorial house of representatives or on the council, at the special convention called in 1910 to draft a constitution for the proposed state, Morris Goldwater and Jacob Weinberger played prominent roles.[9]

How influential Jews continued to be in Tucson at the end of the nineteenth and early years of the twentieth century is a matter of speculation. The arrival of the railroad in the early 1880s had stimulated an economic boom, but a ten-year depression that began in the late 1880s led to a decrease in the city's population, which fell from seven thousand at the beginning of the decade to five thousand ten years later.[10] In the Tucson area during the depression of the nineties, silver mines cut down production, railroads raised rates and curtailed activities, and the general business climate became dismal, leading to further population decline.

That Jews continued to live in Tucson there is no doubt. *The Tucson City Directory 1899–1900* listed 61 names that appeared to be Jewish, including an attorney, a chiropodist, and several owners of the Arizona Bank, but there seemed to be no physicians or other professionals among them. Three dry goods and one department store as well as two barbershops, a saloon, a confectionary store, a soda-and-bottling-works establishment, a bakery, a meat market, a tobacco shop, a flour mill, shoestore, and an assayer's office also seemed to be owned by Jews who constituted a tiny fraction of the entire city's population of ten thousand.[11]

The Quiet Years

The period of Jewish history about which we know least extends through the first four decades of the twentieth century, the quiet years. As Arizona's history generally and Tucson's in particular has not been widely researched, the limited information at hand must suffice.

We know that in 1904 the Hebrew Ladies' Aid Society began—the direct successor (perhaps) to the earlier Hebrew Ladies' Benevolent Society—and it proved to be the forerunner of the Sisterhood of Temple Emanu-El, the first formal Jewish religious insititution in Arizona, which was founded six years later and counted twenty-five families among its members. One of its organizers, Sam Drachman, who long had served as lay leader of Tucson Jewry, died the following year.[12]

In the subsequent three decades, every Jew who came to Tucson did so because a family member was afflicted with arthritis or a respiratory disease and benefited from the warm, dry air. The relatives who came along did their best to eke out a livelihood in a city with no major businesses or industries other than the Southern Pacific Railroad, the major employer,[13] and a small university with only a few thousand students, faculty, and staff combined. This in a state still largely rural where cattle, cotton, and copper provided the major sources of income. Beginning in the 1920s, Tucson and Phoenix alike profited immeasurably from the steady stream of winter visitors—tourists, generally from the Midwest, who began arriving in Novem-

The Jacobs' Bloc, Tucson, c. 1900. (Courtesy of the Bloom Southwest Jewish Archives, University of Arizona.)

ber and remained for varying periods of time until the end of April when most of these snowbirds returned home. Indeed, during the depths of the Great Depression, winter visitors provided the economic lifeblood of the two metropolitan areas, leading one writer in the 1940s to refer to Tucson as "probably the only city of any size in the United States that has no visible means of support" and to dub the Old Pueblo "the winter tourist capital of the Southwest—the January suburb of the Mid-West."[14]

Until World War II, the two "big" cities remained relatively small, with Phoenix going from 11,134 to 64,414 in population between 1910 and 1940 and Tucson from 13,193 to 35,752.[15] Jewish population growth proved even less impressive increasing from 1,150 in all of Arizona in 1920 to only 1,847 in 1937.[16] Jewish children were almost always the only Jews in their classes, sometimes in their schools, and one newcomer found that aside from those who had migrated from the East, "nobody even knew what a rye bread was."[17] Another commentator

The Albert Steinfeld department stores, Tucson, c. 1925. (Courtesy of the Bloom Southwest Jewish Archives, University of Arizona.)

may have summed it up best, "If there was a common thread linking those [Jews] who came to Tucson during the twenties, thirties, and for-ties, it was a sense of isolation."[18]

Jewish newcomers, reared in the Orthodox traditions of the East or Midwest, finding the polished style and English prayers of Temple Emanu-El's Reform Judaism utterly foreign, organized a Conservative congregation, Anshei Israel, in 1930 and five years later began renting rooms in the temple for its own services. On September 6, 1939, a Eu-ropean refugee, Marcus Breger, became rabbi of the small congrega-tion of twenty to twenty-five families,[19] and, except for a wartime leave of absence, served at Anshei Israel until his retirement in 1970.

A Time of Growth

World War II transformed Tucson as it did the West. Davis-Monthan Air Force Base, a training ground for pilots and bombardiers, hummed with activity, servicemen and their families came and went, and both retail businesses and military suppliers flourished. Consolidated-Vultee Aircraft, which later became General Dynamics, established a plant in Tucson and further invigorated the economy.[20]

After the war, Tucson continued to prosper. Servicemen from all over the country who had been stationed in Arizona thought they might like to settle there with their families, and those overwhelming attractions—the sun and the dry climate—continued to attract health seekers. Tucson's Jewish population rose from 480 in 1940 to 4,000 in 1948.[21] The accompanying surge in property values throughout the region led a number of newcomers as well as a few oldtimers to invest in land, with the expectation that land values would continue to rise.

Throughout the 1940s Jewish newcomers to Tucson tried to re-create the institutions with which they were familiar. The New Yorker, Jacob Fruchthendler, who arrived in 1940, was instrumental in establishing the Young People's Hebrew Association, where young adults could socialize; helped organize the Jewish Community Council (JCC) in 1942; and participated in the hiring of the JCC's longtime executive director, Ben Brook, in 1949. Other postwar innovations included the inauguration of weekly broadcasts of "The Jewish Hour"[22] in 1946 and the establishment that same year of the *Arizona Post*, the community's Jewish newspaper, a venture called "preposterous and doomed to failure,"[23] by the *Denver Intermountain Jewish News* and the *Los Angeles B'nai B'rith Messenger*. The prognosticators proved wrong and the biweekly *Post* has thrived ever since.

In those years, Jews in Tucson as in other American cities began to institutionalize their activities, establishing local Jewish community relations councils (CRC) and in 1944 the overall umbrella organization, the National Community Relations Advisory Council (NCRAC). Prompted by the Holocaust in Europe and the intensification of anti-Semitism in the United States during World War II, the CRCs worked both alone and along with local groups in a campaign to curb anti-Semitic discrimination and to promote favorable Jewish public relations throughout the nation.[24] The decision to establish the Jewish Community Council of Tucson in 1942 fit the national pattern.

The explosive growth of the Tucson Jewish community in the 1940s, and then again after the Korean War in the 1950s, led to the need for standing institutions where Jews could meet and feel at home.

They found them in the Conservative synagogue, Congregation Anshei Israel, in the Reform Temple Emanu-El, and in the Orthodox
Young Israel. Tucson was, perhaps, the only city of its size in the
United States with Orthodox, Conservative, and Reform congregations and a Jewish Community Council that served as the umbrella
organization for a host of Jewish groups.

The one thing many people cannot forget are the great number
of Jewish transients who came to town from the 1930s to the 1950s.
Often roaming the streets in search of work and housing, they were
provided with meals and temporary shelter by members of the Jewish
Ladies' Aid Society, which subsequently merged with the professionally directed Jewish Family Service. The synagogue and temple also
looked out for the wanderers, as Rabbis Marcus Breger of Anshei Israel and Albert Bilgray of Temple Emanu-El added social services to
their other responsibilities.

In these years of rapid growth, Breger and Bilgray, along with Ben
Brook, who each served over twenty-five years, provided the stable
leadership that the Jewish community needed. Although a majority
of the city's Jews may not have had any formal association with Jewish
organizations, the synagogue, temple, community council, and women's
groups, such as Hadassah and Pioneer Women, allowed Jews to participate in Jewish life in their own way. These Jewish institutions also
served as reference points for the general community at the same
time that Breger, Bilgray, and Brook helped bring Christians and Jews
together.

Characterized by one old-timer as "a giant of a man," Breger was
Orthodox by training and inclination and wise in the ways of the world.
Although he lead a Conservative synagogue, he realized that if it were
not for the Reform Temple few Jews would have remained in Tucson.
He also knew that if the Jewish community were to grow, the temple
had to be strong and that Jewish leaders had to participate in community affairs. He joined the Rotary Club, always eating a vegetarian
or fruit plate, and appeared on many a platform along with Albert
Bilgray, the rabbi of the temple; he also built Anshei's membership
from twenty-four families in 1939 to over six hundred in 1969. During
Breger's service, Anshei moved into two new buildings, one in 1946
and an even more impressive edifice in 1969, the year he retired, thus
leaving his successor, Arthur Oleisky, a strong and thriving Conservative synagogue.

A more formidable task confronted Albert Bilgray, who successfully guided the temple from 1947 to 1972, for he replaced the dyna-

mic and outspoken Joseph Gumbiner who had frightened many of the temple's members by his "radicalism." He had allowed the National Urban League to meet at the temple, had called for desegregation, and was an outspoken supporter of Henry Wallace, the Progressive party candidate for the U.S. presidency in 1948. As director of the Berkeley Hillel Foundation at the University of California in the 1960s, Gumbiner would go to Jackson, Mississippi, to help integrate that city's facilities and be arrested and imprisoned.

Many temple members—several of whom had been raised in Arizona and who were comfortably ensconced in Tucson—were disturbed by an outspoken religious leader whose views on the issues of the day differed from their own. Arizona was a conservative state where public schools and theaters were segregated and most Tucson Jews felt that their leaders should not challenge community standards publicly. To be sure, in subsequent decades, with the growth of both the Jewish population in Tucson and a more tolerant atmosphere in America, Jews taking controversial public positions would no longer be viewed as a threat to the Jewish community. But in the late 1940s, a period of intense agitation over the impact of communism in the United States, fears of possible attacks on Jews as Communist fellow travelers or subversives caused many Tucson Jews to be wary of a religious leader who expressed opinions in public not generally acceptable to a majority of the community.

In many ways, Tucson and Arizona were good-old-boy communities in the southern tradition, places where the leading families knew one another and where people avoided public controversy. It was one thing for an Episcopalian of an old Arizona family to say something shocking or uncouth, but it was quite another for a Jew, like Gumbiner, who thought like a New Yorker, to do so.

As Gumbiner's successor, Bilgray faced delicate problems when he took over the spiritual leadership of the temple,[25] for the new rabbi had to contend with an acculturated Jewish congregation, including assimilationists, of whom a small minority actively supported the American Council for Judaism (ACJ), an organization that regarded Judaism solely as a religion and, therefore, opposed a Jewish state in Palestine. Although weak nationally, in the more conservative regions of the South and West, the ACJ had influential supporters.

But the wind was at the rabbi's back. Within a few months of his arrival in Old Pueblo, his congregants sent Bilgray to Washington to meet with elected Arizona officials and to tell them of the Jewish community's vigorous support for the establishment of the State of Israel. One of the senators with whom he spoke was caught by surprise, for

Carl Hayden assumed that the outspken members of the ACJ in Tucson as well as in Phoenix represented Arizona's "Jewish" point of view.

In addition to presiding over temple affairs, Bilgray also participated actively in the life of the community. He helped create the Family Service Agency of Tucson and the Child Guidance Center; was instrumental in developing the first Tucson Police Juvenile Center, a separate holding area for young people awaiting a court appearance, and served as chairman of the Tucson chapter of the American Red Cross and president of the Tucson Community Council. Moreover, he belonged to numerous organizations. He became a charter member of the Tucson Commission on Human Relations in 1956 (remaining there until the city abolished the agency in 1969), president of the Tucson Ministerial Association in 1954, and a member of the Arizona State commission on Penology and Rehabilitation. In 1965, the Tucson chapter of the National Conference of Christians and Jews chose him as its Man of the Year; that very same year, he gave the benediction at the inaugural of Samuel S. Goddard as governor.[26] One of the accomplishments of which he has been particularly proud was his role in forming and developing the Jewish Studies Program at the University of Arizona. Bilgray's public activities not only brought wide recognition to the man and the rabbi but increased his value to the Jewish community because many Jews believed that his successes enhanced the image of all Jews.

The third pillar of stability in the community, Ben Brook, a trained social worker, helped develop and shape the Jewish secular institutions. Coming to Tucson after serving for three years in Italy as the head of the American Jewish Joint Distribution Committee, he was an excellent administrator with a keen insight into how to get people to work together for common goals and a determination to build a variety of organizations that eventually provided the nuclei for a network of programs beneficial to the city's Jews.

With Brook's leadership, the Jewish Community Council integrated the major Jewish activities under its control and developed new agencies. A refugee resettlement program helped the European displaced persons who arrived in Tucson; Jewish Family Service, directed by Brook's wife, Betty, professionalized the work heretofore done voluntarily by the Jewish Ladies' Aid Society; and a community center, a nursery school, and an old-age home eventually followed. Easiest to support was the center and nursery school. "You can always get the Jews to do things for their children," one interviewee observed.

Brook had the ability to get people to work together and encouraged newcomers to participate in community activities. Brook also knew how to work with the officers of the Jewish Community Council, who were elected for short terms, and how to reward those who worked in almost any capacity. Heavy fund-raisers, donors, or community leaders were honored as Jewish Man or Woman of the Year, as Young Jewish Man or Woman of the Year, as Student of the Year, and so on. Everyone wanted some kind of recognition or reward, and Brook saw to it that the meritorious received their due, even if it was only a picture in the *Arizona Post*. Then and now, seniority counted for little in the development of whatever Jewish power structure existed. Wealth, talent, and a willingness to devote oneself to Jewish concerns were what was important. Inevitably, there was a considerable turnover, but Brook remained ever-present to guide and aid those who needed it. By the time he retired in 1978, the institutional structures had been solidly set in place.

Coping with Anti-Semitism

Old-timers of the pre–World War II era rarely acknowledged themselves to be victims of anti-Semitism in Tucson. As small proprietors and businessmen trying to earn a living in an economically depressed community—where Jews accounted for slightly more than 1 percent of the population of 35,000 in 1940 (approximately one-third of which was Hispanic)—they did not concern themselves too much about social discrimination.

Prejudice was taken for granted and the absence of physical and verbal abuse were all that they thought they could expect. Banks, law firms, and utilities, like their counterparts elsewhere in the nation, did not hire Jews. Examinations in public schools took place on Jewish holidays and, until 1950, the University of Arizona maintained a "New York" quota. Resorts such as the Arizona Inn, the White Stallion Ranch, and the Lodge on the Desert discouraged Jewish patronage until the 1960s, but, as one interviewee told me with a shrug: "We couldn't afford those places anyway." But the frontier spirit still prevailed in Tucson and there was a certain respect for those people and those groups who went their own way. Thus an easy fellowship and regnant gentility softened intergroup relations.

The first major public snub occurred in the 1950s when the establishment of the "restricted" Tucson Country Club became the focal point for Jewish concerns over anti-Semitism. The El Rio Golf Club, slightly to the west of the downtown area, had accepted almost everyone who chose to belong—WASPs, Jews, Mexicans—but then the WASPs left to form the Tucson Country Club beyond the eastern boundaries of the city. For more than a decade, Jews talked about the club and deliberated about how to get it to lift its restrictions. Ostensibly, the reason for the concern was that Jewish businessmen were precluded from meeting their economic peers, but essentially the practice of anti-Semitism was galling and provided a concrete focus for the Jews who were beginning to stand up and fight discriminatory barriers.

But the Tucson Country Club was not the major battleground for many Jews actively engaged in fighting anti-Semitism. Behind the scenes they faced serious obstacles in the city, however, because William Matthews, the editor of the *Arizona Daily Star*, Tucson's morning newspaper, was an outspoken anti-Zionist and arch conservative. The Jewish community challenged Matthews on many occasions and did not shrink from doing bitter battle with him, but many questioned the wisdom of confronting so formidable an opponent. Those agitated by the tone and spirit of Matthews's editorials consulted the local Anti-Defamation League (ADL) and the national offices of the American Jewish Committee. The local *shtadlonim*, influential Jews who interceded on the community's behalf with the Gentile power brokers, as well as the firebrand newcomers, all expressed their concerns. In that battle, S. R. Kaufman, a merchandiser who organized the ADL chapter, played an important role as did Jack Sarver who succeeded in getting the Tuscon Country Club to open its doors to Jews.

Anti-Semitism also clearly existed in the professions. Jewish law school graduates could not get jobs in the major law firms, and several people recalled that in 1960 Marvin Cohen was the first Jew to be hired by a Gentile firm. Nationally, barriers against Jewish lawyers seemed to tumble after 1964, and thereafter the problem no longer seemed significant. Obviously, the impact of the 1964 Civil Rights Act barring discrimination and the national civil rights movement in general affected Tucson.

More disgraceful was the plight of prospective dentists, but this was a statewide problem. Jewish applicants taking the state dental examination would do very well on the written portions, but almost invariably would fail in the practical aspects. This obvious discrepancy troubled Jews in Arizona who believed that the licensing commission was deliberately failing Jewish applicants. Jewish delegations from Tucson began petitioning the governor, beginning with Sidney P. Osborne, right after World War II, but as late as 1961 there were still only three Jewish dentists in the city. Some changes occurred during Paul Fannin's term in the early 1960s, but only after Sam Goddard assumed office in 1965 and learned of the situation from a few of his Jewish supporters in Tucson was the problem finally resolved.[27]

Economic Growth and Decline

In the 1950s and 1960s a number of changes occurred at every level of American society that laid the groundwork for a dramatic transformation in the Jewish community in the following decades. Nationally, the fifties had been a period of social and political stability and economic growth, the sixties an era of social revolution. The Civil Rights Act and the mass protest against injustice led to irreversible societal changes that ultimately affected Arizona, particularly Phoenix and Tucson, which were bursting with people and ideas drawn from other areas of the country.[28] Phoenix, always more conservative than Tucson, reflected the sentiments of the state's renowned Senator Barry Goldwater. The more liberal Tucson area thought along the lines of its own congressmen, Stuart and then Morris Udall. Thus people with a more conservative outlook found a congenial home in the Salt River Basin of Phoenix, whereas more adventurous and socially conscious people wound up in Tucson.

The climate of expansion proved congenial to social change. Several factors propelled growth in Arizona after World War II, in addition to natural beauty, healthful climate, and a relaxed way of living. But none proved more critical than the general availability of evaporative cooling in the 1940s and then air-conditioning in the 1950s, for these technological innovations made the ghastly summer heat, with temperatures often reaching over one hundred degrees daily, more tolerable and certainly more livable.[29] Without cooling systems built into all but the most modest homes, none of the state's other attractions would have sufficed to draw large numbers of people to Arizona. With them, the economy took off.

Tucson of the 1950s and 1960s witnessed both boom and bust. First, there was an enormous construction binge between 1954 and 1961 accompanied by a fivefold growth in the city's population, which went from 45,545 at the beginning of the fifties to 212,892 ten years later.[30] Although the Jewish population increased by only 50 percent (going from 4,000 to 6,000), the larger numbers, the stable Jewish community infrastructure, and the movement of most Jews into the solid middle and upper-middle classes combined to make Tucson's Jews more confident. Then in 1961–1962, with the end of the construction boom, economic reversals hit the city hard and the lean years lasted until 1967 when the economy revived.

Instrumental in helping the economy reverse itself were two Jews, Jack Sarver and Stanley Abrams, among others, who wanted the Tucson City Council and community leaders to be more aggressive in pursuing economic development. As a result of their efforts, city and county officials established the Development Authority for Tucson Expansion (DATE), which later become the Development Authority for Tucson Economy. By 1974, DATE's efforts attracted more than fifty new industries to the area, including Burr-Brown. After 1978, DATE was absorbed by the Tucson Economic Development Corporation, IBM arrived, and National Semiconductor and VELCO Instruments came the following year.[31]

One of the key movers for DATE, Jack Sarver, arrived in Tucson in 1960. During the next two decades, he was the single most dynamic force in Tucson Jewish life. A number of people have identified him as perhaps the key figure in making the Jewish community more alive and more assertive. Investing in hotels, motels, and real estate and later opening a bank, he also was willing to take strong stands on issues important to him personally and to the Jewish community in general. Sarver believed that economic growth was the lifeblood of the community and fought hard to help the area prosper. He also objected to every vestige of discrimination and was willing to tackle the restrictionist policies of the Tucson Country Club. Fortunately, his personal style allowed him to take risks that others might not have; the changed attitudes toward bigotry in the nation and the growing self-confidence of the Jewish community itself proved supportive.

Beginning in the late 1960s, Sarver brought the issue of the Tucson Country Club from the talking to the doing stage. Before then, the community had not acted on the club matter because it was an issue with a low priority. Despite the lackluster economy through much of the decade, the 1960s had been a period of rapid population growth. The city needed classrooms, hospital beds, and basic social service institutions. The Jewish community required new buildings for its Conservative and Reform congregations and for its new community center; in addition, many Jews, caught up in the civil rights movement of the late 1960s, were actively involved in eliminating segregation and discrimination from all walks of life. With so many major tasks facing the relatively small Jewish population at the same time, few felt the need to divide the community over a relatively minor irritant like discrimination at a country club.

That does not mean that the Tucson Country Club issue was ignored. The Tucson Rotary Club and the American Red Cross rejected invitations to hold functions at the club, and when an outsider came to town to set up a new Ford dealership, he was promptly informed that if he held a big gala at the Tucson Country Club, he could forget about any business from the members of the city's Jewish community.

Among Jews themselves, moreover, there was general agreement that the club should stew in its own juice until a propitious time came to move ahead.

That time came while Jack Sarver served as president of the Jewish Community Council. When the Jewish Community Center swimming team was invited to a meet at the Tucson Country Club, the mother of one of the participants complained to Sarver about how inappropriate it was for any kind of communitywide activity to be held in a segregated facility. Sarver agreed and wrote to officials of the club asking them for a policy statement that would specify that applicants would be accepted as members simply on the basis of merit rather than on extraneous matters like religion.[32] Officials of the club refused to do so, even though some members wanted to end what they considered an embarrassing and unjust limitation. Not getting the kind of response he wanted, Sarver authorized that letters be sent by the Jewish Community Council to prominent political, civic, and business officials to inform them of the Tucson Country Club's discriminatory policies and to request that they avoid authorizing events or sponsoring corporate memberships there. In the meantime, the story broke in the Tucson newspapers in late July 1971 that Tucson community leaders were said to be "extremely offended by the discriminatory membership policies in the Tucson Country Club." A few days later the *Arizona Daily Star* editorialized:

> If the Tucson Country Club wishes to remain anti-Semitic, which apparently some of its members want it to do, then let it exclude Jews in its constitution and bylaws, and let the chips fall where they may. To pretend to be an open club but actually closed by "gentleman's agreement" is so transparent, so archaic socially and so filled with hypocrisy that the club's membership does not deserve the stigma resulting thereby.[33]

Sarver followed up the *Star* editorial with an "Open Letter to Tucsonans"[34] demanding the end to public events at the Tucson Country Club; editor Martha Rothman continued the discussion in the *Arizona Post* on October 1 when she stated that what is at issue "are questions of fundamental bigotry and hypocrisy";[35] and the Jewish community was reminded of the situation on several occasions when the *Arizona Post* identified officers of the club and their business affiliations.[36]

The collective pressure finally achieved its desired goal when on May 5, 1972, the *Arizona Post* reported that Jack Sarver had received a letter from M. J. Lang informing him that henceforth the Tucson Country Club would no longer discriminate in screening new applicants.[37] Afterward a few Jews joined the club, but most, of course, had no desire to go where they were not wanted. Since then, there have been signs that the Tucson Country Club may still not be completely open to Jews, but its importance in the city is so diminished that questions about whether or not it still discriminates are of almost no significance.

The Tucson Country Club issue marked a major victory for Sarver's efforts, which came at almost the same time that the national Jewish community was engaged in the same kind of battle. In 1969, the *Los Angeles Times* printed a story about how the American Jewish Congress, the American Jewish Committee, the ADL, and local community relations councils across the nation had been studying the problem of private club discrimination for a decade. Many young Jews believed that they could not be promoted in their corporations because they could not gain admission into the important clubs where major business transactions were conducted.

The efforts of Jewish Tucsonans coincided with the national Jewish trend in America,[38] but local conditions cannot be ignored. The victory over the Tucson Country Club came at a time when the Jewish community was feeling enormously proud and increasingly confident after Israel's spectacular victory in the 1967 Six Day War and a more hospitable atmosphere had developed for Jews. The growth of the University of Arizona and its medical school, founded in 1964, attracted Jewish physicians both to the school and the community. Jewish graduates were moving directly from the University of Arizona law school into positions of responsibility, and a new breed of Jews, confident in their professional and business acumen, was coming to town. These newcomers came primarily in response to professional and career opportunities, not for health reasons. Finally, what proved most decisive, the real estate explosion had begun and people who had "held onto their land by their teeth" suddenly began realizing millions in profits. Throughout the 1970s and into the 1980s, several Jewish real estate developers and speculators realized great fortunes, and they exerted an enormous impact in the community and the political arena.

One indication of the new wealth of the Jewish community was the changed fortunes of the Combined Jewish Appeal (CJA). As population grew and Jews prospered, contributions to the CJA mounted. After a downturn in the mid-1960s, CJA figures once again soared, tripling from 1967 to 1971, almost quadrupling after that date. Informants attribute this rise primarily to the success of real estate investors, whose sizable contributions began to make a big difference, the greater commitment to Jewish causes by physicians who used to be chastized for their lack of generosity, and the arrival in the 1980s of some especially affluent persons who promptly associated themselves with Jewish organizations and began to make annual donations in excess of one hundred thousand dollars. By 1986, the goal of the CJA exceeded $2.7 million, almost four times the contributions of 1972.[39]

Political Involvement

Jews, like other minority groups in the United States, have pointed with pride to fellow ethnics elected to political office, for political recognition has given them a sense of community acceptance when they still did not feel secure. Tucson's Jews were pleased that Harry Ackerman and David Wine were elected to the Arizona State Senate, that Jacob Fruchthendler won a seat on the local school board, and that Lew Davis was mayor of the city from 1963–1967. (The current mayor, Tom Volgy, is also Jewish and a Hungarian immigrant who arrived in the United States as a boy in the mid-1950s, but he has never been significantly involved with Jewish community life.) Where political influence really counted, such as easy access to the highest elected and political officials, the Jewish community had a more formal relationship; in the 1940s and 1950s, it often worked thorough intermediaries like Arizona native Aaron Levy, co-owner of the city's largest department store, and longtime resident Elmer Present, a jeweler. There were no specifically Jewish issues aside from curbing anti-Semitism and support for the State of Israel; in general Tucson's Jews had relatively little political influence. As late as 1966, in fact, a letter from Marvin Volk, a prominent member of the Jewish community, to Paul Fannin on the issue of a constitutional amendment allowing prayer in school elicited a totally impersonal response from the senator. "It was good of you to let me have your views on this matter."[40] To be sure, Morris Udall, county attorney and then congressman, had many Jewish friends, associates, and supporters and was responsive to their concerns, but otherwise Jews as a group were not a major factor in the political arena. Somewhere between 1967 and 1971, however, things changed.

By the early 1970s politicians in Tucson and later on throughout the state began paying much more attention to the Jews as a group. The reasons for this were many. The population was increasing and a large number of well-educated and politically sophisticated people, reared elsewhere, were arriving in the state and were having an impact on both the Jewish and general communities. Younger people who grew up in Tucson were becoming more mature and more secure economically and felt comfortable dealing directly with political officials. Governor Goddard, a Tucsonan with many friends in the community, had invited Rabbi Bilgray to give the invocation at his inauguration and had brought an end to the anti-Semitic practices of the dental-licensing examiners, thus signaling to Jews that he was alert to their needs. After pushing through DATE and backing successful candidates for the city council in 1967, politically minded Jews were encouraged to continue their activities; Jack Sarver's vigorous leadership and determination galvanized others. Not to be ignored either was Jewish pride in Israel's smashing victory in the Six Day War in June 1967 and the self-confidence that followed. The more tolerant atmosphere that pervaded the nation and to some extent Tucson, as well, made Jews more assertive in the political arena. Most important, some Jews were moving from the comfortable upper middle class into the millionaire class. And as they did so, their interests compelled, encouraged, or allowed them to participate more actively in politics.

In the late 1960s and 1970s, when real estate speculators and developers began amassing almost undreamed-of wealth, their need for favorable zoning and other legislation coincided with the developing importance of television and the astronomical rise in the cost of political campaigns. Real estate developers sought friends in government and politicians smiled on supporters able to fill their coffers. The connection between politicians and members of the Jewish community was certainly not as crass or as simple as that, for Jews do not support candidates for national office unless they are friendly to Israel, no matter what their other attributes. Neverthleless, the dovetailing of resources and needs helped promote a cooperative relationship, at first with Democrat Mo Udall, already an ally, and Dennis DeConcini, who was elected to the U.S. Senate in 1976, but subsequently with both Republican and Democratic candidates for offices at every level of government.

The changed atmosphere in the state and the relationship between Jews and politicians has been noticeable in a number of symbolic ways. Arizona's Carl Hayden, a member of the U.S. House of Representatives from 1912 to 1929 and the U.S. Senate from 1929 to 1967, paid almost no attention to Jewish issues, but he usually got the Jewish vote, negligible as it was, and had no close relationships with Tucson Jews. Senator DeConcini, on the other hand, chose a Jewish administrative assistant and at one point selected Jews to head both his Tucson and state offices. Moreover, there are any number of Jewish people who have had easy access to the senator and to both of Tucson's congressmen, Udall and Democrat Jim McNulty—who served one term between 1983 and 1985—and his successor, Republican Jim Kolbe.

In the early 1970s, Jews chaired both the Republican and Democratic state parties, but until the 1980s few Tucson Jews had much contact or influence with the Republicans who represented the state in Washington, DC.

The Desert Caucus

Perhaps the single most important political issue uniting an overwhelming majority of American as well as Tucson Jews is Israel. Since its inception in 1948, American Jews have always supported the state. But the 1967 Six Day War and the Yom Kippur War in 1973, in which the Arabs took the Israelis by surprise and initially won some sweeping victories, alerted American Jews to the fact that Israel was extremely vulnerable and reaffirmed their convictions that they had to be ever-vigilant. Moreover, the subsequent Arab oil embargo disturbed all American Jews, for they feared that the political reverberations might generate anti-Israeli feelings. As Jewish groups began to coalesce both nationally and locally in search of the appropriate policies to pursue, a new vehicle for action, known as the political action committee (PAC), came into being.

Tucson Jews wrestled with the best methods for supporting Israel and Jack Sarver, himself totally dedicated to the cause, also began to broaden his horizons. After developing a close friendship with Senator Henry Jackson of the state of Washington, he helped Jackson and other candidates raise money for their campaigns in 1976, serving as national finance chairman of Jackson's unsuccessful bid for the Democratic presidential nomination. Sarver also argued, correctly, that Tucson's Jews could help Israel to a far greater extent by winning allies in Congress who would then favor federal appropriations of loans and grants far greater in value than the sum total of individual contributions.

Sarver's combination of political ambition and savvy led in 1977 to the organization of Tucson's Desert Caucus, a political action committee dedicated to supporting candidates, primarily for the U.S. Senate, who could be relied on to be friendly to Israel. Sarver may have seen the Desert Caucus as a way of furthering his own political ambitions as well as aiding the Democratic party financially. In any case, after his death in 1980, the Desert Caucus evolved into far more than just a political action committee.

Today the caucus has perhaps two hundred members whose fortunes have been made primarily in real estate. As a special interest group, committed to aiding Israel, its members are sophisticated enough to recognize that they have strength in numbers and collective action. Many of them joined the caucus because they saw a real threat

The Desert Caucus and friends, Tucson, c. 1976. From left to right: Ben Brook, Jack Sarver, Governor Raoul Castro, Mrs. Henry Jackson, Senator Henry Jackson, Mrs. Dennis DeConcini, Senator Dennis DeConcini, Al Stern. (Courtesy of the Bloom Southwest Jewish Archives, University of Arizona.)

to Israel in shifts in American foreign policy and, especially after 1978, in the tremendous growth of Arab influence in Washington. Highly visible in its support of candidates for national office, the caucus does not seek public recognition.[41] Members meet monthly to hear speeches by prominent political candidates, such as West Virginia's John D. Rockefeller IV, Tennessee's Albert Gore, and Wisconsin's Robert Kasten, and the caucus makes five-thousand-dollar contributions, the maximum allowable under federal law, to the primary and election campaigns of their invited guests. They support both Democrats and Republicans, mostly the former, and caucus members often make additional individual private contributions. "We like to get in early," volunteered one member, "where our money is noticed and has an effect."

But the Desert Caucus serves more than just a political purpose. An organization composed of many of Tucson's most prominent Jewish leaders, it offers Jews an opportunity to meet one another in a convivial atmosphere. One member pointed out that the caucus not only embraces a good cause but provides a pleasant social diversion with lively people. "You're learning while socializing," she stated. For some members, there are other benefits, like getting to hobnob with important Jews in the community and prominent politicians whom they would not ordinarily encounter. In addition, "the more you're together," remarked an interviewee, "the more likely it is you'll do business together." But this last factor does not seem to loom large.

The More Recent Past

Since 1970 the population of the Tucson area has more than doubled, going from 250,000 to over 500,000 people. At the same time, the number of Jews has more than tripled growing from around 6,500 to 20,000 or more. Most of this growth has come about as a result of economic opportunities, although the desire to spend one's declining years in the Sunbelt or to join close relatives ought not to be discounted.

During these years, Jewish community growth continued apace. In the religious sphere, additional Orthodox and Conservative groups have formed and a quasi-Reform *Chavurah* has encouraged do-it-yourself family religious activities. Rabbis Arthur Oleisky and Joseph Weizenbaum, the successors in the early 1970s to Rabbis Breger and Bilgray, respectively, have presided over the continuous growth and development of Anshei Israel and Temple Emanu-El. Rabbi Oleisky has been particularly concerned with youth and education programs and has broadened the adult education efforts of Anshei, which has garnered national awards, and helped develop a day school at the synagogue. Rabbi Weizenbaum—a throwback to Rabbi Gumbiner—is an articulate advocate of liberal political causes and is willing to challenge some of his more conservative congregants. He is particularly proud of the role that he and Temple Emanu-El have played in the Sanctuary movement that has assisted political refugees from Central America. Rabbi Weizenbaum also enjoys appearing on the local public television station and soliciting contributions. The fact that he participates in such public activities is a sign of Jewish acceptance in Tucson.

In 1990, the Jewish community in the city is far too large to be referred to as a single entity. It is too diverse religiously, socially, and occupationally to be categorized. Newcomers find the institutions they need and want to help them adjust to the city, but old-timers— and that includes people who have been here for only ten or fifteen years—have already formed their own networks and social groupings, some of which do not involve institutional associations. Jewish women's organizations, which used to have considerable influence within the Jewish establishment, are now composed primarily of senior citizens. The younger women are more often than not gainfully employed and no longer have the time or the need that their older sisters and mothers once had for active community involvement.

In the 1980s, a number of major resorts opened in the city, with golf courses and condominiums that anyone can join—if they can afford to do so. There are no observable residential or employment restrictions against Jews, and anti-Semitism, which was never that much of a community concern even when it was a formidable barrier, is of almost no consequence. Jewish businessmen, physicians, and attorneys may still interact primarily with one another, but their social, political, and economic opportunities are rarely restricted by their heritage.

The federal government's expenditures in the West during World War II introduced millions of people to the region and the sunny, dry, and healthful climate of Tucson sparked the growth of its population. Unlike the urban ghettos of the Northeast and Midwest, where immigrants in search of economic opportunities were virtually deposited, people came to the Southwest first for their health and later because of the relaxed lifestyle. Not until the 1970s did Jews in other areas of the nation recognize the enormous economic potential of the Sunbelt. Tucson in particular benefited from the professionalization of the University of Arizona, the development of its medical school, and the establishment of high-tech industries. And these developments led to the greatest Jewish growth spurt since the end of World War II.[42]

Unlike the postwar era, however, a mature Jewish community is now in place. Changes in American and Arizona society have allowed Jews to function independently, and perhaps two-thirds of them have no formal association with synagogue, temple, or any other Jewish group. But for Jews who have religious and other Jewish needs and find comfort among Jews in a Jewish setting, the institutional infrastructure is there. At no time has any member of the JCC (now the Jewish Federation) or any other Jewish institution in Tucson spoken for all of the city's Jews—such an assumption of authority would be preposterous—but an outsider looking in would see a variety of well-functioning agencies and committees ready to serve any Jews who wish to partake as well as ready to speak out on any important issue that any group of Jews believes needs institutional backing.

A frontier atmosphere no longer prevails. Tucson's Jews have access to the same amenities as coreligionists have elsewhere in the country, and their ambition seems to be to make the city a more desirable urban center than exists in some of the older areas of the East and Midwest. The climate and geography set the city apart. But the telephone, television, and airplane, national and international business and political connections as well as frequent trips to other cities keep Tucsonans—especially Jewish residents who follow developments about Israel in Washington and maintain ties to Israelis and interest in Jewish groups with problems in the Soviet Union and elsewhere—in much closer contact with the rest of the nation and the world than was possible even a generation ago. Tucson's Jewish community is mature and, therefore, much like Jewish groups in other parts of the country. It is no longer a western outpost but a vital part of the larger American and Jewish scene.

Notes

In the absence of a significant collection of primary sources I have turned to oral history as an appropriate medium for initiating this community study. No effort was made by me to scientifically select a representative sample of interviewees; I simply started with people I knew and went on to others they recommended. I believe that all of them responded with integrity, although the lack of corroborative documents regrettably must be acknowledged. All of the interviewees and a few others knowledgeable about Tucson Jewish history were sent a draft of the essay for review. I take this opportunity to thank all the persons I interviewed: Judy Abrams, Stanley Abrams, Jack August, Pete Bateman, Allan Beigel, Joan Beigel, David Ben-Asher, Eugene Bernstein, Albert Bilgray, Clara Bilgray, Leon Blitzer, Bertha Breger, Ben Brook Abe Chanin, Mildred Chanin, John Crow, Ruth Dickstein, David Dolgen, Norma Feldman, Stanley Feldman, Jacob Fruchthendler, Vincent Fulginiti, Don Golos, William Gordon, Don Hall, Conrad Joyner, Harry Karchmer, Paula Karchmer, Carol Karsch, Ted Koff, David Leonard, Judy Leonard, Alan Levenson, Jack Levkowitz, Esther Levy, Selma Scora Paul Marks, Arthur Oleisky, Betejoy Oleisky, Jonathan Oleisky, Charles Plotkin, Bob Present, Irene Sarver, Helen Schaefer, John Schaefer, Selma Scora, Art Solomon, David Steele, Tom Volgy, Leonard Weiner, Joseph Weizenbaum.

1. Earl Pomeroy, *The Pacific Slope: A History of California, Oregon, Washington, Idaho, Utah, and Nevada* (New York, 1965), 297; Gerald D. Nash, *The American West Transformed: The Impact of World War II* (Bloomington, IN, 1985), 58. Also see Bradford Luckingham, *The Urban Southwest: A Profile History of Albuquerque-El Paso-Phoenix-Tucson* (El Paso, 1982).

2. Rudolph Glanz, "Notes of Early Jews in Arizona," *Western States Jewish Historical Quarterly*, 5 (July 1973), 249–50; Joseph Stocker, "Arizona's Century of Jewish Life," in "Arizona Days and Ways," *Arizona Republic* November 14, 1954, 15; Floyd Fierman, "The Drachmans of Arizona," *American Jewish Archives*, 16 (November 1964), 136, 156, 159; Floyd Fierman, "The Goldberg Brothers: Arizona Pioneers," *American Jewish Archives*, 18 (April 1966), 3–19; Joseph Stocker, "Jewish Roots in Arizona," prepared under the auspices of the Tercentenary Committee of the Phoenix Jewish Community Council (1954), 26; Gerald Stanley, "Merchandizing in the Southwest: The Mark I. Jacobs Company of Tucson, 1867 to 1875," *American Jewish Archives*, 23 (April 1971), 86–102; Harriet Rochlin and Fred Rochlin, *Pioneer Jews: A New Life in the Far West* (Boston, 1984), 57, 69; Harriet Rochlin, "Pioneer Jews in Arizona," *Hadassah*, (October 1976), 2, in Clipping Folder, "Ethnic Groups—Jews—Arizona—Tuscon." Arizona Historical Society. Tucson; Larry Fleischman, "The Memories Linger On," *Arizona Post*, September 5, 1980, 4–5; Edward J. Baumgart, "An Evaluation of Banking in Arizona," *Journal of Arizona History*, 3 (Winter 1962), 45.

3. *American Jewish Year Book*, 16 (1914–1915), 352, Elizabeth L. Ramenofsky, *From Charcoal to Banking: The I. E. Solomons of Arizona* (Tucson, 1984), 104.

4. Glanz, "Notes of Early Jews." 252.

5. Blaine Peterson Lamb, "Jewish Pioneers in Arizona, 1850–1920" (Ph.D. diss., Arizona State University, 1982), 308; *Tucson Citizen*, November 12, 1982, in Clipping

Folder, "Ethnic Groups . . . ," Arizona Historical Society, Tucson; H. Rochlin, "Pioneer Jews in Arizona," 2–3; Janet Ann Stewart, "The Mansions of Main Street," *Journal of Arizona History*, 20 (Summer 1979), 206–7.

6. Norton B. Stern, "Mayor Strauss of Tucson," *Western States Jewish Historical Quarterly*, 12 (July 1980), 347–69; Jay J. Wagoner, *Arizona Territory, 1863–1912* (Tucson, 1970), 508, 511, 512, 517; Baumgart, "An Evaluation of Banking," 45; Clipping, *Tucson Citizen*, November 12, 1982; H. and F. Rochlin, *Pioneer Jews*, 11, 141; Lamb, "Jewish Pioneers," 245, 279; Bernard Postal and Lionel Koppman, *American Jewish Landmarks* (New York, 1979), v. 2, 41.

7. Stocker, "Jewish Roots," 27, 28; Fred C. Lockwood, *Pioneer Days in Arizona* (New York, 1932), 255, 256, 258; Wagoner, *Arizona Territory*, 212; H. Rochlin, "Pioneer Jews in Arizona," 3; Lamb, "Jewish Pioneers," 307, 308.

8. Lamb, "Jewish Pioneers," 307, 308.

9. Ibid., 284.

10. C. L. Sonnichsen, *Tucson: The Life and Times of an American City* (Norman, 1982), 129.

11. *Tucson City Directory, 1899–1900* (n.p., n.d.)

12. Tucson Emanu-El, *Commemorative Book* (Tucson, 1970); Ramenofsky, *From Charcoal to Banking*, 197; H. and F. Rochlin, *Pioneer Jews*, 203.

13. Nash, *The American West*, 110.

14. June Caldwell, "Tucson: The Folk Industry," in Ray B. West, Jr., ed., *Rocky Mountain Cities* (New York, 1949), 208; see also *Arizona Daily Star*, March 8, 1946, 2.

15. *Arizona Yearbook, 1985–1986: A Guide to Government in the Grand Canyon State* (Sisters, Or, 1985), 127.

16. "Statisics of Jews" in *American Jewish Year Book*, 25 (1923–1924), 338; ibid., 42 (1940–1941), 227.

17. Fleischman, "The Memories Linger On," 5.

18. Ibid.

19. Gilbert Kushner, "The Jewish Community in Tucson: Structure and Forms of Jewish Self-Identification" (M.A. thesis, University of Arizona, 1958), 41; *Arizona Daily Star*, September 20, 1959, 11.

20. Nash, *The American West*, 29, 56, 58, 83; see also Pomeroy, *The Pacific Slope*, 298.

21. H. A. Linfield, "Jewish Communities of the United States," in *American Jewish Year Book*, 42 (1940–1941), 227, 236, 237; Ben B. Seligman and Harvey Swados, "Jewish Population Studies in the United States," in ibid., 50 (1948–1949), 671. One of my informants, after reading a draft of this essay, told me that he thought there were only fifteen hundred to two thousand Jews in Tucson in 1948.

22. Kushner "Jewish Community in Tucson," 34, 62.

23. Quoted in the *Arizona Post*, September 5, 1980, 5.

24. See Leonard Dinnerstein, "Anti-Semitism Exposed and Attacked, 1945–1950," *American Jewish History*, 71 (September 1981), 137.

25. *Commemorative Book*, 87, 528.

26. Ibid., 29, 89; *Arizona Daily Star*, February 24, 1954, 10; *Arizona Post*, June 16, 1972, 1.

27. The sources for this material prefer to remain anonymous. I have been unable to find written documentation for the facts presented.

28. *Arizona Yearbook, 1985–1986*, 127; Nash, *The American West*, 110.

29. Sonnichsen, *Tucson*, 283; Michael Konig, "Phoenix in the 1950s: Urban Growth in the Sunbelt," *Arizona and the West*, 24 (Spring 1982), 22.

30. *Arizona Yearbook, 1985–1986*, 127.

31. Sonnischsen, *Tucson*, 284.

32. "Minutebook," JCC Executive Board, housed in the offices of the Jewish Federation of Southern Arizona, Tucson, January 6, 1967.

33. Clippings from the *Arizona Daily Star*, July 30, 1971; August 3, 1971.

34. *Arizona Post*, August 20, 1971, 5.

35. *Arizona Post*, October 1, 1971, 1.

36. Ibid., October 1, 1971, 4; October 29, 1971, 2; December 10, 1971, 19; March 3, 1972, 11; March 24, 1972, 19; "Minutebook," February 18, 1972.

37. *Arizona Post*, May 5, 1972, 1.

38. *Arizona Post*, January 30, 1970, 11.

39. Sandra Heiman, "Dr. Benjamin Brook, Exec. Dir. of the Jewish Community Council, 1949–1979," *Arizona Post*, September 5, 1980, 10; "Minutebook," April 25, 1950, May 17, 1951, May 14, 1965, June 16, 1966; Memos from Ben Brook to Jack Sarver, September 7, 1967, April 23, 1968, March 3, 1972, housed in the offices of the Jewish Federation of Southern Arizona, Tucson,; *Arizona Post*, January 17, 1972; some figures were supplied by Charles Plotkin of the Jewish Federation of Southern Arizona.

40. "Minutebook," Paul Fannin to Marvin Volk, September 22, 1966.

41. The development and growth of Jewish efforts to support the State of Israel by working within the American political system have drawn increasing attention. Works that explore the role of the Jewish lobby and AIPAC (American Israel Political Action Committee) and that set the historical context for understanding the activities of the Desert Caucus are: Cheryl A. Rubenberg, *Israel and the American National Interest: A Critical Examination* (Urbana and Chicago, 1986); Edward Tivnan, *The Lobby: Jewish Political Power and American Foreign Policy* (New York, 1987); Bernard Reich, *The United States and Israel: Influence in the Special Relationship* (New York, 1984); M. Margaret Conway, "PACS, the New Politics and Congressional Campaigns," in Allan J. Cigler and Burdette A. Loomis, eds., *Interest Group Politics* (Washington, DC, 1983); Yossi Lapid, "Ethnic Political Mobilization and U.S. Foreign Policy: Current Trends and Conflicting Assessments"; and Peter Y. Medding, "Segmented Ethnicity and the New Jewish Politics," in Ezra Mendelsohn, ed., *Studies in Contemporary Jewry: Jews and Other Ethnic Groups in a Multi-ethnic World* (New York, 1987), v. 3, 3–25 and 26–48, respectively. Ex-congressman Paul Findley, an opponent of AIPAC who was regarded by many as being pro-Arab, discusses the activities of the Tucson Jewish community and its efforts to counter the perceived pro-Arab bias of the University of Arizona's Near Eastern Center in *They Dare to Speak Out: People and Institutions confront Israel's Lobby* (Westport, CT, 1985) 212–37.

42. *American Jewish Year Book*, 77 (1977), 230, 233; ibid., 85 (1985), 180, 183.

Chapter 7

Intermarriage
and the Urban West:
A Religious Context
for Cultural Change

WILLIAM TOLL

Introduction

William Toll's essay on intermarriage in the West explores a theme that has always been of great concern to the Jewish community but that has become a major issue for American Jewish social scientists only in the past two decades. Concern over increasing rates of intermarriage in western cities and elsewhere, rates that in some instances appear to challenge Jewish survival, have brought the matter into the open and have led to efforts to understand the full dimensions of the phenomenon. Toll is the first to place the analysis of intermarriage into the broadest historical context. His survey of patterns of intermarriage in the West since the late nineteenth century includes comparisons with selected European Jewish communities as well as with Jewish communities on the East Coast.

As extraordinary rates of intermarriage in western cities in the current generation have been disclosed, especially by the population studies undertaken by the Jewish communities of Los Angeles, Phoenix, and Denver, the question has arisen whether the West has always been a region in which intermarriage between Jew and Gentile was more frequent than in the East. Was the West, for whatever reasons, more hospitable to Jews and thus an area in which a higher incidence of intermarriage than elsewhere might be expected? Or were Jews in the West less committed to the preservation of a Jewish identity and, therefore, more prone to intermarriage?

Toll's discussion of the existing data that relate to these questions is revealing. Although the evidence is spotty and hard to come by, Toll argues that in the nineteenth century the marriage of Jewish men with Gentile women in the sparsely settled and isolated frontier regions may have been common because of the absence of prospective Jewish partners. On the other hand, data from the western urban centers and the small towns in which most Jews lived seems to indicate that intermarriage was no more prevalent in the West than elsewhere.

Indeed, Toll has discovered an interesting pattern in second- and third-generation western Jews for whom the larger centers of Jewish population, such as San Francisco and Denver, provided marriage marts to which the Jewish young men from the smaller communities, such as Portland or Trinidad, Colorado, might turn in their quest for suitable mates. The decline of the German Jewish families of the West, noted by Dinnerstein in Tucson, is explained by Toll as the outcome not of intermarriage, but of a reduced birthrate and the apparent deliberate choice by a significant number of middle-class second- and third-generation Jews of both sexes not to marry. Toll's argument, then, is that generally Jews in the West in the nineteenth century did not intermarry with any greater frequency than Jews elsewhere. Furthermore, he contends that middle-class western Jews chose faithfully to maintain their ethnic and religious identity.

When Toll undertakes investigation of the more recent trends in intermarriage as reported in the population surveys for Los Angeles, Phoenix, and Denver, he does note that intermarriages have increased dramatically in the fourth generation of western Jews and that the incidence of intermarriage is higher in the West than in the Jewish communities of the East. But, Toll cautions, "trends in the West . . . differ in magnitude but not in direction from trends elsewhere." The questions that now arise, therefore, are: what are the characteristics that Jews in every region share that explain the increase in intermarriage? Are those traits most prevalent of all in the West? In answer to the first question, Toll points to the high levels of education and of occupational choice of the present generation of Jews as factors that have led to closer contact with non-Jews at the workplace than had been the case for previous generations. Also friendships that cross ethnic and religious boundaries encourage more intimate social contact and increase the likelihood of intermarriage. In answer to the second question, Toll points out that western Jewish communities after World War II received an influx of young, well-educated Jewish professionals and corporate managers from across the country, people who are precisely those most prone to intermarry. What is distinctive about the West, according to Toll, is the large pool of just those people. When it comes to intermarriage, the West is like the East—only more so.

In the concluding section of his paper, Toll offers an additional argument to explain the magnitude of intermarriage among western Jews. Drawing on a distinction between ethnicty (Jewishness) and religion (Judaism), Toll contends that "the surveys of Denver and Phoenix indicate that among the larger Jewish communities in the West, young people perceive Jewishness very differently than was true twenty years ago." These intermarried young people in large part apparently reject Jewishness as ethnically parochial and inappropriate in a world more open to them than it was to their parents and grandparents. But they also retain vestiges of Jewish loyalty that express themselves in a commitment to Judaism as a religion; this is signified by the growing number of conversions of non-Jewish spouses, synagogue membership, and the choice to raise children as Jews.

The implication of Toll's analysis is that American Jewry at large, particularly Jews in the West, should be challenged to explore and renew the sources of strength in Judaism and show less concern for an ethnic Jewishness that may be impossible to sustain among a young and transient population. If Toll is correct, the West may be expected to take the lead in fashioning a Judaism that meets the spiritual needs of a younger generation more prone to intermarry than its predecessors. Clearly, the implications for the future of American Judaism and American Jewry are both promising and formidable.

INTERMARRIAGE AND THE URBAN WEST

Over the past twenty years throughout the United States, nowhere more so than in the cities of the West, Jewish intermarriage rates have risen to their highest point in modern times. As Charles Silberman has written, "intermarriage rates are so far higher in the West than in the East and Mid-West . . . that we almost seem to be talking about two separate phenomenon [sic]."[1] What the meaning of intermarriage might be to the community and, less so, to the individuals involved has become the subject of intense debate. Sociologists might tabulate the trend, but its meaning as a symptom of deep change in the values and organization of the community is not yet understood.[2] In 1970, Marshall Sklare, the sociological spokesperson for Conservative Judaism, wrote, "Intermarriage is the quintessential dilemma for the American Jew. It calls into question the very basis on which American Jewish life has proceeded—that Jewish survival is possible in an open society."[3] Thirteen years later, Calvin Goldscheider and Alan Zuckerman added, "No other issue symbolized more clearly the conflict between universalism and particularism, between the American melting pot and pluralism, between assimilation and ethnic continuity."[4]

To appreciate the various meanings that one can give to intermarriage, especially in the West, we must examine three interrelated issues. First: How must intermarriage be linked to broader questions of social and ideological change that affect successive generations of Jewish settlers? Herein the statistical techniques and intensive interviews used by practitioners of the New Social History will, in modified forms, be applied to measure and interpret intermarriage patterns.[5] Second: Has the western locale (as Silberman has assumed) in some way caused a massive defection from Jewry? Examined historically, the issue is related to Frederick Jackson Turner's thesis that the social, economic, and political pressures of extending the market economy westward led settlers to modify their cultural traditions and to interact democratically with one another.[6] Third; any effort to measure the meaning and consequences of intermarriage must not only consider demographic changes among those who intermarry but also must examine the dual character of Jewish tradition.[7] The ethnic and religious poles of Jewry, which to immigrants and their children seemed inseparable, present to their grandchildren significant alternatives. Once these three issues are sorted out, we shall be better able to identify what in the Jewish tradition is disintegrating and what is being revitalized.

The study of intermarriage has usually relied on statistical series that measure changing rates over several decades in specific places. Scholars assume that if we know the age, sex, occupation, or place of birth as well as the number of the intermarried, we can infer something about the circumstances that lead to intermarriage. Reliance on statistical correlation to describe a community's structure has also typified the New Social History. Over the past twenty years in the writing of American history and over the past ten in American Jewish history, scholars have shifted attention from leaders and even institutions to trace basic changes in the way ordinary people formed and sustained families, moved within or between cities, changed occupations over a lifetime or a generation, and generally participated in the American saga of social mobility.[8] The Federal Manuscript Census, as it has been released periodically, has allowed us to gather information on otherwise inarticulate individuals, so we may take account of their lives and compare them with others. Although many gaps in American Jewish family and community history remain, we can begin to see the accumulation of changes that lead from decisions to reduce family size in one generation, to move to predominantly Gentile neighborhoods in the next, and rapidly to increase the rate of intermarriage in the third and fourth generation.[9] Whereas correlations and accumulating patterns of change do not constitute a causal chain, they do suggest the specific conditions that lead to a measurable outcome. Perhaps even more important, they help disprove popular theories that rest on wish rather than fact.[10]

Regrettably for the study of intermarriage, the Bureau of the Census does not collect data on individual religious affiliation, so we must rely on less-complete studies conducted by local Jewish federations. But as we correlate such data with other trends that can be reconstructed from the manuscript census, we may better understand how intermarriage has entered the lives of families. As we observe how federations have changed the data they correlate with intermarriage and, thus, how they interpret intermarriage, we gather clues to the changing light in which the Jewish community views the subject. In addition to relying on statistical data, the New Social History has also turned to extensive interviews (oral histories) so we might better understand the meaning that ordinary people give to their lives. Federations have generally not conducted such interviews in their social surveys, and they have not attempted to integrate individual meanings into their presentation of intermarriage. But to begin to understand the spectrum of meanings that intermarriage holds for its participants and to understand its possible meaning for the community, individual perceptions must be balanced against statistical correlations and official communal pronouncements.

To understand the context of contemporary intermarriage in America we should first review its recent history in Western Europe. Efforts to explain Jewish intermarriage through the Nazi era have usually emphasized the force of pervasive anti-Semitism. Jewish young people pursuing economic opportunities often saw their Jewish identity as a stigma and, when given the choice, converted to Christianity. Indeed, the very concept of conversion connoted Jewish apostasy.[11] In Germany from the 1890s through World War I, social trends became manifest that have ever since accompanied the emergence of Jews from social isolation. By then the majority of Jews had been concentrated in the largest cities for two generations, their families had become the smallest of any religious denomination in the country, they held white-collar jobs, their children attended universities in large numbers and aspired to professional employment, and their intermarriage rate accelerated. From 1901 to 1905, for every one hundred marriages between two Jews, there were eighteen intermarriages. Calculated differently, 8.5 percent of the Jews married a non-Jew. By the 1920s, the proportion of intermarriages had tripled, so that for every one hundred marriages between two Jews, there were fifty-four intermarriages.[12] Again, calculated alternately, 21 percent of the Jews chose a non-Jewish mate.

In France, which from the 1880s through the 1930s experienced a significant Jewish immigration to its large cosmopolitan cities, legal restrictions against Jewish access to the civil service, the army, and universities had been abolished. Social anti-Semitism, however, persisted. In this ambiguous milieu, intermarriage became a minor social drama, and scholars disagree on its incidence. Michael R. Marrus, in his impressive study of French Jewry in the era of the Dreyfus affair, claims that it was infrequent. David Weinberg, in his history of Paris Jewry during the 1930s, argues that intermarriage among native French Jews had been very high since the mid-nineteenth century, though low among recent Jewish immigrants.[13] The data, however, remain sketchy and inconclusive.

A new study of Viennese Jewry by Marsha Rozenblit has disclosed more complex trends and speculates on the mixed motives for intermarriage. Austrian law prohibited marriage between persons of different religions, so that one prospective partner had to choose the religion of the other. Under the circumstances, the number of Jews converting to Christianity increased between 1870 and 1910, but the rate seems to have been only about half as high as in Berlin. In addition, almost half as many Christians converted to Judaism, thus indicating more complex social patterns than scholars had previously imagined.[14] Individual reasons for intermarriage are not available, but the social backgrounds of the two groups suggest different mobility routes within the Jewish community. The majority of the Jews converting to Christianity were men, often civil servants or professionals from middle-class families already residing outside areas of heavy Jewish residential concentration. Their apostasy represented a further search for status, a retreat from the stigma of Jewish origins. The great majortiy of Christians converting to Judaism, however, were working-class women who were not deterred from such a change in social identity, despite the increase in Viennese anti-Semitism.[15] The pressure of Austrian law deflected personal choice into patterns of conversion, though what the meaning of conversion either to, or away from, Judaism might have been to the participants is not known. Ms. Rozenblit suggests, quite plausibly, that individual intermarriage decisions may simply have arisen from increased contacts between Jews and non-Jews as the Jewish population grew to almost two hundred thousand or 10 percent of the city's total.[16]

In Italy, where Jews have been a tiny minority in modern history, the majority have been members of urban elites in Rome, Milan, Turin, and elsewhere. Among them intermarriage has been common for generations. Current estimates for Milan indicate that half the young Jews intermarry, though the figure is much lower for Rome's larger Jewish community.[17] H. Stuart Hughes, in a recent study of Italian Jewish novelists, argues that intermarriage with a Jew for many Italians constitutes an instance of upward social mobility,[18] and for the Jew does not lead to legal separation from the Jewish community.

In a new society like the United States, explanations for intermarriage were ascribed initially not to social status or apostasy, but to ecological variables. As a corollary to Frederick Jackson Turner's frontier thesis, Jewish scholars noted how the isolation of small communities or the proportionally large numbers of potential non-Jewish spouses in the smaller towns broke down traditional constraints.[19] Later scholars turned to more fashionable psychological explanations that saw the choice of a non-Jewish spouse as an expression of adolescent rebelliousness, for well-adjusted persons, presumably, would have acceded to communal authority and accepted proper limits on mate selection.[20] The most popular of the psychological explanations, imported from Germany by the émigré psychologist, Kurt Lewin, represented intermarriage as a form of Jewish "self-hatred" that expressed an introverted resentment at a stigmatized minority status.[21] However, actual data on Jewish intermarriage in the United States prior to 1950 are very rare, and the motives of individual Jews for marrying non-Jews have never been thoroughly investigated.[22]

Whether intermarriage in the West exceeded rates in other parts of the country in the nineteenth century is not really known. The study of Jewish pioneers by Harriet and Fred Rochlin cites the exotic cases of pack mule traders who married Indian squaws and explains these unions as examples of frontier isolation. More important, they cite a rate of 25 percent for Jewish intermarriage in Los Angeles in 1876.[23] If this figure refers to individuals rather than marriages (or couples), it would be extremely high. The figure would apply to pioneer merchants of high status whose motives for intermarriage would largely be propinquity and personal choice, not a desire to escape stigma. My own work on Portland, Oregon, uncovered only one prominent nineteenth-century Jew who intermarried, though several Jews lost interest in their religion and flirted with others.[24] Documenting intermarriage is difficult because relevant public documents do not record either religion at birth or at the time of marriage. Synagogue records are more helpful. Temple Beth Israel in Portland, for example, recorded 269 marriages between November 1884 and August 1912. About 11 percent of these may have involved a non-Jew. One woman was recorded as a convert, and 28 others, primarily women, had English surnames—Holt, Hamilton, Laurence, Dean, Taylor, Holister, and Mc-Farlane—that could not be traced to local Jewish families. Several of the marriages were civil ceremonies conducted in towns, such as Boise and Lewiston in Idaho; Spokane, Washington; and Baker, Oregon.[25]

Because the bulk of the Jewish men resided in remote towns, these unions seem to follow a common pattern of the male search for companionship on frontiers where Jewish women were scarce.

Nevertheless, the dominant theme in late nineteenth- and early-twentieth-century family formation in the Pacific Northwest was a localized social network in which sons and daughters of German or Polish Jewish families married one another. The frontier tradition that opened economic and political opportunities also minimized the stigma attached to Judaism elsewhere and thus diminished the social utility of intermarriage. If the West cultivated tolerance, it also encouraged the maintenance of ethnic communities. The most successful Jewish pioneer merchants were accepted into the fraternal and civic institutions of the developing elite, yet they also expected to retain their own intimate social networks. Their names already appeared in elite directories, their synagogues stood adjacent to elite Protestant churches, and their rabbis shared pulpits with liberal Protestant ministers.[26] The Jewish elite in the West was maintained through an elaborate institutional network for women as well as for men, created largely by the first and second generations from the 1870s through 1900. It rested solidly on an interlocking mercantile supply network, with its Pacific coast hub in San Francisco and its Mountain States' center in Denver.

Just as the pioneer merchants before 1870 had often returned to German villages for brides, so the young men of the late 1880s and 1890s turned to the regional supply centers for brides. Just after 1900, for example, an increasing proportion of marriages were between residents of Portland and San Francisco, thus suggesting that deliberate efforts were being made to extend the Jewish marriage market to insure ethnic continuity. Between 1903 and 1910, the Levi, Ackerman, Sonnenberg, and Harris men of San Francisco came to Portland to marry Hirsch, Friendly, Blumenthal, and Lippitt women.[27] Likewise in a small town like Trinidad, Colorado, in 1900, it is almost impossible to detect intermarriages. Most of the Jewish men constituted an interlocking network of brothers and friends, many of whom had emigrated from Alsace. Of those men married to American-born women, almost all selected wives born in states with the largest Jewish populations. The fathers of these women had all been born in Germany, and most women themselves belonged to the local Hebrew Ladies' Aid Sociey, which was open only to Jewish women.[28]

The demographic decline of German Jewish families that occured after 1900 cannot be attributed to extensive intermarriage. Instead, it was the consequence of a more general pattern of modern urban middle-class behavior found throughout the United States and Western

Europe. Men and women defined new life options for themselves, as second-generation women of German descent married later and had far fewer children than did their immigrant mothers. A few of their sisters sought careers and either greatly delayed marriage or, like a surprising number of men, never married at all. In Portland a pattern emerged similar to that in late-nineteenth-century Germany in which fully 17 percent of second-generation women over age twenty-five and 13 percent of the men over age thirty remained single. Although a few women and many men did marry at a later age, they tended to have very few children. Often unmarried sisters and brothers shared the parental house after the immigrant generation had died or they rented a large apartment suite in a fashionable hotel. Although men usually outnumbered women in rapidly growing western towns, the absence of Jewish men of suitable standing as potential mates did not lead Jewish women to intermarry.[29]

The years from 1910 through 1945 saw western Jewish communities dominated demographically by immigrants of Eastern European descent, and then by their children. Data subsequently collected for cities, such as Los Angeles and San Francisco, indicate that their older Jewish residents had very low rates of intermarriage, which did not differ from elsewhere in the country. Similarly, in Portland in 1910, Russian immigrants had very large families, larger than those of the Italians with whom they shared the city's only "immigrant district."[30] Like their German predecessors, Russian Jews in the urban West found the economic opportunities and social tolerance that sustained them in their communal traditions when seeking a mate. As several older residents of Denver and Portland recollect, even socializing between German and Russian Jews was frowned on by parents.[31]

Just after World War II, local Jewish welfare associations began to gather data to assess social needs so they might allocate funds more efficiently. Initially, these surveys did not consider intermarriage sufficiently widespread to be worth examining. Where information was gathered, it was not correlated with data on the social characteristics of the intermarried Jews or of their Gentile partners. Indeed, the study of Portland in 1947 was more significant for its description of a pattern common throughout the country in which older and poorer Jews had been left behind in decaying neighborhoods, whereas couples married during the Great Depression had had very few children.[32]

Studies of Los Angeles in 1953 and of Long Beach in 1962 by Fred Massarik finally began to present systematic data and to infer relationships between the intermarriage of individuals and the broader changes in local Jewish communities. The Los Angeles study created a general context by noting that its Jewish community was growing so rapidly that it had become the second largest in the country, so that what occurred there could well be a portent of national trends. And intermarriage rates did seem to be growing. In a sample of six hundred households, intermarriage was tested against what was called religious identification, which, in turn, was measured by ritual observance. Among the four hundred households that considered themselves "observant," only 1 percent were intermarried. Among the approximately two hundred households that considered themselves "unobservant," almost 12 percent had intermarried, a proportion at that time well above the national average.[33] Having defined Jewishness as religious identity marked by degrees of ritual piety, Massarik was not surprised to find that the least observant were the most likely to break ethnic bonds as well. But individual motives for intermarriage were not elicited.

A breakdown of the sample according to geographical district, however, suggested an acceleration of intermarriage rates according to generation and income. In the older Los Angeles immigrant districts, such as Boyle Heights and City Terrace, intermarriage was virtually unknown. In other areas of early Jewish settlement, like Beverly–Fairfax and Wilshire, rates were well under the national average. In the newer and wealthier districts, like Beverly Hills and in the new suburb of Glendale, however, rates reached from 10.4 percent to almost 15 percent. Although the study did not directly correlate generation, occupation, or income with intermarriage, the data clearly suggest that the wealthier element in Beverly Hills and the younger upwardly mobile couples settling in the San Fernando Valley were over twice as likely to intermarry as second-generation middle-class people in older Jewish districts.[34]

The Long Beach study of forty-five hundred households (about 14,500 persons) did not break the population down into districts, instead, it reported an overall intermarriage rate of 9 percent, about the same as in nearby Los Angeles suburbs, like Mar Vista and South Los Angeles, but substantially lower than for the San Fernando Valley. Again, intermarriage as a subject was not discussed in detail, but a clue to the social background of those who intermarried was provided by forms of Jewish identification and income. The largest proportion of local Jews identified themselves as Conservative and the next largest as Reform, whereas fewer than 5 percent of the household heads considered themselves Orthodox. And at a time when ten thousand dollars a year was considered a solid middle-class income, 61.6 percent of Long Beach households fell below that figure. Only 9.5 percent earned more than twenty thousand dollars annually. These characteristics suggest a predominantly second-generation community whose denominational distribution and rate of intermarriage were not very different from the suburban patterns of Providence, Rhode Island, studied at the same time by Goldstein and Goldscheider.[35] When denominational affiliation, generation of residence in the United States, and income level were held constant, the location of the Long Beach Jewish community on the West Coast seems to have had little effect on the distribution and rate of intermarriage.

A very different picture emerged from a study by Massarik of the San Francisco area in 1959. Intermarriage rates and disaffiliation from synagogues seemed so high there that Jewish spokespersons commented ominously on their implications for the next decade. In San Francisco, which had a Jewish population of 46,000 and where over 13 percent considered themselves Orthodox, 17.2 percent of the households were intermarried. In the more affluent peninsula communities, like Menlo Park and Palo Alto, where only 3 percent considered themselves Orthodox, 20 percent of the couples were intermarried. In Marin County, with a very small Jewish population of 2,700 and where only 1 percent considered themselves Orthodox, 37 percent of the households were intermarried, and 43 percent of the Jews did not identify with any Jewish denomination.[36] Again, regrettably, Massarik did not correlate intermarriage with social or economic variables. Neither did he directly measure its incidence in different neighborhoods—even though in 1959 San Francisco had a very high proportion of older Jews compared with twenty years before—nor with surveys of other western cities.[37] Nevertheless, it seemed clear that Orthodoxy and very low rates of intermarriage could be associated with the downtown neighborhoods where so many older and smaller households clustered. In the newer districts, like the Western Addition and Park Merced, where children were far more conspicuous, the intermarriage rate may have been substantially higher, perhaps approaching levels akin to Marin County. Though Massarik did not guess at the causes for intermarriage, general surveys in the 1960s attributed the high rate to San Francisco's special status as a national center for professional and managerial personnel who were prone to divest themselves of ethnic identification and to acquire other criteria for evaluating achievement and status.[38]

A follow-up study of Oakland, Berkeley, and the East Bay completed in 1968 demonstrated that whereas rates of intermarriage were steadily increasing, they were associated with two apparently contradictory patterns: a failure to affiliate, which had been consistently noted in prior studies, and the new phenomenon of conversion to Judaism. In Oakland, where the Jewish population had grown very little since 1951, the proportion of married people and especially of widows was higher than elsewhere in the region, but the proportion of single people, including children, was much lower. The intermarriage rate was about 10 percent, about the same as in Long Beach six years earlier. In Berkeley, however, not only had the Jewish population tripled since 1951, but its proportion of single persons, including children, was more in line with that of the other expanding Jewish communities in the East Bay. Its intermarriage rate of 16 percent was about the same as San Francisco. An additional question, however, elicited the information that many born Jews as well as persons born into another religion but currently heading households with Jews now considered themselves to have no religious affiliation.[39]

Apparently running counter to this trend, however, was the finding that almost 6 percent of the heads of households had not been born Jewish but had converted. (Whether any nonheads of households had converted was not recorded.) The significance of this data or its implications for the Jewish community as a whole were not drawn out. Interestingly, Goldstein and Goldscheider had also discovered a new incidence of conversion in their study of Providence, Rhode Island. Perhaps because it had previously been rare and was increasing at a much more rapid rate than that of intermarriage, they were much struck by it. Without examining how converts or their spouses defined Jewishness or how they felt about conversion, the authors came to the conclusion that Judaism had achieved such an elevated status in America that conversion was no longer a source of stigma. Furthermore, they found that most children of mixed marriages were being raised as Jews.[40] By 1972, the *National Jewish Population Study* seemed to corroborate their findings. A national sample indicated that 27 percent of intermarrying Gentile women had converted and that most children of intermarrying Jewish women were being raised as Jews.[41]

The most recent studies of such western Jewish communities as Phoenix, Denver, and Los Angeles, completed in the early 1980s, take us to a very different social world. By comparison, two studies of Boston in 1965 and 1975 show gradual and predictable increases in patterns of cultural assimilation. The incidence of higher education, especially the acquisition of graduate degrees, had increased; young men had shifted from independent businesses to salaried professional employment; ritual observance had decreased; and intermarriage had increased.[42] In particular the incredibly low intermarriage rate of salaried professionals, which stood at 1 percent in 1965, had increased to 8 percent in 1975, and the intermarriage rate of salaried workers had increased from 3 percent to 20 percent during the same ten-year period. But Boston was a large, old Jewish community segmented into many social clusters, from Orthodox immigrants to transient professionals attracted to the array of local universities. Phoenix and Denver, by contrast, were largely new communities for Jews. The surveys revealed Denver and nearby Boulder had over 42,000 Jews and Phoenix and its suburbs over 43,000, but over 50 percent of those in Denver and over 60 percent of those in Phoenix had arrived less than ten years prior to the surveys.[43] Thus, in social composition both the Denver and Phoenix communities were similiar to the San Francisco community studied by Massarik almost twenty-five years earlier. All three were virtually identical in size and were diffused over the urban area. Each had some population clusters, but none had an intensively Jewish neighborhood. All three had large cohorts of children, with Phoenix ranking slightly higher and Denver slightly lower than San Francisco. In addition, the proportion of persons over age sixty-five was about 5 percent lower than for San Francisco, even though Phoenix attracted many retired persons.[44] Although the rates of intermarriage seemed exceptionally high in San Francisco where almost 20 percent of the households were intermarried, the rates in contemporary Denver and Phoenix, especially for persons under age forty were higher still.

The Denver study recognized forthrightly that intermarriage was only one aspect of a revolution in family life that has overtaken Jews as well as Gentiles. A section, "Marriage, Remarriage, and Intermarriage," was devoted to new personal choices in family configuration that included those living together, the divorced, the single parent, and multiple households. Intermarriage seemed so important to the federation because in Phoenix 24 percent and in Denver 30 percent of all marriages were between born Jews and non-Jews. This already high figure, however, represented all couples, including a large contingent of retired people, among whom relatively few were intermarried. Among the younger cohorts, the intermarriage picture was unprecedented. For persons in their thirties, in Denver 43 percent and in Phoenix 53 percent of the marriages joined a born Jew to a born Gentile. And for the first time the intermarriage rate for Jewish young women was almost identical with that for Jewish young men. But in conjunction with this apparently further loosening of ethnic constraints has come an increase in voluntary affiliation with the Jewish religion. Following up on the 1972 *National Jewish Population Study,* both the Denver and Phoenix studies recorded dramatic increases in conversion to Judaism. The spouses of 17 percent of born Jews then in their thirties in Phoenix and of 13.4 percent in Denver had converted to Judaism. For those Jews in their twenties in mixed marriages, the conversion figure for the Gentile spouse was much lower. However many Gentile women, especially at a later stage in the life cycle, convert to Judaism.[45] The picture of extensive intermarriage has most recently been corroborated for Los Angeles, the West's largest Jewish community, where the rate for young people is identical with that for Denver.[46] The phenomenon of conversion, however, was not discussed in the Los Angeles study.

How are we to interpret this extraordinary increase in intermarriage as well as the social and ideological changes that accompany it? As the literature over the past twenty years indicates, intermarriage constitutes a crisis for Jewish communal leaders. As late as the 1960s, when Jewish scholars discussed the intermarried, they invariably deemed such a choice of spouse a personal and social disaster. The majority of the intermarried Jews, they argued, either left the community, created families that would be isolated from it, or would see their marriages end in divorce. In the early 1960s, the great majority of Hillel rabbis surveyed felt that intermarriage must lead to divorce.[47] Although divorce rates for the intermarried at the time were much higher than among endogamous Jews, the actual causes of divorce were simply unknown.[48] Scholars have since learned—by studying the incidence of divorce in every segment of American society—that the relatively high rate of divorce among the intermarried often has little to do with the differing religious origins of the partners.

Until recently, rabbis and counselors writing on intermarriage have stressed their own professional dilemmas in approaching what they perceived to be a serious social problem. As counselors they wished to assist young people to find happiness, but as rabbis they wished to strengthen the Jewish community, which they were sure would be weakened by intermarriage. In the mid-1970s Gerald Bubis, director of the School of Jewish Communal Services at Hebrew Union College in Los Angeles, explained the rabbis' dilemma in the following terms: "The rabbi works toward an accommodation between group expectations and communal demands. He is caught in the clash and conflict which sometimes results, and always must be guided by what's good for Jews and Judaism."[49] Many well-known rabbis have simply resigned themselves to intermarriage as the price Judaism must pay for the privilege of living in a liberal democracy.[50] Others have suggested that a more intense Jewish education, classes for potential converts, or even procedures for arranging contacts between young Jewish men and women, might curb intermarriage.[51]

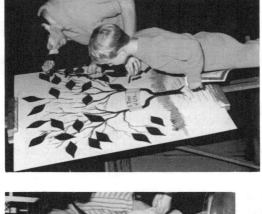

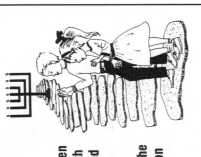

A community project to build Jewish identification for children of unaffiliated inter-faith families. Developed and implemented by Congregation Emanuel and funded in part by the Allied Jewish Federation of Denver and private contributors.

Stepping Stones: Congregation Emanuel, Denver: A community-sponsored educational program for children of intermarried couples, Denver, 1987. Right: Stepping Stones' logo and mission. Center: Her first matzah ball. Left: Looking at the Tree of Life. (Courtesy of Stepping Stones.)

The extraordinary increase of intermarriage in the West in recent years, however, requires more imaginative thinking not only about individual motives and communal consequences, but also about the implications for Jewish identity. Despite occasional anti-Semitic incidents, Jews in the West have not been stigmatized nor even challenged by a politics of ethnic conflict. Instead, liberal social circumstances and broad economic opportunities have encouraged contacts between Jews and Gentiles in residential areas, business, school, and in secular voluntary associations. Steven Cohen has argued that as Jews have been integrated at various contact points into American society, traditional Judaism has been reduced in scope and intensity, and major innovations have occurred in Jewish practices.[52] Almost twenty-five years ago, Judith Kramer and Seymour Leventman noted that in societies like the United States, which encourage religious and ethnic diversity and also promote economic growth, the social and cultural synthesis produced by one generation provides merely the point of departure for the next.[53] For parents, intermarriage may represent the ultimate intrusion of secularism into Jewish family relations. But for the children, it usually culminates after a series of breaks from the intensive ethnic network actually initiated by the parents. Furthermore, in a culture that has come to value rather than denigrate Judaism, neither the Jewish nor the Gentile partner need relinquish pride or status because of his or her religious origins or new religious choice.

To interpret the new context and implications for Jewish intermarriage let me offer three suggestions. First, young American Jews settling in western cities are participating in a general pattern of friendship selection and the construction of new support networks with non-Jews of the same age, education, and occupation. In a study of the effects of urbanism on the formation of social networks in northern California, Claude Fischer found that men and women in their twenties and thirties with advanced degrees and high incomes were the most likely to cut ties with the social world of parents, neighbors, and church so that they might seek opportunities in core cities. The large city itself did not leave individuals isolated and rootless, as some sociologists said. Instead, it offered unprecedented opportunities to build new support networks to meet personal needs. The immigrant grandparents of these young people had themselves constructed support networks of married siblings, cousins and *landsmen* to replace the families that had initially been broken by immigration. Their descendants, equipped with advanced degrees and high incomes, now had the resources to create entirely new kinds of networks with segments both within the ethnic context and with others quite separate from it, that is, persons of diverse ethnic origin. According to Fischer, Catholics, Jews, and blacks are more likely than white Protestants to establish friendships with persons of their own ethnic background. But young people in general, Jews among them, have resorted to cities like San Francisco or Sacramento to build extensive social networks based largely on friendship rather than on family.[54] Because the majority of young Jews in Denver and Phoenix had arrived less than ten years prior to the surveys and because they selected "partners" in unprecedented degrees from nontraditional sources, one can safely conclude that they were adapting to social patterns common to non-Jews of their generation.[55]

Second, trends in the West, Charles Silberman notwithstanding, differ in magnitude but not in direction from trends elsewhere. Indeed, surveys do not reveal how many of the intermarried couples now residing in western cities were actually married in the East. The San Francisco study of 1959 yielded intermarriage rates that did not differ markedly from those for Washington, DC, in 1956. At the time, the sociologist C. B. Sherman pointed to the similar occupational structures of the two cities, which, because of the high proportion of salaried professionals, attracted persons who in smaller numbers everywhere were prone to break from the ethnic community's social conventions.[56] Even in the very large and old Jewish community of Philadelphia, the educational and occupational mobility of the young has produced a similar trend. In a new study in which data are presented only for couples rather than individuals, 23 percent of those couples with a husband in his thirties included a Jew and a Gentile, approximately 17 percent less than in Denver, but only 3 percent less than in Phoenix. For couples in their twenties in Philadelphia, 34 percent included a Jew and a Gentile, compared with 66 percent in Denver and 60 percent in Phoenix.[57] Denver and Phoenix present much steeper trends among young people than does Philadelphia and the respective federations do not present interview data that might explain the discrepancies. Perhaps the much larger pool of prospective spouses and the denser Jewish institutional network made endogamous marriage more likely in Philadelphia. But whatever influenced intermarriage in the West also operated in the East.

Third, the surveys of Denver and Phoenix indicate that among the larger Jewish communities in the West, young people perceive Jewishness very differently than was true twenty years ago. In a paper comparing Jewish with Japanese marriage patterns in the West, Paul Spickard has catalogued those sociological variables that predispose one generation to widen boundaries for selecting suitable mates compared with its immediate predecessor. Because both Japanese and Jewish immigrants valued education, each succeeding generation increased the proportion in attendance at college. Consequently, in a society that progressively accepted minorities, both young Jews and young Japanese came to share more interests with contemporaries beyond their respective groups and less with older people within them.[58]

Spickard's argument, however, glides over two points that provide a more complex explanation for the acceleration of Jewish intermarriage and for the new importance of conversion. First, he assumes that American Jews are an ethnic group. Conventionally, this characterization is acceptable, but what permits continuity in Jewish life, despite uprootings and resettlement, is the constant tension between Jewry as an evolving cultural entity and Judaism as a religious ideology that gives a historically conscious people a sense of moral purpose. Indeed, because Jews have largely defined themselves through a religious ideology, non-Jews can become "Jewish" by accepting it, or "converting" to it. Through a personal search for spiritually satisfying ritual forms both converts and born Jews can counter a seemingly inevitable process of cultural assimilation.[59] Joel Crohn, in a series of interviews with intermarried couples in the Bay Area, found that the Gentile or converted spouse inevitably had to wrestle with the ethnic versus the religious component of Jewishness. During the course of what he terms ethnotherapy sessions, Crohn found that, "While many of the Jewish partners were caught between the wish to reaffirm their Jewish identities and the desire to hide them, many of their spouses were struggling with the idea of adopting some aspect of a Jewish identity for themselves."[60] And those aspects most readily available were religious rituals, especially those normally practiced in the home.

Second, Spickard is indifferent to what remains of Jewish identity for the intermarried. He recognizes that more Jews might marry white Protestants than Catholics or blacks, but he incorrectly infers that this implies something about Jewishness. Specifically, he does not examine the spiritual appeal of Judaism. Nor does he suggest how a new ethnicity for Jews can, or perhaps must, include a revitalized religious core. By the late 1950s, Will Herberg and Marshall Sklare had both noted how religion had replaced ethnicity as the basis of social identity for most Americans. However, for them religion itself had become a social, that is an ethnic, rather than a spiritual experience.[61] Charles Liebman identified this preoccupation with social solidarity as a "folk religion" in which social convention took precedence over ritual piety, and in which ethnic solidarity became the basis of identity.[62] More recently, though, Milton Plesur has perceptively noted that, with the move of the third generation to the suburbs, Jewishness became a fragment of identity associated with specific religious acts.[63] Corroborating Claude Fischer's work, Plesur found that Jews no longer assumed that their social contacts would be confined to one another. The new variety of social contacts has led an increasing number to select partners with little regard to ethnic origins who, nevertheless, sought in marriage some sense of spiritual support. This has led the Jewish partner to suggest, or the Gentile partner to seek, conversion. Recognizing the unfamiliarity of the older generation with the phenomenon of conversion to Judaism, the Conservative movement has recently issued a pamphlet that seeks to separate folk beliefs about the convert from rabbinic teachings. Converts, the pamphlet argues, are as genuinely Jewish as are born Jews. Jews are "chosen" not because God endowed their ancestor with a unique psychological makeup, but because Jews chose a uniquely pious way of behaving. Those now choosing to become Jews are simply following a pattern established by the ancestors of those now born into the Jewish community. Any challenge to the authenticity of Jews by choice comes not from *halacha*, but from folk prejudices.[64]

For the intermarrieds in America, what persists of religious expression derives largely from moments in the life cycle that tie generations together. Recent sociological studies demonstrate that Judaism remains identified with the home and synagogue and is most intensively expressed by parents and their school-age children.[65] For the intermarried especially, who have many non-Jewish friends, conscious efforts to behave Jewishly now entail synagogue activity rather than spontaneous Jewish social intercourse. Indeed, because the synagogue seems to focus religion on child rearing, women and men seem willing to develop their Jewishness around it. Several converts found a much more intensive nurturing atmosphere in synagogues than they had experienced in Protestant churches. One woman, the daughter and sister of Episcopal ministers, taught music to children in a Hebrew school and served as an officer in a synagogue. Another woman, married to a Gentile, had been raised in the folk *shul* tradition and was fluent in Yiddish. She learned Hebrew as an adult and teaches regularly in a Hebrew school.[66] Still other converts have initiated *havuroths* that study Jewish literature and current events. The synagogue itself not only offers classes for converts but emphasizes family participation in festive rituals, like Succoth, Chanukah, Purim, and Passover.

The strong affective ties that have held families together have led most intermarried persons to desire to tie the moral education of their children to their own psychological roots. The graduate of an Orthodox yeshiva who has become a thoroughly secular clinical psychologist married to a Protestant woman stated the point most clearly. In a view that he characterized as irrational, he argued that he wanted his daughter to appreciate the sense of compassion and the social conscience that Judaism had taught him, but he did not necessarily want her to join a Jewish community, which he still associated with compulsive ritual.[67]

The several dozen interviews I have conducted suggest that intermarried persons reflect most of the broad range of attitudes toward religion that one finds in the general population of the same age. But like their Gentile peers, they perceive the traditional ethnic network of kin, neighbors and synagogue as constrictive. As many sociologists have found, intermarriage by itself does not threaten the Jewish community because it is merely a symptom of growing dissatisfaction with exclusively ethnic social affiliations that had marked prior generations.[68] Even the effects of intermarriage on communal size depend on a host of complex variables: the relative fertility of conversionary marriages, the ratio of women to men among born Jews who intermarry, and the rate of conversion of born Gentiles to Judaism.[69] Bernard Lazerwitz found almost twenty years ago that as rabbis reach out to convert Gentiles in mixed marriages, the proportion of children in such marriages who are raised as Jews increases dramatically. And the data from Phoenix and Denver indicate that conversion has greatly increased under far more enlightened circumstances than even ten years ago.[70] Intermarried couples are not in search of some sentimentalized symbolic ethnicity, which is how Herb Gans characterized Jewish behavior in the 1970s.[71] Instead they seek an ethical tradition rich in symbolic expression that they can transmit to their children. Major segments of Jewry, especially in western cities, can best be conceived of as persons joined by a sense of ethical need.[72] Put another way, the identity of many American Jews now depends on a belief that a religious tradition brings spiritual buoyancy to a personality that derives from diverse cultural traditions.

Notes

1. Charles Silberman, *A Certain People: American Jews and Their Lives Today* (New York, 1985), 294.

2. Clifford Geertz, *The Interpretation of Culture* (New York, 1973), 87–125.

3. Marshall Sklare, *America's Jews* (New York, 1971), 193.

4. Calvin Goldscheider and Alan S. Zuckerman, *The Transformation of the Jews* (Chicago, 1984), 178.

5. The application of new statistical methods to American Jewish history is discussed in William Toll, "The New Social History and Recent Jewish Historical Writing," *American Jewish History*, 69 (March 1980), 325–41; Marc Lee Raphael, "The Utilization of Public, Local and Federal Sources for Reconstructing American Jewish Local History: The Jews of Columbus, Ohio," *American Jewish Historical Quarterly*, 65 (September 1975), 10–35. A somewhat different approach is outlined in Deborah Dash Moore, "The Construction of Community, Jewish Migration and Ethnicity in the United States," in Moses Rischin, ed., *The Jews of North America* (Detroit, 1987), 105–17.

6. The literature on Turner and the frontier is enormous. See Ray A. Billington, ed., *Frontier and Section: Selected Essays of Frederick Jackson Turner* (Englewood Cliffs, NJ, 1961), 37–62; Lee Benson, *Turner and Beard: American Historical Writing Reconsidered* (Glencoe, IL, 1960), 42–91; Richard Hofstader, *The Progressive Historians: Turner, Beard, Parrington* (New York, 1969), 47–164.

7. Mordecai M. Kaplan in *The Future of the American Jew* (New York, 1967), 3–8, defines the inner conflict somewhat differently: as between "affirmative" Jews he identifies as religiously observant and those "marginal" Jews who see their ethnic origins as a misfortune and are obsessed with anti-Semitism.

8. As examples see Thomas Kessner, *The Golden Door: Italian and Jewish Immigrant Mobility in New York City, 1880–1970* (Cambridge, MA, 1977); Olivier Zunz, *The Changing Face of Inequality: Urbanization, Industrial Development and Immigrants in Detroit, 1880–1920* (Chicago, 1982).

9. This was certainly the pattern in Portland, Oregon. See William Toll, *The Making of an Ethnic Middle Class: Portland Jewry over Four Generations* (Albany, NY, 1982). In an older city, with a larger Jewish population, the neighborhoods inhabited by second-generation Jews were more visibly ethnic. See Sidney Goldstein and Calvin Goldscheider, *Jewish Americans: Three Generations in a Jewish Community* (Englewood Cliffs, NJ, 1968), 44–48.

10. The case for the importance of framing "verifiable" propositions "which can be tested through the gathering of quantitative data" is clearly stated in Lee Benson, *Toward the Scientific Study of History* (Philadelphia, 1972), 3–11. An application that sets Jewish settlement into the broader context of urban social and geographical mobility is that of Howard Chudacoff's "A New Look at Ethnic Neighborhoods: Residential Dispersion and the Concept of Visibility in a Medium-Sized City," *Journal of American History*, 60 (June 1973), 76–92.

11. Uriel Tal, *Christians and Jews in Germany: Religion, Politics and Ideology in the Second Reich, 1870–1914* (New York, 1972), 5, 14–15, 138, 143; Marjorie Lamberti, *Jewish Activism in Imperial Germany: The Struggle for Civil Equality* (New Haven, CT, 1978), 179; Todd Endelman, *Jewish Apostasy in the Modern World* (New York, 1987), 9–18.

12. Daniel Niewyk, *The Jews in Weimar Germany* (Baton Rouge, LA, 1980), 98; Louis A. Berman, *Jews and Intermarriage: A Study in Personality and Culture* (New York, 1968), 123, cites intermarriage data.

13. Michael R. Marrus, *The Politics of Assimilation: A Study of the French Jewish Community at the Time of the Dreyfus Affair* (New York, 1971), 60–63; David H. Weinberg, *A Community on Trial: The Jews of Paris in the 1930s* (Chicago, 1977), 48–50.

14. Marsha L. Rozenblit, *The Jews of Vienna, 1868–1914: Assimilation and Identity* (Albany, NY, 1984), 129, 140.

15. The same pattern of Gentile working-class women marrying Jewish men is

noted for Berlin in Marion A. Kaplan, "Priestess and Hausfrau: Women and Tradition in the German-Jewish Family," in Steven Cohen and Paula Hyman, eds., *The Jewish Family: Myths and Realities* (New York, 1986), 73.

16. Rozenblit, *Jews of Vienna*, 5, 138–42.

17. S. Della Pergola, *Jews and Mixed Marriages in Milan, 1901–1968* (Jerusalem, 1972), 24, 37, 43, 47–48; idem, "A Note on Marriage Trends Among Jews in Italy," *Jewish Journal of Sociology*, 14 (December 1972), 198–200.

18. H. Stuart Hughes, *Prisoners of Hope: The Silver Age of Italian Jewry* (Cambridge, MA, 1983), 27.

19. Berman, *Jews and Intermarriage*, 86, 93; Peter I. Rose, *Mainstream and Margins: Jews, Blacks and Other Americans* (New Brunswick, NJ, 1983), 56–58; I. Harold Scharfman, *Jews on the Frontier* (Chicago, 1977), 280–81.

20. The literature on adolescent rebellion is criticized in Berman, *Jews and Intermarriage*, 112–13, 118–19.

21. Kurt Lewin, *Resolving Social Conflicts: Selected Papers on Group Dynamics* (New York, 1948), 186–89; Albert I. Gordon in *Intermarriage: Interfaith, Interracial, Interethnic* (Boston, 1964), 63, attributed the decline of self-hatred in the 1960s to a new mood of tolerance in the country.

22. J. S. Slotkin, "Jewish-Gentile Intermarriage in Chicago," *American Sociological Review*, 7 (1942), 34–36, interviews with 146 Jews in 1937. Slotkin found that perhaps 32 percent had married for "anti-social" reasons, though his categories for sorting motives were highly subjective.

23. Harriet Rochlin and Fred Rochlin, *Pioneer Jews: A New Life in the Far West* (Boston, 1984), 90.

24. "Judge Deady in Relation to B. Goldsmith," December 3, 1889; manuscript in Bancroft Collection, Bancroft Library, University of Cailfornia, Berkeley.

25. Congregation Beth Israel, Portland, Oregon, Marriage Licenses, 1884–1912, American Jewish Archives, Cincinnati.

26. Toll, *Ethnic Middle Class*, 23–26; Peter R. Decker, "Jewish Merchants in San Francisco: Social Mobility on the Urban Frontier," in Moses Rischin, ed., *The Jews of the West: The Metropolitan Years* (Berkeley, 1979), 21–22.

27. Beth Israel marriage licenses show a slight annual increase in marriages and in unions between Portland and San Francisco families after 1900. The number of marriages, however, is too small to allow for broad generalizations.

28. Data on places of birth have been gathered from the Federal Manuscript Census, 1910, Las Animas County, Colorado. Membership data for the women are gathered from Trinidad, Colorado, Hebrew Ladies' Aid Society, Minutebooks, American Jewish Archives, Cincinnati.

29. Toll, *Ethnic Middle Class*, 52–53.

30. William Toll, "Ethnicity and Stability: The Italians and Jews of South Portland, 1900–1940," *Pacific Historical Review*, 54 (May 1985), 180.

31. Interview with Tyllie Levy, Denver, May 19, 1978, Rocky Mountain Jewish Historical Society, Denver; interview with Mrs. Gladys Trachtenberg, Dec. 11, 1973, Jewish Historical Society of Oregon, Portland.

32. Papers Relating to Portland, Oregon, Jewish Population Census, March 1947, Table 6, Western Jewish History Center, Berkeley; S. Goldstein and Goldscheider, *Jewish Americans*, 51, 182.

33. Fred Massarik, "A Report on the Jewish Population of Los Angeles," (1953), 49, Western Jewish History Center, Berkeley.

34. Ibid., 11.

35. Fred Massarik, "A Study of the Jewish Population of Long Beach, Lakewood, and Los Alamitos," (1962), 27 [Table 20], Western Jewish History Center, Berkeley; Goldstein and Goldscheider, *Jewish Americans*, 51, 182.

36. Fred Massarik, "A Report on the Jewish Population of San Francisco, Marin County, and the Peninsula," (1959), 29 [Table 13], 44 [Table 24], Western Jewish History Center, Berkeley.

37. *A Study of the Jewish Community in the Greater Seattle Area* (Seattle, 1979), 23 [Table 6] shows 13.3 percent over age 65; Portland, Oregon, Jewish Population Census, March 1947, Tables 6 and 7 show only 7.5 percent over age 65.

38. C. Bezalel Sherman, "Demographic and Social Aspects," in Oscar Janowsky, ed., *The American Jew: A Reappraisal* (Philadelphia, 1964), 40; Gordon, *Intermarriage*, 204–6; Judith Kramer and Seymour Leventman, *Children of the Gilded Ghetto: Conflict Resolution of Three Generations of American Jews* (New Haven, CT, 1961), 14–15, 202–3.

39. Fred Massarik, "A Report on the Jewish Population of Alameda and Contra Costa Counties, California" (1970), 11 [Table 2], 16 [Table 7], 85 [Tables 58, 59], Western Jewish History Center, Berkeley.

40. Goldstein and Goldscheider, *Jewish Americans*, 156–57.

41. Fred Massarik and Alvin Chenkin, "United States National Jewish Population Study: A First Report," *American Jewish Yearbook, 1973* (Philadelphia, 1973), 292, 296.

42. Steven M. Cohen, *American Modernity and Jewish Identity* (New York, 1983), 37.

43. Bruce A. Phillips and William S. Aron, "Phoenix Jewish Population Study: Part 1, Demographic Overview" (1983), 5, 24; Bruce A Phillips and Eleanore P. Judd, *The Denver Jewish Population Study, 1981* (Allied Jewish Federation, Denver, 1981), iii, 29–30 [Table 15].

44. "Phoenix Jewish Population Study," 8; *Denver Jewish Population Study*, 3 [Table 2].

45. "Phoenix Jewish Population Study," 14–15; *Denver Jewish Population Study*, 44–46. A less sophisticated study of Seattle in 1979 found that 44 percent *of marriages* involving at least one born Jew included a born Gentile. This translated into an individual intermarriage rate of 28 percent. See *Jewish Community in the Greater Seattle Area*, 16. However, this study provides no breakdown of age groups.

46. Neil C. Sandberg, *Jewish Life in Los Angeles: A Window To Tomorrow* (Lanham, MD, 1986), 53–54.

47. Berman, *Jews and Intermarriage*, 178; Gordon, *Intermarriage*, 186.

48. Gordon, *Intermarriage*, 4.

49. Gerald D. Bubis, "Intermarriage: The Rabbi and the Jewish Communal Worker," in Gerald D. Bubis, ed., *Serving the Jewish Family* (New York, 1977), 72.

50. Arnold Schwartz, "Intermarriage in the United States," *American Jewish Year Book, 1970* (Philadelphia, 1970), 101; Robert Gordis, *The Root and the Branch: Judaism and the Free Society* (Chicago, 1962), 132.

51. Stuart E. Rosenberg, *The Search for a Jewish Identity in America* (New York, 1965), 275–76; Erich Rosenthal, "Jewish Intermarriage in Indiana," *American Jewish Year Book, 1967* (Philadelphia, 1967), 263–64.

52. S. M. Cohen, *American Modernity*, 37.

53. Kramer and Leventman, *Children of the Gilded Ghetto*, 4; Cohen, *American Modernity*, 21, comments on the emergence of the concept "generation" in American sociological literature.

54. Claude S. Fischer, *To Dwell Among Friends: Personal Networks in Town and City* (Chicago, 1982), 56–58, 65, 80, 83, 204–6. On immigrant family adjustments, see Judith E. Smith, *Family Connections: A History of Italian and Jewish Immigrant Lives in Providence, Rhode Island, 1900–1940* (Albany, NY, 1985).

55. Sandberg in *Jewish Life in Los Angeles*, 83, reports that of Jews "unaffiliated" with Jewish institutions, 60 percent still reported that their closest friends were Jews, but he provides no breakdown by age, education, and so forth.

56. Sherman, "Demographic and Social Aspects," 40; Gordon, *Intermarriage*, 204–6.

57. William Yancey and Ira Goldstein, "Jewish Population Study of Greater Philadelphia" (Federation of Jewish Agencies of Greater Philadelphia, 1985), 132.

58. Paul S. Spickard, "Intermarriage and Ethnic Identity: Jews and Japanese Americans in the Western United States." Paper delivered at the American Historical Association meeting, San Francisco, December, 1983, 5–7 in author's possession.

59. On the role of the American social environment in encouraging diversity of self-definition, see Martin Cohen, "Structuring American Jewish History," *American Jewish Historical Quarterly*, 57 (December 1967), 140.

60. Joel Crohn, *Ethnic Identity and Marital Conflict: Jews, Italians, and WASPS* (American Jewish Committee, New York, 1986), 24–25.

61. Will Herberg, *Protestant, Catholic, Jew: An Essay in American Religious Sociology* (New York, 1960), 186–95; Sklare, *America's Jews*, 110.

62. Charles S. Liebman, *The Ambivalent American Jew: Politics, Religion and Family in American Jewish Life* (Philadelphia, 1973), 66. The most subtle analysis of the shift in the meaning of family loyalty and of responsibility from the immigrant to the second generation is found in Sylvia Junko Yanagisako's *Transforming the Past: Tradition and Kinship Among Japanese Americans* (Palo Alto, 1985), especially see 186–92.

63. Milton Plesur, *Jewish Life in Twentieth Century America: Challenge and Accommodation* (Chicago, 1982), 158.

64. Merton K. Siegel, *Convert or Genuine Jew* (United Synagogue, New York, 1981), 11, 13–16.

65. Plesur, *Jewish Life*, 187; S. M. Cohen, *American Modernity*, 55–63.

66. Interviews with Marge T., Eugene, OR, September 17, 1984; Alberta W., Eugene, OR, August 2, 1984; Rachel T., Eugene, OR, August 23, 1984; and Yonah A., Eugene, OR, August 9, 1984.

67. Interview with Mitchell S., Eugene, OR, September 20, 1984.

68. Bernard Lazerwitz, "Intermarriage and Conversion: A Guide for Future Research," *Jewish Journal of Sociology*, 13 (June 1971), 50, 60; Schwartz, "Intermarriage in the United States," 110; S. M. Cohen, *American Modernity*, 122–24.

69. Yancey and Goldstein, "Jewish Population Study of Greater Philadelphia," 152–62.

70. Lazerwitz, "Intermarriage and Conversion," 52; "Phoenix Jewish Population Study," [Table 91]; Egon Mayer, *Intermarriage and the Jewish Future* (American Jewish Committee, New York, 1979), 30–33; Silberman, *A Certain People* 307–21.

71. Herb Gans, "Symbolic Ethnicity: The Future of Ethnic Groups and Cultures in America," *Ethnic and Racial Studies*, 2 (January 1979), 1–18.

72. Joseph R. Rosenbloom, *Conversion to Judaism: From the Biblical Period to the Present* (Hebrew Union College, Cincinnati, 1978), 135, 145.

Chapter 8

On Becoming a Westerner:
Immigrants and Other Migrants

EARL POMEROY

Introduction

Most of the essays in this collection have made the point, in one way or another, that the significance of western Jewish history can best be appreciated when compared with the history of Jews in other regions of the country. What is distinctive to western Jewish history emerges when we juxtapose it with the Jewish experience in the Northeast, South, or Midwest. Earl Pomeroy, the dean of Western history, brings the comparative perspective to bear on the western Jewish experience in a way patently different from that of the other contributors. To Pomeroy, Jews have been a vital element in the peopling of the western territories where all inhabitants, except the Indians and pioneer Hispanics, have been newcomers. Although he differentiates between immigrants and emigrants, Pomeroy emphasizes those features that westerners held in common rather than those that have set them apart. In placing the history of Jews within the shared context of all those peoples who settled in the West, Pomeroy compares the Jewish experience not with the Jewish experience elsewhere, but with the experiences of the Chinese, Scandiavians, Irish, Italians, and Anglo-Americans. He argues that in a new land distinctive cultural institutions, such as newspapers and schools, were as necessary to the foreign-born as to the native-born, for all were migrants in need of associational supports of their own devising.

Pomeroy's investigation of the Jewish experience in the West in the nineteenth century emphasizes the climate of acceptance they enjoyed; other scholars, too, have been struck by the relative absence of anti-Semitism in the Far West. The explanation Pomeroy offers for western receptivity to Jewish settlers centers on the observation that many Jews arrived with precisely those skills that were most in demand in the newly developing communities. Merchants, whether Jew or Gentile, were essential in the unstructured towns and cities of the

West if local economies were to flourish. Recognized as valuable additions to their communities, Jewish merchants, welcomed by their neighbors, became well integrated into the western mercantile society. Furthermore, the Jewish migrants to the West in the nineteenth century were predominantly from the German states and benefited from the high esteem in which German culture was held in the United States. Even if, as some historians have demonstrated, the reports on Jewish merchants submitted by local observers to the New York credit-rating firm of Dun & Bradstreet included references that can be interpreted as anti-Semitic, the prominence of Jewish merchants in the West indicates that religion and ethnicity were no barriers to commercial success.

Pomeroy's essay offers additional evidence that Jews shared readily in the western experience by pointing to their role in politics. In greater numbers and earlier than in the East, Jews were elected to public office (local, state, and national), which was especially notable when it is recalled that Jews made up so small a percentage of the qualified voters.

If the West in the nineteenth century was a region remarkably open to Jews and other foreigners, it certainly was a long way from being a democratic society. Emigrants from China and Japan, native Indians and Hispanics, and the few black migrants, who differed in race as well as culture, surely were not received in the way that European immigrants were, for the West could be as racially intolerant as any region of the country. Nevertheless, the presence of the Chinese and Japanese and the western fear of "the yellow peril" cannot, insists Pomeroy, account for the favorable treatment afforded Jews. There is no evidence to sustain the speculation that anti-Asian sentiment in the West defused the potential for anti-Semitism. Indeed, in California, before the Chinese arrived in large numbers, Jews were integral to mercantile life and were among the first to be elected to political office. Unlike the Jewish merchants, whose economic functions were so valued, Chinese laborers working for a pittance competed directly with resentful white workers. By contrast, the welcome afforded Jews in the West reflected the fact that they arrived at the right time, were in the right place, and had the right skills. Only since World War II would Asians and other peoples of non-European origin begin to receive the same treatment in the West as did peoples of European origin.

Pomeroy also reminds us that migration to the West has continued to the present day. If the proportion of newcomers is less marked than it was in the nineteenth century, the total number of migrants has been more formidable than ever. And Jews, of course, have been participants in this ongoing westward movement that has made Los Angeles the second largest Jewish community in the country. A full understanding of the western Jewish experience in the twentieth century yet remains a challenge. Pomeroy demonstrates how much can be gained by comparing the history of Jews in the West with the history of other groups of migrants.

ON BECOMING A WESTERNER

Historians have for many years neglected the ethnic and cultural variety of the American West, among others of its varieties. Like western films and novels, general accounts commonly show Asians, continental Europeans, and Africans as sojourners rather than residents, as passive victims of discrimination rather than actors in their own right. They are depicted as workers in no more than marginal capacities in the more transitory occupations—imported under contract to trap beaver, lay railroad tracks, or harvest seasonal crops—whereas the old-stock Americans pioneer labor in raising livestock, growing crops, and building commonwealths. As Moses Rischin pointed out two decades ago, scholars and librarians at Berkeley—long the capital of Far Western academic historical studies—traced in loving detail the movements and labors of early Jesuit and Franciscan missionaries in New Spain but neglected to preserve much of the record of the cosmopolitan American California about them.[1] Until recently, graduate students writing theses seldom ventured much beyond the gold rushes that brought the world into San Francisco Bay.

The proportions of most recorded western history, whether popular or scholarly, were strangely inconsistent with the visible realities of western life. In his essay on the significance of the frontier in American history, which westerners shortly regarded as defining their field, Frederick Jackson Turner emphasized the ascendancy of non-English immigrant stock beyond the eastern counties of the thirteen colonies and recalled the prospects that his own state of Wisconsin could have become a German-speaking commonwealth.[2] When the German-born population of Wisconsin peaked in 1860 at nearly 16 percent—the highest level in the United States—Milwaukee's population was 35.3 percent German-born.[3] Although the census figures overstated the German presence by including all emigrants from Prussia (Poles as well as ethnic Germans), they understated it by excluding Swiss Germans, Alsatians, and after the organization of the North German Confederation and the German Empire, Austrians and Luxemburgers. At the time Turner wrote in 1893, Wisconsin was still more foreign-born than New York, and the children and grandchildren of immigrants so reinforced immigrant traditions that in Milwaukee—the German Athens, as its citizens liked to call it—many English speakers felt obliged to learn German.[4] The foreign-born were smaller-than-average fractions of the population in only three of the then-sixteen Far Western states and territories west of the Missouri River, including New Mexico, which was still predominantly Spanish-speaking. The percentage of foreign-born in San Francisco—metropolis of the Far West—was higher than in any other American city of its size and exceeded only by the percentages in Duluth, Minnesota, and five New England milltowns among other cities.[5] San Francisco was not only the most Chinese of American cities but also more French than any of them, except New Orleans, and one of the most Irish and most Italian. Migrations over the last century have submerged some such concentrations but perpetuated and even reinforced others. Moreover, Americans of most immigrant stocks, especially those that came in large numbers in the nineteenth and twentieth centuries, have not distributed themselves evenly over the country but concentrated in a few states. Although Jamaicans, Haitians, Dominicans, and Ecuadorians, for instance, have favored the Northeast, others more numerous have gone disproportionately to the West, including Scandinavians, East Asians, Filipinos, Armenians, Mediterranean peoples, and Mexicans, of course.[6]

But numbers and proportions of populations seldom define roles, especially in the early Far West where census taking was notoriously inexact. Moreover, although many newcomers soon moved on, many others remained, concentrated both by occupation and region. Ethnic minorities comprised large parts of western labor forces under Anglo-American as well as Spanish, Mexican, French, and Russian rule; turbulence in relations between laborers and employers may have followed more on resentment at the treatment of minority workers than on traditional American or frontier individualism.[7] Over large sectors of western economies, employers long depended on successions of low-paid newcomers who, until they learned to exact better terms, lived on the peripheries of the dominant society.

Immigrants also comprised large parts of western entrepreneurial and property-holding populations. Immigrant Jews, at first primarily German, predominated among merchants in the mountain and Pacific states and territories soon after the mid-nineteenth-century gold and silver rushes; Germans, Czechs, and Scandinavians persisted more than older stock Americans as farmers in Wisconsin, Minnesota, and the high plains.[8] In contrast with successions of wage-earners who were classically marginal in most dimensions of life (often marginal in being single),[9] these men immigrated in the sense of seeing themselves as residents and as commanding recognition as solid citizens, even as leaders when they chose to give time to public affairs.

In parts of the West where immigrants established themselves economically they also established themselves politically by the test of officeholding—in general more rapidly than in the East. By the time New York had its first of three immigrant mayors in 1893, Los Angeles had had five of its six, San Francisco one of its three, and the next year San Francisco elected its first immigrant Jewish mayor, Adolph Sutro (1895–1897). Sutro was not, however, the first of a substantial number of Jewish immigrants who became mayors in western cities: Los Angeles had had one (1878–1880) and Portland two of its three (1869–1873 and 1909–1911, respectively).

Of twenty-nine foreign-born governors of states, eight served in Wisconsin and Minnesota, all but one from the dominant German and Scandinavian stocks. Of the rest, all served in states even farther to the west—with the exception of one elected in an eastern state who was born of American parents living temporarily in Paris, so not legally an immigrant. They included the first Jewish governors of states, Moses Alexander of Idaho (1915–1919) and Simon Bamberger of Utah (1917–1921). By Mormon terminology, Bamberger was the first Gentile governor of that state as well as the third immigrant governor and the first Jewish governor. West of Minnesota and Wisconsin, immigrant officeholders seldom had constituents of similar origin numerous enough to account for their successes. Like Alexander and Bamberger, the first immigrant Jewish western U.S. Senator, Joseph Simon of Oregon (1898–1903)—later mayor of Portland—was elected in a state with a small Jewish population. A second western Jewish senator—not an immigrant but the son of recent immigrants—Simon Guggenheim of Colorado (1907–1913) was elected forty-one years before an eastern state first chose a Jewish senator, Herbert H. Lehman of New

York. Well before New Yorkers began electing the first of a series of remarkably durable representatives—including Emmanuel Celler and Sol Bloom, who began their long service in 1923—Julius Kahn, a German immigrant, began the first of twelve terms from San Francisco in 1898. On his death in 1924, his widow, Florence Prag Kahn, succeeded him for six more terms. Like most immigrants who went far in politics, Kahn had been brought west in early childhood; on the other hand, both Alexander and Bamberger, among others from continental Europe, had had their schooling abroad. All of these early Jewish officeholders won election in states that had recently had strong Populist movements. Sutro ran on the Populist ticket as the hero of the workingmen in a city where they were used to having their way politically. Although Joseph Simon was a Republican, he had significant Populist support in a state whose previous governor had been a Populist. Their careers do not confirm later theories of western nativism and anti-Semitism. Oregonians subsequently, in 1930, elected the fifth western Jewish governor, Julius L. Meier, as an independent write-in candidate—advanced by the advocates of public power and supported by farmers and laborers—two years before the election of the first Jewish governors in nonwestern states.

That many immigrants moved ahead in politics as in business and the professions in western states does not mean that leaving or even staying was easy or that those who tried were likely to succeed. The records of developing western settlements chronically exaggerate success; although winners everywhere tend to be more visible than losers, losing in the West often meant failing to remain or even to become a westerner, thus leaving nothing of their contributions among the records of those who succeeded. Until recently, historians tended to dwell on the processes rather than on the victims of discrimination —on the Irish who cried that the Chinese must go rather than on the Chinese who went or stayed. And historians still say more about those who visibly and effectively pressed on imposed barriers than of those who did not, about Japanese and Mexicans rather than Filipinos and East Indians.[10] They are just now beginning to note the extent of reverse international migration: The departure of immigrants who returned to their old homes.[11] They singled out the Chinese as exceptional in their intention to stay only temporarily.[12] But they have been slow to recognize that others, long assumed to have cut their ties completely and intending when they came to remain, in fact, also made the return voyage in large numbers, as Jonathan Sarna has shown for Eastern European Jews before 1908[13] and other scholars have shown for Scandinavian and Italian immigrants.[14]

We may better understand why some new westerners commanded the esteem of their neighbors, whereas others did not, if we look at them in the context of both the stresses and demands of migration as well as the objects of migration. Similarities between the experiences of newcomers from other states and the experiences of newcomers from other countries ran beyond achievements in fortune and influence. Whatever their origins, once they had to move west of tidewater along the eastern seaboard in order to find free or cheap land—as all newcomers had to do from the early eighteenth century—distances and differences between old and new settlements made for significant changes in ways of life. Soon after the American Revolution, as settlers moved into the Ohio Valley, distances between generations grew to perhaps three hundred miles. By the 1840s, they grew for some to three thousand miles, and the idea that moving from the older states across the Great Plains was like moving from Europe to America appeared metaphorically in the use of the terms *emigrant, emigrant wagon,* and *emigrant trail* as well as in comparisons of the plains to the ocean.[15] The costs and rigors of the trip to the Pacific slope by either land or sea in the early years—involving risks of cholera on the Great Plains or the risks of tropical fevers on the Isthmus—contributed to a sense of final separation among emigrants from the older states—a feeling of separation that was declining among emigrants from Europe to North America over these same years as steamships came into transatlantic service. Single men went for the prospect of quick returns large enough to justify traveling both out and back, as American forty-niners indicated in calling themselves Argonauts: gold in the Sierra Nevada and the profits of speculation in real estate at San Francisco Bay. The analogies of passage and emigration overseas persisted well outside literary circles and endured even after transcontinental railroad service reduced the costs and discomforts of travel: railroads ran emigrant and (later) colonist trains for settlers recruited through emigrant and colonization bureaus; travelers compared social relations among passengers to those at sea, the motion of the cars to that of a ship; insurance companies exacted extra premiums for travel in the Rocky Mountains and beyond as late as the 1880s, just as for travel by sea.[16]

As the experience of emigrating from older to newer states resembled that of emigrating from Europe or Asia to America, so, too, the developing relationships of the two kinds of newcomers—domestic and foreign in origin—to the communities they had come to also resembled each other. Both came and settled in groups when they could, clustering by language, national and local origins, religious commitment, and above all family. In establishing themselves at their new homes, temporarily or permanently, both depended heavily on managers and purveyors of transportation, capital, information, and education, those who by design or without it served as agents of acculturation. Institutions that helped one kind of newcomers to survive and put down roots were much like those that helped another kind, occasionally the same. For instance, similarities between, newspapers and schools in western cities with large migrant (emigrant) populations seem more than coincidental. Arguing that institutions that gave immigrants the reassurance of association with kin and kind became instruments of Americanization, Horace Kallen noted that much of the immigrant press was like the American yellows, which had sprung up simultaneously to serve different readerships on the two coasts.[17] Although Abraham Cahan edited the *Jewish Daily Forward* at a higher intellectual level than the Hearst papers, in the years when Arthur Brisbane edited the *New York Journal* for Hearst, Cahan's use of illustrated Sunday supplements, headlines, and feature material earned him the sobriquet of the Yiddish Brisbane.[18] The sociologist Robert E. Park quoted a saying that the *Journal* gained a new body of subscribers every six years, mainly from among immigrants, Park's marginal men. Many of the immigrants had been barely literate when they arrived in the United States, having relied on village gossip rather than newspapers in the old country. In the city, where they had to read to survive,[19] they began by scanning the headlines of the immigrant press they saw in crowded subway and elevated cars. As heirs to a regional style of journalism whose essence was reportorial and editorial mayhem, Hearst and his editors in the West reached a wider spectrum of readers, including many who had known more sober journalistic traditions but responded most readily to news of communities they did not regard as home when it appeared in large type.[20] Years before Hearst brought to the *San Francisco Examiner* the techniques and personnel Joseph Pulitzer had employed in New York, Californians knew their kind. The *San Francisco Chronicle*, which generally supported Republican candidates and causes (the *Examiner* supported Democratic ones) represented the businessmen and larger propertyholders of the city rather than the Irish labor unionists, and it anticipated the *Examiner* of Hearst's time in its reckless sensationalism. Beginning as a daily announcement of threater programs rather than as a newspaper in the ordinary sense, it filled out its columns with fragments of humor, satire, and scandal before it added general reporting in similar spirit.[21]

As newspapers introduced both kinds of newcomers informally

to new cultures and communities, schools and colleges introduced them formally. Public education beyond elementary levels varied widely among states and cities well into this century. This may not have concerned many immigrants as long as most Americans left school by the eighth grade and most states required no more than that education for teachers. As Americans moved into cities, however, access to education increasingly represented opportunity, even more than access to land. Western states, including some with the most immigrants, led in the founding of public colleges, although for many years most of these were less than they pretended to be, offering chiefly preparatory work comparable to work in the secondary schools of the larger northeastern cities and professional training for prospective public school teachers. Eastern states lagged, probably because most of them were well endowed with privately supported colleges. In New York, the legislature did not establish a full-fledged state university system until 1948, the year after President Truman's Commission on Higher Education noted that the state of California already exceeded the commission's main recommendations. But in New York City, site of two major private colleges—King's (1754), later Columbia, and the University of the City of New York (1832)—the New York Free Academy offered a full college-level course from its beginning in 1849, seventeen years before it took the name of College of the City of New York.[22] By the early twentieth century, substantial educational opportunity was open to immigrants and migrants and their children in the states and cities where most of them went, and both they and their teachers testified to the results. In *Little Citizens* (1904), Myra Kelly wrote the urban counterpart to Edward Eggleston's *Hoosier Schoolmaster* (1871). She described the experiences of one generation of immigrants leading the next through the New York public school system in her accounts of Miss Constance Bailey and the best of boys, Morris Mogilewsky, nine months out of Russia—thus anticipating the experiences of nisei teachers with Southeast Asian and Filipino students in Hawaii several decades later. By 1903, Jewish students, most of recent Eastern European origin, comprised about three-fourths of the enrollment of City College.[23] Surveying the progress of children of immigrants in American public schools in 1908, the U.S. Immigration Commission found that in both eastern and western cities children of some immigrants, led by German and Polish Hebrews—as the commission called them— went farther and less often fell behind in moving through the grades than did children of native-born parents.[24]

Public schools affected even those who never attended them and those who at first rejected them. As in New York and other cities where immigrants concentrated, the B'nai B'rith, the Young Men's Hebrew Association, the Knights of Columbus, and their purely social and recreational counterparts developed in response to organizations that were too Christian, too Protestant, or otherwise too exclusivist for various newcomers. The Hebrew Free School Association and comparable institutions of heavily immigrant origin devised their programs not merely to counteract and supplement programs of public schools but also to emulate them. In western rural communities where public school teachers were not much more literate than the pupils from whose ranks they came, parents interested themselves in politics: some to demand better education; some to oppose change lest it increase their taxes; others to resist laws requiring attendance and the use of English. Correspondingly, school and college administrators learned to cultivate widening circles of clients if only to protect their budgets.

American newspapers and schools became extraordinarily successful in reaching both eastern and western migrants and seemed to help to draw them into closer relations with their neighbors, but not all migrants fitted into the larger community. In the nineteenth century, those who did not fit often escaped general attention by returning to their old homes — some may have failed to fit because they had expected to return home. Later many migrants long remained outside or on the fringe in urban slums that were more visible than the earlier rural slums; those who had gotten inside the community reproached the outsiders for not trying harder or argued that their kinds of migrants should not have been allowed to try. Attempts to explain differences that concentrate on the migrants themselves, their preparations for migration, and their relationships with their cohorts promise to be more fruitful than attempts that concentrate on the efforts of outsiders to draw them in — as through the schools, whose advocates sometimes have claimed much credit — or on prejudice against other minorities in the dominant society. The view that blacks were "the lightning rod for prejudice" against Jews in the South, inviting or facilitating what editor and writer Harry Golden and others have called philo-Semitism,[25] may suggest that the Chinese served similarly in the West. Yet the case is no more than circumstantial at best for either region, especially the West, and the circumstances of prejudice against one group and acceptance of another do not stand out significantly above other circumstances. For example, the southern state where Jews most often won high elective office in the nineteenth century, Louisiana, was no more of a lightning rod in the shape of a rejected minority than any of its neighbors. It was, however, the most cosmopolitan of southern states, its white majority being Spanish, French, and Roman Catholic, as were the majorities of Florida and Maryland—where Jews also won high office—but to lesser extents Spanish and German. On the other hand, although California led the West in numbers of Chinese and in anti-Chinese agitation as well as in election of immigrants to office, it also led in white immigrant population and in immigrants and old Californians of Mexican descent who were winning office well before the Chinese became a major political issue in the 1870s—other western states where Jews and other immigrants won office included some with few or no Chinese. Moreover, a few Jews were prominent enough among progressive Republicans in California so that their leading journalist opponent made a point of calling Meyer Lissner, chairman of the party's state central committee, Three Ball Lissnerski (referring to his operation of a jewelry and pawnshop as a teenager) and saying that he acted "true to the traditions and precepts of this race."[26] And it was only well after labor unionists urged it on them that Governor Hiram Warren Johnson and other progressive Republican leaders endorsed anti-Asian legislation.

The historian of immigration who investigates old-country backgrounds may find that some immigrants, like David Levinsky, anticipated their new life psychologically before they entered it physically. But the circumstances of the society that migrants entered or failed to enter also may partly explain their experiences, including cordiality toward some of them and hostility toward others.

Migration everywhere was occasion for someone to make a sale and turn a profit. Thus newcomers were especially welcome in the nineteenth-century West, above all in villages and towns ambitious to become cities. Elites were less jealous of their turf and more hospitable to strangers in new and expanding communities than in old ones. As businessmen they commonly thought of newcomers as potential customers and fellow promoters in an expanding economy rather than as competitors in a static one; as landholders, which most of them were, they counted on new buyers to drive up prices of urban real estate. Many of them, having come from eastern commercial centers and having learned to mingle with Europeans during the gold rushes, tended to be more cosmopolitan in their social expectations than residents of older rural communities. Even the Mormons of Salt Lake City, who had rejoiced at leaving Missourians behind them when they left Babylon for Zion, were glad to accommodate the assorted emigrants of other religious persuasions and moral principles who stopped to refresh themselves on their way to Oregon and California.

Yet, in such settings, immigrants of some origins and habits were more welcome than others. Businessmen who had organized vigilance committees to run herd on inconveniently assertive and disorderly Irishmen and Australians during the California gold rush came to terms with the Irish and even went far in soliciting their favor after they had staked out monopolies in strategic fields of employment, as in the Montana copper towns as well as in San Francisco. Politicians could not afford to ignore Irishmen who became citizens, registered, and voted out of proportion to their numbers.[27] The Chinese, who shared with the Irish the hard work of building the overland railroad, fared very differently. Whereas racial prejudice seems to explain much or most of the friction between the two groups, the immediate forms of protest against the Chinese corresponded also to the special circumstances of new settlement, especially to changes in the western economy that affected migrants among other newcomers. Whites had attacked Chinese in the mines from the early 1850s, and both the California legislature and local authorities, including those in San Francisco, had discriminated against them. But the first attack by a western mob on a group of immigrants was not on Asians, but on Europeans in 1865 after the assassination of President Lincoln when rioters sacked the quarters of a French-language newspaper at San Francisco.[28] The Chinese first came to San Francisco in large numbers to stay—rather than merely to pass through on their way to the mines or the railroad construction camps—in the 1870s and after, arriving in the midst of a severe economic depression, the first that American California had experienced. Labor suddenly was in surplus, and laborers of older immigrant stocks—for the first time facing the dearth of opportunity for employment that Irish immigrants had faced in Boston and other eastern cities in the 1840s[29]—resented the competition. First persuading Congress to exclude Chinese immigrants in 1882, unionists persuaded it to extend exclusion indefinitely twenty years later when economic conditions had improved after the depression of the 1890s but when employers on the West Coast were trying to break unions and Asian immigrant labor became the symbol of their designs.[30] By then the symbol included Japanese immigrants, even though they rapidly developed their own enterprises and moved out of the general labor market, especially as farm operators. Far from saving them from antagonism, their move became a grievance and prompted other grievances. It coincided with hopes that national programs of irrigation would open new opportunities for family farmers on small tracts of land. Instead, when rates of failure on irrigated land ran high, whites, predisposed to dislike Asians, blamed the Japanese for what they considered white flight in parts of rural California where family farming had developed so late and so slowly that there was widespread concern over this backwardness.[31] Further, by retreating to locales and opportunities in parts of the West and in parts of western economies that whites had neglected and by cultivating their own resources when they could not get access to those that whites enjoyed, the Japanese accepted segregation and helped those who had segregated them to believe that this was their destiny and thus that they were incapable of becoming westerners more like their neighbors.

The quite different reception of Jewish immigrants in the West also corresponds to the special circumstances of a society developed through continuing migration. The "happy union of America's economic needs and the industry and attributes of the Jewish peddler and shopkeeper" by which Naomi Wiener Cohen explains much of the experience of German Jews in the United States[32] seems to have been especially close in the cities of the Pacific and mountain states and territories. Esteem for immigrant Jewish merchants ran high. Although in early years Gentile bankers were, at most, cautious creditors—as cool and occasionally slurring references in Dun & Bradstreet ratings suggest—election of Jews to office and their participation in community activities mark them as leading and respected citizens. More than most other newcomers, they brought commercial experience where it was much in demand. Hersch estimates that about one-fifth of all immigrant Jewish breadwinners of 1899–1914 had been in commerce, against less than one-twentieth of all immigrants.[33] When San Francisco, Portland, and their successors were growing most rapidly, they imported much of their food as well as most of their manufactures. Moreover, the kinds of commerce they engaged in were peculiarly well matched to the skills and resources of Jewish immigrants, including those that merchant immigrants improvised to get started. As Rodolf Glanz has observed, Jewish emigrants often pooled their savings to send one member of a family ahead, whereas non-Jewish Germans more often were able to come as whole families.[34] Accordingly, a rising merchant in a new community on the Pacific slope might have close relatives in San Francisco, New York, and Europe on whom he could rely for stocks and credit rather than on wholesalers and bankers. In turn, the remoteness of much of the urban West along with the affluence and cosmopolitan backgrounds and contacts of much its population inclined retail customers to favor goods that came from distant manufacturers and suppliers rather than dressmakers or wholesalers in Missouri. Meanwhile, esteem and success followed on each other as peddlers became resident merchants, general stores became department stores. A town's promoters, who included not only the speculators who had platted it but also nearly everyone who had given hostage by establishing residence, above all its newspaper editors, pointed to the examples of businessmen who thought enough of its prospects to invest their profits locally. Its first brick buildings were showplaces, pictured proudly in the lithographic prints that real estate salesmen displayed.[35]

The German cultural antecedents and traditions of Jewish merchants further contributed to their reputations in communities that valued cultural activity both for its own sake and as evidence of solid growth. Although San Franciscans followed French fashions, developed tastes for French cuisine, and liked to call their city the Paris of Americans, with other Americans they disliked the Emperor Napoleon III, who went further than any other European leader in favoring the Confederacy. Americans correspondingly respected Prussia and Germany, applauding the unification of the German states as comparable to the preservation of the Union and recalling that Germans had bought Union bonds and fought in the Union army. The largest non-British element in the American population, particularly numerous in the West, German-speakers had been accepted and respected since the first German immigrants came to Pennsylvania in the seventeenth century; German scholarship and art had enormous prestige; and German was the standard modern foreign language in schools. As during and after World War I many German Americans did not bother to dispel misunderstanding of the term *Pennsylvania Dutch*, in the nineteenth-century natives of Prussia seldom corrected Americans who assumed that they were German rather than Polish. As carriers of a respected culture, German Jewish immigrants in new western communities had advantages that Italian and Irish immigrants in Boston, for instance, conspicuously lacked.[36] They routinely joined *Vereins* and other societies devoted to German culture; as the traveler Israel Benjamin (Benjamin II, as he like to call himself) noted on visitng San Francisco in 1860–1861, the president of the local German society was a Jew.[37]

Over much of the American experience most Americans have been migrants in some sense or children of migrants, and many of them continued to migrate and to seek the opportunities and suffer the strains of migration and resettlement long after they or their ancestors immigrated from abroad. Thus, considering them as migrants and groups of migrants may suggest how they fared in relationships with members of their own group and in relationships with members of other groups. But it is easier to describe relationships than to explain them and far easier still to describe bad or unfriendly relation-

ships than good. Parties to working relationships soon look beyond
ethnic, religious, or other stereotypes and learn to understand beliefs
and customs that have been strange to them; they come to recognize
that members of a neighboring cultural community vary as much as
members of their own community; and they seldom generalize about
others they know as individuals. When Benjamin wrote that non-Jews
greatly respected Jews and tried to guess why (they supported the
opera house; they always contributed to worthy causes),[38] he illustrated
rather than explained, apparently finding their attitudes more note-
worthy than those of their contemporary San Franciscans, who left
it to historians over a century later to find, for instance, that Jews belonged to Masonic lodges out of proportion to their numbers.[39] Newcomers on the frontier often tagged each other by their origins when
they first met, calling each other John Bull or New York. Frontier jour-
nalists writing up minor events often did not bother to get the names
of foreigners, referring to them only as Frenchmen, Mexicans, or celes-
tials, presumably outside the fellowship of their readers. Yet once
acquainted, they looked beyond labels. Judge Matthew P. Deady, leader
of the Oregon bar, after dining with Bernard Goldsmith, former mayor
of Portland, with whom he had often worked in civic causes, noted
in his diary, "he is no common man,"[40] making no attempt to categorize
Goldsmith relative to his coreligionists.

If the historian exploring attitudes of people who did not generalize about their relations with their neighbors, let alone explain
them, implies that German Jews commanded esteem for qualities that
Americans liked to call characteristically American, he must know
that many westerners later found some of those same qualities offen-
sive in Japanese immigrants.[41] The one group of immigrants may have
fared differently from the other mainly in having fallen outside the
range of differences in appearance and culture that Americans had
become accustomed to when they came: German Jews followed other
German-speakers who already had made their language and customs
familiar fixtures of the American scene. Especially in the Reformed
version that German-speaking immigrants favored, Judaism was com-
prehensible to nineteenth-century American Protestants as Buddhism
was not.[42] Such relationships were not peculiar to the West, as migration itself was not; but in areas where most people were migrants or
had been migrants, the circumstances of migration may have confirmed and reinforced their effects.

Insofar as migration may explain how American society has developed, it may be that along with cheap land, geographical isolation,
and the predominance of rural over urban populations—circumstances

PAST MASTERS R. L. LA PARFAITE UNION, No. 17, San Francisco.

Parfait Union, the French lodge of the California Free Masons, San Francisco, 1898.

The Hon. Benjamin Wisebart, c. 1882. Born in Louisville in 1841, Wisebart came to Central City, Colorado in 1861, was elected mayor in 1876, and was thrice elected Illustrious Grand Master of the Council of Masons. (Courtesy of the Ira M. Beck Archives of Rocky Mountain Jewish History, Center for Judaic Studies, University of Denver.)

that according to Alexis de Tocqueville helped to maintain free institutions in America—migration explains the past more than it explains the present. Despite the notorious footlooseness of Far Westerners, migrants of all kinds, including immigrants, account for smaller fractions of the populations of most western states now than they did in the last century. But gross relative declines do not tell the whole story. Rates of increase in the nineteenth century were far larger, absolute numbers far smaller, than in the twentieth century. In the 1840s, there were so many emigrants on the trails to Oregon and California that they got in each other's way, depleting the forage of draft animals and so fouling sources of drinking water that more of them died from diseases of filth in season than ever died from attacks by Indians. In 1980, however, the Bureau of the Census reported that migration during the previous decade had accounted for only about 10.5 percent of the total increase in population in the Pacific and mountain states but that even net migration, the excess of those who came over those who went, was over 4.5 million persons, a total larger than the population of those same states in 1900. Moreover, like other migrations it was far from evenly distributed and represented far from even samplings of all kinds of migrants. The northernmost mountain states, like the plains states to their east, have been losing more migrants than they have gained since World War I; Arizona, Colorado, and Nevada have been gaining faster than California. Rates of migration by specific race, religion, and occupation diverge sharply from general averages: changes in some individual communities, states, and social groups have been at least comparable with those of pioneer times. For most, if not all, of the United States, and especially of the Far West, ideas of demographic equilibrium and maturity are illusions. The Jewish migration has been one of those that run far above average, the total Jewish population by 1980 in California alone, for instance, having risen to more than three times the total in the entire country at the onset of the great Jewish migration from Europe exactly one hundred years earlier. The processes of assimilating new residents and the responsibilities for accumulating and analyzing the evidence of social change following on their migration show no signs of abating.

Notes

1. Moses Rischin, "Beyond the Great Divide: Immigration and the Last Frontier," *Journal of American History*, 55 (June 1968), 42–53.

2. Frederick Jackson Turner, "The Significance of the Frontier in American History," *The Frontier in American History* (New York, 1920), 22–23.

3. Bureau of the Census, *Population of the United States in 1860* . . . (Washington, 1864), xxxi–xxxii.

4. Joseph Schafer, "The Yankee and Teuton in Wisconsin. 4: Some Social Traits of Teutons," *Wisconsin Magazine of History*, 4 (September 1920), 16–17; Kathleen N. Conzen, *Immigrant Milwaukee: Accommodation and Community in a Frontier City* (Cambridge, MA, 1976).

5. Bureau of the Census, *Report on Population of the United States at the Eleventh Census: 1890*, Pt. 1 (Washington, DC, 1895), xcii–xciii. In 1870, the percentage of foreign-born in San Francisco, at 49.3 percent, was second only to that in Marysville, California. *Statistics of the United States at the Tenth Census (June 1, 1880)* (Washington, DC, 1883), 447.

6. *Ancestry of the Population by State: 1980*, Supplementary Report PC 80-S1-10 (Washington, DC, 1983), 2–3, 21–22.

7. Howard R. Lamar, "From Bondage to Contract: Ethnic Labor in the American West, 1600–1890," in Steven Hahn and Johathan Prude, eds., *The Countryside in the Age of Capitalist Transformation: Essays in the Social History of Rural America* (Chapel Hill, NC, 1985), 293–24.

8. "[The German farmer] tended to hold on . . . as if his farm were the one piece of land in the world for him and his," Schafer wrote. "The Yankee, already given to change in the East, tended in the West . . . to regard land lightly, and to abandon one tract to another." See "The Yankee and the Teuton in Wisconsin. 1: Characteristic Attitudes Toward the Land," *Wisconsin Magazine of History*, 6 (December 1922), 144. On the persistence of Germans in North Dakota, see E. A. Willson et al., *Rural Changes in Western North Dakota: Social and Economic Factors Involved in the Changes in Number of Farms and Movement of Settlers from Farms*, North Dakota Agricultural Experiment Bulletin 214 (Fargo, 1928), 7, 29–30; on the persistence of Czechs in Oklahoma, see Russell W. Lynch, *Czech Farmers in Oklahoma: A Comparative Study of the Stability of a Czech Farm Group in Lincoln County, Oklahoma . . .*, Oklahoma Agricultural and Mechanical College Bulletin, 39, no. 13 (Stillwater, 1942), 7, 33, 35.

9. Note that some wage-earning immigrants were classic examples of success in moving up the agricultural ladder to freehold tenure. German Russians recruited as laborers in sugar beet fields in the Arkansas Valley east of Pueblo, Colorado, acquired their own land so rapidly that growers shifted to Mexican laborers. Kenneth W. Rock, "'Unsere Leute,' The Germans from Russia in Colorado," *Colorado Magazine*, 54 (Spring 1977), 163.

10. Cf. H. Brett Melendy, *Asians in America: Filipinos, Koreans, and East Indians* (Boston, 1977).

11. Theodore Saloutos, *Expatriates and Repatriates: A Neglected Chapter in United States History*, Occasional Paper Series, No. 10 (Augustana College Library, Rock Island, IL, 1972).

12. Gunther Barth, *Bitter Strength: A History of the Chinese in the United States* (Cambridge, MA, 1964), vii, 1.

13. Jonathan D. Sarna, "The Myth of No Return: Jewish Return Migration to Eastern Europe, 1881–1914," *American Jewish History*, 75 (March 1986), 267–79.

14. Odd S. Lovoll, *The Promise of America: A History of the Norwegian-American People* (Minneapolis, 1984), 29; Harald Runblom and Hans Norman, eds., *From Sweden to America: A History of the Migration: A Collective Work of the Uppsala Migration Project* (Uppsala, 1976), 226; Betty Boyd Caroli, *Italian Repatriation from the United States, 1900–1914* (New York, 1973), 16–17, 49–50, and passim.

15. Lieutenant Zebulon M. Pike, reporting on his expedition of 1806–1807, wrote of "tracts of many leagues where the wind had thrown up the sand, in all the fanciful forms of the ocean's rolling wave." Donald Jackson, ed., *The Journals of Zebulon Montgomery Pike . . .* (Norman, OK, 1966), v. 2, 27.

16. Herbert O. Brayer, "Insurance Against the Hazards of Western Life," *Mississippi Valley Historical Review*, 34 (September 1947), 221–36.

17. Horace M. Kallen, *Culture and Democracy in the United States: Studies in the Group Psychology of the American People* (New York, 1924), 160–63.

18. Moses Rischin, *The Promised City: New York's Jews, 1870–1914* (Cambridge, MA, 1962), 126; *Dictionary of American Biography*, Supplement 5, s.v. "Cahan, Abraham."

19. Robert E. Park, "The Natural History of the Newspaper," *American Journal of Sociology*, 29 (November 1923), 275–76; idem, *The Immigrant Press and Its Control* (New York, 1922), 100–102.

20. Will Irwin. "The American Newspaper : The Spread and Decline of Yellow Journalism," *Collier's Weekly*, 46 (March 4, 1911), 20. In 1932, when Hearst's influence had passed its peak, he had 47.6 percent of total circulation in California and 56 percent of Sunday circulation. Rodney Parker Carlisle, "The Political Ideas and Influence of William Randolph Hearst, 1928–1936" (Ph.D. diss., University of California, Berkeley, 1965), 14.

On Becoming a Westerner

21. Irving McKee, "The Shooting of Charles de Young," *Pacific Historical Review*, 16 (August 1947), 271–84; Franklin Walker, *San Francisco's Literary Frontier* (New York, 1939), 246, 247.

22. S. Willis Rudy, *The College of the City of New York: A History, 1847–1947* (New York, 1949), 1, 91.

23. Ibid., 292.

24. U.S. Congress Senate. Immigration Commission, *The Children of Immigrants in Schools*. 61st Cong., 3d sess., S. Doc. 749. Serial 5871–5875. Vol. 2, 554; Vol. 4, 614; Vol. 5, 292–94, 336, 830, and passim.

25. Eli N. Evans, *The Provincials: A Personal History of Jews in the South* (New York, 1980), 212; Leonard Dinnerstein and Mary Dale Palsson, eds., *Jews in the South* (Baton Rouge, LA, 1973), 13.

26. George E. Mowry, *The California Progressives* (Berkeley, 1951), 125.

27. R. A. Burchell, *The San Francisco Irish, 1848–1880* (Berkeley, 1980), 116, 119; Steven P. Erie, "Politics, the Public Sector, and Irish Social Mobility: San Francisco, 1870–1900," *Western Political Quarterly*, 31 (June 1978), 278, 380–83.

28. Oscar O. Wegelin, "Etienne Derbec and the Destruction of His Press at San Francisco, April, 1865," *New York Historical Society Quarterly Bulletin*, 27 (January 1943), 10–17; Abraham P. Nasatir, ed., *A French Journalist in the California Gold Rush* (Georgetown, CA, 1964), 28–42.

29. Oscar Handlin, *Boston's Immigrants, 1790–1865: A Study in Acculturation* (Cambridge, MA, rev. ed., 1959), 59–60, 62–63.

30. Roger Daniels, *The Politics of Prejudice: The Anti-Japanese Movement in California and the Struggle for Japanese Exclusion* (Berkeley, 2 ed., 1977), 1–31. The introduction of Chinese immigrants as factory workers had aroused organized protest in Massachusetts as early as 1870, see Frederick Rudolph, "Chinamen in Yankeedom: anti-unionism in Massachusetts in 1870," *American Historical Review*, 53 (October 1947), 1–29.

31. Interest in family farming was not confined to old-stock Americans or, among Jews, to advocates of projects of colonization financed through the Baron de Hirsch Fund. In California, the Sacramento merchants David Lubin and Harris Weinstock were foremost among the agrarians. Cf. Olivia Rosetti Agresti, *David Lubin: A Study in Practical Idealism* (Boston, 1922).

32. Naomi Wiener Cohen, *Encounter with Emancipation: The German Jews in the United States, 1830–1914* (Philadelphia, 1984), 29 and passim.

33. Earlier statistics are notoriously scanty and unreliable. Liebmann Hersch, "International Migration of the Jews," in Walter F. Willcox, ed., *International Migrations: Interpretations* (New York, 1931), v. 2, 495–96. Kuznets notes that whereas Russian as well as German Jewish immigrants had had substantial commercial experience, they tended to shift from commerce because their specific commercial skills were not adaptable to American conditions. Simon Kuznets, "The Immigration of Russian Jews to the United States: Background and Structure," *Perspectives in American History*, 9 (1975), 107.

34. Rudolf Glanz, "The German-Jewish Mass Emigration: 1820–1880," *American Jewish Archives*, 22 (April 1970), 2.

35. John W. Reps, *Panoramas of Promise: Pacific Northwest Cities and Towns in Nineteenth-Century Lithographs* (Pullman, WA, 1984).

36. Volunteer social workers at the North Bennet Street Boys' Club in 1898 told Italian boys that they "mustn't get excited, chew gum, spit, swear, cheat or talk Italian." Marian Lawrence Peabody, *To Be Young Was Very Heaven* (Boston, 1967), 147.

37. Israel Joseph Benjamin, *Three Years in America, 1859–1862*, 2 vols., trans. by Charles Reznikoff (Philadelphia, 1956), v.1, 241.

38. Benjamin, *Three Years*, v.1, 233.

39. Tony Fels, "Religious Assimilation in a Fraternal Organization: Jews and Freemasonry in Gilded-Age San Francisco," *American Jewish History*, 24 (June 1985), 376, 393; Joseph Friedman, "Jewish Participation in California Gold Rush Era Freemasonry," *Western States Jewish History*, 16 (July 1984), 291–302. Cf. Robert Scott Cline, "Community Structure on the Urban Frontier: The Jews of Portland, Oregon, 1849–1887" (M.A. thesis, Portland State University, 1982), 79–81.

40. Malcolm Clark, Jr., ed., *The Diary of Judge Matthew P. Deady, 1871–1892: Pharisee among Philistines* (Portland, 1975), II, 309.

41. As anti-Semites did in criticizing Jews, though after World War II critics of other minorities reproached them for not emulating Jewish and Japanese immigrants. On duality in stereotypes of Jews, John Higham, *Send These to Me: Immigrants in Urban America* (Baltimore, rev. ed., 1984), 100–101.

42. Discussing the "Protestantization" of American Judaism as influenced by Isaac Leeser (1806–1868) in Richmond and Philadelphia, Lance J. Sussman notes that in the nineteenth-century Protestants tended to look benevolently on Jews and occasionally attended synagogues. See "Isaac Leeser and the Protestanization of American Judaism," *American Jewish Archives*, 38 (April 1986), 5–6. Liturgical convergence went especially far in the West where the leading congregations were Reform; in Portland, San Francisco, and other western cities, Jewish and elite Christian clergymen often fraternized and worked together in civic causes, finding much in common intellectually.

INDEX

tzedakah tradition and, 94, 101–2,
105, 106, 109, 147. *See also* Polish
immigrants; Russian immigrants
East Indian immigrants, 197
Ecuadorian immigrants, 195
Education, 16; intermarriage and, 166,
167, 177, 179, 180, 183, 184–85;
Jewish, 41–42, 54–55, 57, 77, 127,
184; public, 141, 147, 149, 199–201
Eggleston, Edward, 200
Egypt: Jews in, 129
Ehrman, Mrs. Joseph, Jr., 122
Ehrman, Sidney, 128, 129, 131
Elazar, Daniel, 105–6
El Rio Golf Club (Tucson), 149
Emanu-El: San Francisco congrega-
tion, 18, 35 illus., 119, 122, 123,
124, 127; Tucson congregation,
142, 144, 146–48, 159
Emanuel (Denver congregation), 180
illus.
Emigrant trail, 198, 208
European immigrants (Western
Europe), 194, 195, 203
Ex-Patients Association (Denver), 94,
98

Fairbanks, Douglas, Sr., 58
Family Service Agency (Tucson), 148
Fannin, Paul, 150, 155
Federation of Jewish Charities (San
Francisco), 129
Feingold, Henry, 57
Ferrin, Joe and Therese, 139
Fierman, Floyd, 140
Filipino immigrants, 195, 197, 200
Findley, Paul, 163n.41
Fine, Alvin, 127
Fineshriber, William, 121
Fireman, Peter, 38–39
Fischer, Claude, 181–82, 184
Fleishhacker, Mortimer, 128–29
Florida, 82; Jewish officeholders in,
202
France: cultural influence of, in
America, 205; emigrants from, to
America, 195, 203, 207 illus.; in-
termarriage in, 170–71
Franklin, Selim, 141
Free Masons: Parfait Union (San

Francisco lodge), 207 illus.;
Western Jewry and, 206, 208 illus.
French immigrants, 195, 203, 207
illus.
Frey, William, 38
Friedlander, Isaac, 73, 78
Friedman, William, 96–97
Friendly family (Portland), 173
Frisch, Daniel, 130
Fruchthendler, Jacob, 145, 155

Galbreath, Thomas, 100–101
Gan, Robert, 56, 60 illus.
Gartner, Lloyd P., 18, 53
General Dynamics, 145
George, Henry, 34
Gerber, David, 21
German Jewry in America, 20, 31,
98–99, 192, 196, 200, 210n.8;
esteem for, 204–5, 206; and rela-
tionship with East European
Jewry, 98–100, 104, 119, 173; in
the West, 166, 173–74, 197
Glanz, Rudolf, 204
Glazer, Nathan, 53–54
Goddard, Samuel, 148, 150, 156
Goldberg, Robert A., 18
Golden, Harry, 201
Goldenson, Samuel, 121
Goldin, Milton, 101–2
Gold rush, 18, 32–33, 194, 196, 198,
202–3
Goldscheider, Calvin, 168, 176, 177
Goldsmith, Bernard, 206
Goldstein, Israel, 124
Goldstein, Morris, 124
Goldstein, Sidney, 176, 177
Goldwater, Barry, 151
Goldwater, "Big Mike," 58
Goldwater, Morris, 141
Gore, Albert, 158
Goren, Arthur A., 53
Grand Island, N.Y., 82
Grass Valley, Calif., 33
Guggenheim, Simon, 196
Gumbiner, Joseph, 147, 159
Gunnison, Utah, 72, 73, 75, 77
Gurock, Jeffrey S., 57

Haas, Walter, 125, 127

McNulty, Jim, 156
Magnes, Judah, 41–42
Magnin, Edgar, 128
Magnin, Grover, 122
Malamed, Moshe, 78
Mansfeld, Jacob S., 139, 141
Marinoff, Jacob, 103–4
Marriage market, Jewish, 166, 173
Marrus, Michael R., 171
Maryland: Jewish officeholders in, 202
Marysville, Calif., 209n.5
Masonic lodges: Parfait Union (San
    Francisco), 207 illus.; Western
    Jewry and, 206, 208 illus.
Massarik, Fred, 174–76, 178
Matthews, William, 150
Mediterranean immigrants, 195
Meier, Julius, 197
Menuhin, Moshe, 131
Messianism, 31–32
Mexican immigrants, 28, 42, 149, 195,
    197, 202, 210n.9
Meyers, Arthur, 95
Mezvinsky, Norton, 129
Michigan, 80, 83
Migration: patterns of, 15–16, 17,
    20–21, 39–41, 195, 197–99, 201–9;
    westward, post-World War II, 18,
    20, 28, 43, 138, 139, 145, 192–93,
    208–9; westward, pre-World War
    II, 27–28, 37, 39–41, 111–12, 208–9
Milan, Italy, 53, 171
Milwaukee, Wis., 55, 61, 195
Milwaukee Jewish Agricultural So-
    ciety, 83
Minnesota, 195, 196
Missionaries, 194
Moment (periodical), 59
Montana, 203
Montefiore Agricultural Aid Society,
    82, 83
Montefiore Colony, Kans., 83
Mormons, 36, 196, 202; relations with
    Clarion Colony and, 72, 74, 77,
    79, 80, 81
Morocco: Jews in, 129
"Muller gang" (Denver), 103

Napoleon III, 205
Nash, Gerald, 139

National Association for the Study
    and Prevention of Tuberculosis,
    99
National Community Relations Ad-
    visory Council (NCRAC), 145
National Conference of Christians and
    Jews, 148
National Jewish Hospital (NJH),
    Denver: differences with Jewish
    Consumptives' Relief Society,
    98–101, 103, 105, 107, 109; open-
    air treatment for tuberculosis,
    107; Reform community and, 93,
    96–97, 98
National Jewish Population Study, 177,
    178
National Jewish Welfare Fund, 124
National Urban League, 147
Native Americans, 191, 192, 208
NCRAC (National Community Rela-
    tions Advisory Council), 145
Networks: social and institutional,
    173, 181–82, 185, 189n.55
Nevada: population of, 34, 209
Nevada City, Calif., 33
New Mexico: population of, 34, 195
New Odessa Farm Colony, Oreg., 28,
    37–39, 39 illus.
New Orleans Agricultural Society, 82
New Social History, 17, 18, 57–58,
    168–70
New Spain, Calif., 194
New York City, 40, 103–4, 124, 192;
    history of Jews and, 53–54;
    Jewish community in, 18, 22,
    35–36, 43, 54, 55, 61, 63, 71, 82,
    121, 204; Lower East Side, 21, 55,
    58, 63, 69; as magnet, 80, 81, 86;
    public education in, 200
New York Journal (periodical), 199
"New York" quota: University of
    Arizona admissions, 149
New York State: agricultural colonies
    in, 71, 80, 82; immigrant office-
    holders in, 196–97; Jewish
    population of, 27–28, 34, 196–97;
    public education in, 200
NJH. See Jewish National Hospital,
    Denver
Noah, Mordecai M., 82

The Center for Judaic Studies of the University of Denver is privileged to be associated with the publication of Jews of the American West, the first volume in the American Jewish Civilization series to be issued by the Wayne State University Press. Founded in 1975 by Dr. Stanley M. Wagner, the Center has been committed to publishing works of scholarship reaching across the whole gamut of the millennial experience of the Jews. The Center's Rocky Mountain Jewish Historical Society is especially honored, therefore, to lend its support to the publication of this volume, which is devoted specifically to examining the history of the Jews in the region in which the Center has made its home.